كلام كل يوم

Kalaam Kull Yoom 2

Situational Egyptian Arabic

Alaa Abou El Nour
Matthew Aldrich

lingualism

ISBN: 978-1-949650-05-1

Written by Alaa Abou El Nour and Matthew Aldrich
Edited by Heba Salah Ali and Matthew Aldrich
Illustrated by Heba Khater
Audio by Mohamed Ibrahim and Heba Salah Ali
Cover art: © Shutterstock / rafik beshay

website: www.lingualism.com
email: contact@lingualism.com

Table of Contents

Introduction .... *ii*

How to Use This Book .... *iv*

At the **Greengrocer's** 1

At the **Butcher's** 16

Shopping 31

At the **Market** 46

At a **Hotel** 61

Renting an **Apartment** 75

Dealing with the **Doorman** 89

Getting **Laundry** Done 105

At the **Post Office** 120

At the **Bank** 133

Visiting a **Museum** 147

At a **Mosque** 160

At a **Language Institute** 176

Dealing with **Bureaucracy** 191

Dealing with the **Police** 205

Dealing with **Difficulties** 219

Introduction

This is the book I wish I had when I first went to live in Egypt. I had a pretty good grasp on colloquial Arabic grammar. I could conjugate verbs and form basic sentences. I knew "lots of words"... or so I thought. But I would so often find myself in situations unable to express my thoughts and needs and struggling to understand what people were saying to me. I was always worried that my awkward exchanges with locals made me come across as rude because I didn't know the right things to say at the right times. Understandably, I wanted to prepare before I tried to tackle specific communicative challenges–such as getting my hair cut. But how? I found myself flipping through various course books and pocket dictionaries looking for words and phrases to use with the barber. I would bring lists to my teacher. How do you say "not too short"? What's the word for "sideburns"? How do I make small talk with my barber? (I knew that Egyptian barbers were chatty!) It was a lot of research to accomplish a simple task I'd taken for granted back home.

Kalaam Kull Yoom: Situational Egyptian Arabic was written to help intermediate learners succeed at critical moments during everyday communicative tasks. This is the second of two books in a series. I have divided each book into 16 chapters, which are not meant to be studied in order and do not increase in the level of difficulty. Instead, you should find the chapter to navigate your way through a particular transactional or social situation that is relevant to your needs.

For example, are you planning to rent an apartment soon? Then check out the chapter *Renting an Apartment* on page 75. Each chapter has several dialogues, vocabulary lists, bonus expressions, footnotes, and cultural information. (See How to Use This Book on p. iv to learn more about the organization and features of the chapters.)

I am deeply grateful to Alaa Abou El Nour, who carefully wrote the dialogues with an eye to reflect authentic, everyday Egyptian

Arabic as well as to include high-frequency vocabulary and phrases likely to be heard and used in specific situations. I wrote the texts on cultural tips and information based on my own experiences living in Egypt and information from several Egyptian and expat friends alike who were kind and patient enough to share their advice and feedback. I would also like to thank Heba Salah Ali for her help proofreading the dialogues and vocabulary lists (ensuring the tashkeel and phonemic transcriptions are accurate). Special thanks also to Heba Khater for providing illustrations and to Mohamed Ibrahim and Heba Salah Ali for producing the audio of the dialogues.

Matthew Aldrich

Audio

Visit www.lingualism.com/audio, where you can find the free accompanying audio to download or stream (at variable playback rates).

Anki Flashcards

Enhance your learning with our Anki digital flashcards, available for separate purchase on our website. This comprehensive deck features all the vocabulary and expressions from this book, complete with audio, to help you memorize and master the material more effectively.

How to Use This Book

This is not a coursebook with chapters that build on each other and need to be studied in order. Use the **Table of Contents** at the front of the book (also located on the back cover of the paperback edition, for your convenience) to find the topic that interests you for your immediate or future communicative goals. Of course, you're not going to go out into the real world and have conversations with people that follow the dialogues line by line. The purpose of the dialogues is to teach you different words and phrases that you can use and that you may hear. Synonyms, alternative expressions, and supplementary vocabulary are provided to help you form your own sentences to express yourself and to be prepared for the variety of possible things you may hear Egyptians say to you.

Introductory Paragraph

On the first page of each chapter, you will see an illustration above the chapter's title in English and Egyptian Arabic. An introduction to the topic follows and presents some key vocabulary.

Mini-Dialogues

Next, we have several short dialogues. Each dialogue has a title that shows you the goal of the specific "subtask"–for example, paying the bill, offering your seat to someone, reporting a theft.

Symbols

Notice that the lines of dialogue are preceded by symbols.

○ You–the foreigner, the customer. (Things you might need to say.)

◇ An Egyptian person–merchant, barber, waiter, landlord, friend, etc. etc. (Things you might hear other people say.)

The symbols are there to help you decide whether you need to memorize the phrases so you can actively use them yourself, or if you just need to be able to passively understand them when you hear them.

Arabic Script

Each dialogue appears three times on the page. The first is written in Arabic script with tashkeel (diacritics). At first glance, it may seem that many letters are missing diacritics. A final consonant is assumed to take sukuun, as Egyptian Arabic does not have case endings as MSA does.

We write كِتاب *kitāb* **book** (and not كِتَابْ). Non-final consonants without diacritics are understood to take the short vowel fatha (َ): شمْس *šams* **sun** (and not شَمْسْ). This was done intentionally to keep the texts from being cluttered with redundancies and streamline fluent reading. You can find a detailed online guide with printable PDFs on Egyptian Arabic pronunciation and Lingualism's system of orthography in the Resources section of this book's product page on our website.

Phonemic Transcription

Each dialogue also appears as phonemic transcription. This can be helpful for learners who are not yet comfortable enough with the Arabic alphabet. Some of the phonemic characters may seem unfamiliar and confusing, but by investing just a short time learning the sounds each character represents, you will find the system intuitive and easy to read. The Arabic script does not adequately show all of the sound changes (vowel lengthening, shortening, and elision) and shifts in word stress that occur in Egyptian Arabic. So even learners who prefer Arabic script can benefit by referring to the phonemic transcription. Follow the link above for a guide to Lingualism's phonemic transcription system.

English Translation

Between the dialogues of Arabic script and phonemic transcription, English translations appear to help you understand the dialogues and quickly find words and phrases you want to learn. Some style was sacrificed in the translations to keep them direct and true to the original Egyptian Arabic. This allows you to easily match up phrases and words by comparing the translations to the Arabic.

Footnotes

Underlined words and phrases are followed by superscript numbers that reference footnotes:

- Synonyms are preceded by equal signs (=). These show you words and expressions which can replace those in the dialogue without significantly changing the meaning.
- Alternative expressions show examples of other things you might want to say or might hear instead. These are followed by English translations.

Culture and Information Notes

The real focus of the book is, of course, the language itself. Other information–on culture and services in Egypt–is provided as a bonus. Hopefully, you will find some information useful and interesting, but keep in mind that the comments on culture are generalizations–there are always exceptions. Likewise, the information on services (companies, procedures, transportation options, etc.) is subject to change. You should always double-check such information from other sources, especially Egyptian friends and acquaintances.

The Extended Dialogue

The mini-dialogues in each chapter are followed by a longer dialogue that combines several of the subtasks into a full communicative exchange.

Vocabulary

Vocabulary lists in three columns (English, phonemic transcription, and Arabic script) follow the dialogues. These are not glossaries containing all of the words from the dialogues, but rather lists of keywords related to the topic and those likely to be needed in various circumstances–that is, they are there to save you time searching in dictionaries for the words you need.

Expressions

Expressions are divided into two sections, preceded by the same symbols used in the dialogues. First are expressions you may need to use, and second are statements and questions you may hear others say.

Audio

All of the dialogues have been recorded by professional voice artists from Cairo, Egypt. You can download or stream the audio free of charge from our website.

At the Greengrocer's عنْد الخُضري

A فكهاني *fakahāni* **fruit seller** specializes in selling fruit but may also sell some vegetables. A خُضري *xúḍari* **vegetable seller**, likewise, sells mainly vegetables but may also sell some fruit. Both terms can be translated as **greengrocer** in English. Prices in shops, not to mention supermarkets, are set and are clearly displayed. Most fruit and vegetables are sold by the kilogram. Vendors use traditional scales and will try to weigh out whole kilograms. (In supermarkets, where digital scales are used, you can buy produce without worrying about making the weight an even kilo.) Some fruit is sold by the piece. Ask when in doubt, as shown in the dialogue on the next page. Prices in small greengrocer's shops and supermarkets alike are set. However, you may be able to haggle a bit with vegetable cart vendors or at farmers' markets. Prices fluctuate depending on the season, demand, and inflation. Tomatoes are especially infamous for fluctuating prices, so there is a running joke about 'crazy tomatoes' (See dialogue 4 on p. 5).

1

Buying fruit

○ المانْجة دي بِالكيلو وَلّا بِالواحْدة[1]؟

◇ الكّيلو بِـ ١٥ جِنيْهْ بسّ شوف اللي إنْتَ عايْزُه.

○ طب، اِوْزِنْلي الاِتْنينْ دوْل.

◇ دوْل عامْلين كيلو إلّا رُبْع. نِزوِّد[2] الصُّغيّرة عليْهُم عشان يِكْمل كيلو؟

○ تمام، مفيش مُشْكِلة.

○ Are these mangoes sold by the kilo or by the piece?

◇ A kilo is 15 LE, but you can pick them out yourself.

○ Okay. Weigh these two [mangoes] for me.

◇ They weigh three-quarters of a kilo. Shall we add this small one to them to make an even kilo?

○ All right, no problem.

○ *ilmánga di bi-kkīlu wálla bi-lwáħda[1]?*

◇ *ikkīlu bi-xamastāšar ginēh bassᵊ šūf íll- ínta 3áyzu.*

○ *ṭab, iwzínli -lʔitnēn dōl.*

◇ *dōl 3amlīn kīlu ílla rub3. nizáwwid[2] iṣṣuɣayyára 3alēhum 3ašān yíkmal kīlu?*

○ *tamām, ma-fīš muškíla.*

1 = بِتْبيع بِالكّيلو وَلّا بِالواحْدة؟ *bitbī3 bi-kkīlu wálla bi-lwáħda?*

2 = نِحُطّ *niħúṭṭ*

Greengrocers will deliver. A tip is expected for the delivery service.

Many Egyptians pull along a عربيةْ خُضار *3arabīt xuḍār*, a small, two-wheeled folding wire shopping cart to transport their vegetables back home in. Note that this word is also used to refer to a mobile vendor's vegetable cart.

2

BUYING VEGETABLES

○ الخُضار ده طازة؟
◇ أُمّال[1] يا مدام. لِسّه جايّ مِن شُوَيّة.
○ طب، ناوِلْني[2] كيس كِده. أنقّي بِراحْتي.
◇ اِتْفضّلي. المحلّ كُلُّه تحْت أمْرك.
○ تِسْلم! اِوْزِنْلي دوْل كِده شوفْهُم طِلْعوا[3] قدّ أيْه.
◇ هاتي واحْدة كمان عشان يِكْملوا[4] كيلو.

○ Are the vegetables fresh?
◇ Of course they are, ma'am. They just came in a little while ago.
○ Okay, hand me a plastic bag so I can pick the ones I want.
◇ Here you are. The entire shop is at your service.
○ Thank you! Weigh these for me and let me know how much they come out to.
◇ Add one more to make an even kilo.

○ *ilxuḍār da ţāza?*
◇ *ummāl*[1] *ya madām. líssa gayyᵊ min šuwáyya.*
○ *ţab, nawílni*[2] *kīs kída. anáʔʔi bi-ráħti.*
◇ *itfaḍḍáli. ilmaħállᵊ kúllu taħtᵊ ámrak.*
○ *tíslam! iwzínli dōl kída šúfhum ţíl3u*[3] *ʔaddᵊ ʔē.*
◇ *hāti wáħda kamān 3ašān yikmálu*[4] *kīlu.*

[1] = طبْعاً *ţáb3an*

[2] اِدّيني *iddīni* **give me**

[3] يِعْمِلوا *yi3mílu* **they make**

[4] = يِبْقوا *yíbʔu*

3

Buying organic

o عنْدك خِيار أوْرْجانيك؟

◇ صِوَب يَعْني؟ آه فيه بسّ الكّيلو بـِ ٢٣ جِنيْه.

o تمام أيّ حاجة[1]، المُهِمّ مَيْكونْش مرْشوش.

◇ لا متقِلْقيش، ده مفيهوش أيّ مُبيدات.

o طب، اِوْزِنْلي نُصّ كيلو. و فيه فاكْهة أيْه في الموسِم دِلْوَقْتي[2]؟

◇ فيه قِشْطة و كاكا زيّ السُّكّر[3].

o Do you have organic cucumbers?

◇ Greenhouse ones, you mean? Yes, we do, but a kilo is 23 LE.

o That's fine, whatever [you have], as long as they're not sprayed [with pesticides].

◇ No, don't worry. These don't have any pesticides.

o Okay, weigh half a kilo for me. And what fruits do you have in season now?

◇ We have nice and sweet sugar apples and persimmons.

o *3ándak xiyār ōrganīk?*

◇ *ṣíwab yá3ni? āh fī bass ikkīlu bi-talāta w 3išrīn ginēh.*

o *tamām, ayyᵊ ḥāga*[1]*, ilmuhímmᵊ ma-ykúnšᵊ maršūš.*

◇ *lā, ma-tiʔlaʔīš, da ma-fihūš ayyᵊ mubidāt.*

o *ṭab, iwzínli nuṣṣᵊ kīlu. wi fī fákha ʔē fi -lmūsim dilwáʔti*[2]*?*

◇ *fī ʔíšṭa wi kāka zayy issúkkar*[3]*.*

[1] = زيّ بعْضُه *zayyᵊ bá3ḍu* = مِش مُشْكِلة *miš muškíla*

[2] اليومينْ دوْل *ilyumēn dōl* **these days**

[3] زيّ العسل *zayy il3ásal* (lit. like honey)

Organic produce is usually sold in supermarkets and in some high-quality greengrocers.

4

ASKING ABOUT PRICES

- ○ بِكام كيلو القوطة[1] النّهارْده؟
- ◇ بِـ ٧ جِنيْه.
- ○ نطِّت[2] ليْه كِده؟ ده أنا لِسّه جايِبْها[3] بِـ ٤ جِنيْه مِن يومين.
- ◇ مجْنونة يا قوطة![4] هنِعْمِل أيْه؟
- ○ طب، عايِز كيلو بسّ جامْدة عشان السّلطة.

- ○ How much is a kilo of tomatoes today?
- ◇ 7 LE.
- ○ Why did [the price] jump so much? I just bought some for 4 LE a couple of days ago.
- ◇ Crazy tomatoes! What can we do?
- ○ Okay, I'd like a kilo, but hard ones for a salad.

- ○ *bi-kām kīlu -lʔūṭa*[1] *-nnahárda?*
- ◇ *bi-sáb3a gnēh.*
- ○ *náṭṭit*[2] *lē kída? d-ána líssa gayíbha*[3] *bi-3árba3a gnēh min yumēn.*
- ◇ *magnūna ya ʔūṭa!*[4] *haní3mil ʔē?*
- ○ *ṭab, 3āyiz kīlu bassᵊ gámda 3ašān issálaṭa.*

[1] = (Alexandrian) الطّماطِم *iṭṭamāṭim*

[2] = زادِت *zādit;* غِلْيِت *ɣílyit* **got expensive**

[3] = شارْياها *šaryāha*

[4] مجْنونة يا قوطة! *magnūna ya ʔūṭa!* **Crazy tomatoes!** is a playful expression common among greengrocers to explain fluctuating prices of tomatoes. You may even hear tomato vendors shouting this as they go through neighborhoods on their horse-drawn carts.

Quality varies from one greengrocer's to another and from one supermarket to another. While fruit and vegetables look cleaner and higher in quality in supermarkets, there's no guarantee that they will be tasty or sweet.

5

ASKING WHAT IS IN SEASON

○ كُنْت عايْزة اعْرف[1]، أيْه الفاكْهة المَوْجودة اليومينْ دوْل؟

◇ خيرْ ربِّنا كِتير! فيه مانْجة و بطّيخ و تين شوْكي.

○ أَيْوَه، أيْه التّين الشّوْكي ده؟

◇ خُدي اقشّرْلِك واحْدة و دوقيها[2]. ده لازِم يِتّاكِل كِده[3].

○ طب، عايْزة كيلو[4].

◇ لا ده بِيِتّاخِد[5] بِالواحْدة، الكِّبيرة بِـ ٣ جِنيْه و الصُّغيرّة بِـ ٢ جِنيْه.

○ I wanted to know what kinds of fruit there are these days.

◇ God's bounty is great! We have mangoes, watermelon, and prickly pears.

○ Yeah? What is this 'prickly pear'?

◇ There you are. Let me peel one for you to taste. It has to be eaten like this.

○ Okay, I'll take a kilo.

◇ No, this is sold by the piece. A large one is 3 LE and a small one is 2 LE.

○ *kunt^{ə} 3áyza á3raf*[1]*, ʔē ilfákha ilmawgūda ilyumēn dōl?*

◇ *xēr rabbína ktīr! fī mánga wi baṭṭīx wi tīn šōki.*

○ *áywa, ʔē ittīn iššōki da?*

◇ *xúdi -ʔaššárlik wáḫda wi duʔīha*[2]*. da lāzim yittākil kída.*[3]

○ *ṭab, 3áyza kīlu*[4]*.*

◇ *lā, da byittāxid*[5] *bi-lwáḫda, ikkibīra bi-talāta gnēh wi -ṣṣuɣayyára bi-tnēn ginēh.*

[1] مُمْكِن تِقوليّ *múmkin tiʔúlli* / [2] = جرّبيها *garrabīha* / [3] دي طريقةْ أكْله. *di ṭarīʔit áklu.* **This is the way to eat it.** / [4] اوْزِنْلي كيلو *iwzínli kīlu* / [5] = بيِتْباع *biyitbā3*

Prickly pears are rarely sold in greengrocers' shops, but rather on carts in the street.

6

RETURNING A PURCHASE

o أنا اشْتريْت[1] البطّيخة دي مِنّك إمْبارِح و عايز أرجّعْها.

◇ ليْه بسّ؟

o طِلْعِت قرْعة[2] يا حاجّ[3]، و أنا اشْتريتْها على ضمانْتك.

◇ وَلّا يِهِمّك. تاخُد واحْدة تانْيَة بدالْها و أشُقّهالك[4]؟

o لا خلاص، هرجّعْها و آخُد فِلوسْها[5].

◇ تمام، اللي إنْتَ عايْزه.

o I bought this watermelon from you yesterday, and I want to return it.

◇ Why is that?

o It turned out to be tasteless, Haji, and I bought it with your guarantee.

◇ Never mind. Take another instead, and shall I split it open for you?

o No, no. I want to return and get my money back.

◇ Okay, as you wish.

o *ána -štarēt*[1] *ilbaṭṭīxa di mínnak imbāriḫ wi 3āyiz aroggá3ha.*

◇ *lē bass?*

o *ṭíl3it ʔár3a*[2] *ya ḫagg*[3]*, w ána ištarítha 3ála ḍamántak.*

◇ *wálla yihímmak. tāxud wáḫda tánya badálha w ašuʔʔahālak*[4]*?*

o *lā, xalāṣ, haraggá3ha w āxud filúsha*[5].

◇ *tamām, íll- ínta 3ayzu.*

[1] = أخدْت *axádt*

[2] أقْرع *áʔra3* (f. قرْعة *ʔár3a*) specifically describes watermelons that are not sweet enough or unripe.

[3] حاجّ *ḫagg* **Haji, pilgrim** is a polite form of address to an elderly man. To an elderly woman, it's حاجّة *ḫágga.*

[4] أقْطعْهالك *aʔṭa3hālak* = أفْتحْهالك *aftaḫhālak* **I'll cut it [open] for you**

[5] = تمنْها *tamánha* = حقّها *ḫaʔʔáha*

Extended Dialogue

○ صباح الفُلّ. عنْدك قوطة يا ريِّس[1]؟

◇ صباح النّور. آه عنْدي يا مدام.

○ بِكام الكّيلو؟

◇ بِـ ١٠ جنِيْهْ.

○ طب، هاتْلي نُصّ كيلو بسّ جامْدين عشان السّلطة.

◇ حاجة تانْيَة؟

○ آه عايْزة كمان اِتْنينْ كيلو بطاطِس.

◇ طبيخ وَلّا تحْمير؟

○ لا بطاطِس تحْمير، مِش عايْزاها تِشْرب الزّيْت.

◇ تمام، اللي إنْتي عايْزاه بسّ الكّيلو مِنْها بِـ ٥ جِنيْهْ.

○ ماشي اِوْزِنْلي اِتْنينْ كيلو. فيه بصل أبْيَض؟

◇ لا عنْدي بصل أحْمر، بِـ ٣ جِنيْهْ الكّيلو.

○ طب، اِوْزِنْلي اِتْنينْ كيلو بصل بِالمرّة. عنْدك فاكْهة طازة أيْه بقى النّهارْده؟

◇ عنْدي خوْخ لِسّه جايِّلي[2] زيّ العسل، و فيه مانْجة ألْفوْنْس زيّ الزِّبْدة[3].

○ بِكام كيلو الخوْخ و كيلو المانْجة؟

◇ الخوْخ الكّيلو بِـ ٢٤ جِنيْه، و المانْجة الكّيلو بِـ ٣٥.

○ الخوْخ غالي كِده ليْه؟

◇ ده مُسْتَوْرد يا مدام. خُدي مِنُّه و مِش هتِنْدمي[4].

○ طب، اِوْزِنْلي نُصّ كيلو بسّ أجرّبْه و خلّي المانْجة مرّة تانْيَة[5].

◇ مِن عينيّا... حاجة تانْيَة يا مدام؟

○ لا تِسْلم. كِده الحِساب كام؟[6]

◇ كِده كُلُّه ٣٣ جِنيْه.

o معاك بقيةْ ٥٠؟

◇ آه معايا فكّة. اِتْفضّلي.

o Good morning! Do you have any tomatoes, boss?

◇ Good morning! Yes, I do, ma'am.

o How much is a kilo?

◇ 10 LE.

o Okay, bring me half a kilo, but hard ones for a salad.

◇ Anything else?

o Yeah. I'd like two kilos of potatoes.

◇ For cooking or French fries?

o I want them for French fries. I don't want them to absorb the oil.

◇ Okay. As you wish, but a kilo of those is 5 LE.

o That's fine. Weigh two kilos. Are there any white onions?

◇ No, I've got red onions for 3 LE a kilo.

o Okay, weigh two kilos of onions, too. By the way, what fresh fruit have you got today?

◇ I've got nice, sweet peaches that have just came in. And there are also Alphonso mangoes, smooth as cream.

o How much is a kilo of peaches or mangoes?

◇ One kilo of peaches is 24 LE, and a kilo of mangoes is 35 LE.

o Why are the peaches so expensive?

◇ They're imported, ma'am. Try them and you won't regret it.

o Okay, weigh out just half a kilo so I can try them. And leave the mango for another time.

◇ My pleasure. Anything else, ma'am?

o No, thank you. How much is total then?

◇ altogether it's 33 LE.

○ Do you change for a 50?
◇ Yes, I have change. Here you are.

○ *ṣabāḫ ilfúll. 3ándak ʔūṭa ya ráyyis*[1]*?*
◇ *ṣabāḫ innūr. āh, 3ándi ya madām.*
○ *bi-kām ikkīlu?*
◇ *bi-3ášara gnēh.*
○ *ṭab, hátli nuṣṣᵊ kīlu bassᵊ gamdīn 3ašān issálaṭa.*
◇ *ḫāga tánya?*
○ *āh, 3áyza kamān itnēn kīlu baṭāṭis.*
◇ *ṭabīx wálla taḫmīr?*
○ *laʔ, baṭāṭis taḫmīr, miš 3ayzāha tíšrab izzēt.*
◇ *tamām, íll- ínti 3ayzā bass ikkīlu mínha bi-xámsa gnēh.*
○ *māši iwzínli itnēn kīlu. fī báṣal ábyaḍ?*
◇ *lā, 3ándi báṣal áḫmar, bi-talāta gnēh ikkīlu.*
○ *ṭab, iwzínli itnēn kīlu báṣal bi-lmárra. 3ándak fákha ṭāza ʔē báʔa -nnahárda?*
◇ *3ándi xōx líssa gayyíli*[2] *zayy il3ásal, wi fī mánga alfōns zayy izzíbda*[3]*.*
○ *bi-kām kīlu -lxōx wi kīlu -lmánga?*
◇ *ilxōx ikkīlu bi-arbá3a w 3išrīn ginēh, wi -lmánga ikkīlu bi-xámsa w talatīn.*
○ *ilxōx ɣāli kída lē?*
◇ *da mustáwrad ya madām. xúdi mínnu wi miš haṭindámi*[4]*.*
○ *ṭab, iwzínli nuṣṣᵊ kīlu bassᵊ agarrábu, wi xálli -lmánga márra tánya*[5]*.*
◇ *min 3ináyya... ḫāga tánya ya madām?*
○ *laʔ, tíslam. kída -lḫisāb kām?*[6]
◇ *kída kúllu talāta w talatīn ginēh.*
○ *ma3āk baʔīt xamsīn?*
◇ *āh, ma3āya fákka. itfaḍḍáli.*

[1] Greengrocers tend to have a very casual way of dealing with customers, and this is reflected in the language. For example, يا ريّس! *ya ráyyis!* **boss!** is customarily used between a greengrocer and the customer.

[2] لِسّه واصِل *líssa wāṣil* **just arrived**

[3] زيّ الزِّبْدة *zayy izzíbda* is an expressions to describe anything creamy, soft, and mushy

[4] = جرّبيه و هتِدْعيلي *garrabī w hatid3īli*

[5] = بعْديْن *ba3dēn*

[6] = كِده عايِز كام؟ *kída 3āyiz kām?*

Vendors will sometimes have a piece of fruit cut in half and on display. Otherwise, you can sometimes get the vendor to cut open a watermelon, etc. in front of you, so you can see how ripe his produce is inside.

Vocabulary

greengrocer, vegetable seller	*xúḍari*	خُضري
fruit seller	*fakahāni*	فكهاني
greengrocer's cart, vegetable cart; two-wheel shopping cart	*3arabīt xuḍār*	عربيةْ خُضار
fruit shop	*maḫáll*ᵊ *fawākih*	محلّ فَواكِهْ
fruit and vegetable shop	*maḫáll*ᵊ *xuḍār wi fákha*	محلّ خُضار و فاكْهة
produce section (of a supermarket)	*ʔism ilxuḍrawāt*	قِسْم الخُضْرَوات
change (money back)	*bāʔi*	باقي
small bills, coins	*fákka*	فكّة
kilo	*kīlu*	كيلو
to weigh	*wázan*	وَزن
to select, pick	*náʔʔa*	نقّى
to peel	*ʔáššar*	قشّر

fresh	*ţāza* [invariable]	طازة
to wilt	*díbil*	دِبِل
wilted, dry	*dablān*	دبْلان
squished	*mahrūs* *mifá33aş*	مهْروس مِفعّص
organic	*ōrganīk*	أوْرْجانيك
greenhouse	*şōba (şíwab)*	صوْبة (صِوَب)
sprayed (with pesticides)	*maršūš*	مرْشوش
pesticides	*mubidāt*	مُبيدات
season	*mūsim*	موسِم
herbs	*xúḑra*	خُضْرة
vegetables	*xuḑār*	خُضار
green beans	*faşúlya*	فاصولْيا
broccoli	*brúkuli*	بْروكُلي
carrots	*gázar*	جزر
cauliflower	*ʔarnabīţ*	قرْنبيط
cucumbers	*xiyār*	خِيار
garlic	*tōm*	توْم
romaine lettuce	*xassᵊ báladi*	خسّ بلدي
iceberg lettuce	*kabútši*	كابوتْشي
okra	*bámya*	بامْيَة
red onions	*báşal áħmar*	بصل أحْمر

yellow onions	*báṣal ábyaḍ*	بصل أبْيَض
green onions	*báṣal áxḍar*	بصل أخْضر
peas	*bisílla*	بِسِلّة
potatoes (for boiling)	*baṭāṭis ṭabīx*	بطاطِس طبيخ
potatoes (for frying)	*baṭāṭis taɦmīr*	بطاطِس تحْمير
pumpkin	*ʔár3ᵊ 3ásal*	قرْع عسل
spinach	*sabānix*	سبانِخ
taro	*ʔulʔās*	قُلْقاس
tomatoes	*ʔūṭa*	قوطة
tomatoes (Alexandrian dialect)	*ṭamāṭim*	طماطِم
turnips	*lift*	لِفْت
zucchini (UK: courgette)	*kōsa*	كوْسة
apricots	*míšmiš*	مِشْمِش
bananas	*mōz báladi*	موْز بلدي
beets	*bángar*	بنْجر
cherries	*kirēz*	كِريْز
black dates	*bálaɦ íswid*	بلح إسْوِد
red dates	*bálaɦ zaɣlūl*	بلح زغْلول
figs	*tīn (baršūmi)*	تين (برْشومي)
green seedless grapes	*3ínab banāti*	عِنب بناتي
red grapes	*3ínab áɦmar*	عِنب أحْمر

guava	*gawāfa*	جَوافة
lemon	*lamūn*	لمون
mangoes	*mánga*	مانْجة
creamy, smooth (of mangoes)	*zayy izzíbda*	زيّ الزِّبْدة
navel orange	*burtuʔān bi-súrra*	بُرْتُقان بِسُرّة
sweet orange	*burtuʔān sukkári*	بُرْتُقان سُكّري
peaches	*xōx*	خوْخ
pears	*kummítra*	كُمِّتْرى
persimmons	*kāka*	كاكا
plums	*barʔūʔ*	برْقوق
pomegranates	*rummān*	رُمّان
custard apple, cherimoya	*ʔíšṭa*	قِشْطة
watermelon	*baṭṭīx*	بطّيخ
unripe, tasteless (of watermelons)	*áʔra3 (ʔár3a)*	أقْرع (قرْعة)
sweet (lit. like honey)	*zayy il3ásal*	زيّ العسل
sweet (lit. like sugar)	*zayy issúkkar*	زيّ السُّكّر

Expressions

	○	
Hand me...	*nawílni...*	ناوِلْني...
Put them in my [vegetable] cart, please.	*ḫuṭṭuhúmli fi 3arabīt ilxuḍār.*	حُطُّهُمْلي في عربيةْ الخُضار.

Weigh 3 kilos each in a separate bag.	*iwzínli talāta kīlu kullᵊ kīlu li-wáɦdu.*	اِوْزِنْلي ٣ كيلو كُلّ كيلو لِوَحْدُه.
This is not ripe.	*di miš mistiwíyya.*	دي مِش مِسْتِوية.
This cucumber is shriveled.	*ilxiyār da dablān.*	الخِيار ده دبْلان.
This watermelon is not ripe.	*ilbaṭṭīxa di ʔár3a.*	البطّيخة دي قرْعة.
This watermelon turned out to be no good (lit. like a cucumber).	*ilbaṭṭīxa ṭíl3it zayy ilxiyār.*	البطّيخة طِلْعِت زيّ الخِيار.
The tomatoes are squished.	*iṭṭamāṭam mahrūsa.*	الطّماطم مهْروسة.
I need herbs for stuffed vegetables.	*3āyiz xúḍrit máɦši.*	عايِز خُضْرِةْ محْشي.
Give me two more bell peppers.	*záwwid ʔarnēn fílfil kamān.*	زوِّد قرْنينْ فِلْفِل كمان.

◇

Red or white cabbage?	*kurúmb ábyaḍ wálla áɦmar?*	كُرُنْب أبْيَض وَلّا أحْمر؟
Anything else?	*ɦāga tánya?*	حاجة تانْيَة؟

At the Butcher's عنْد الجزّار

There are two main kinds of butchers in Egypt. The first type of butcher shop is the جزّار *gazzār*, which deals in red meat: كنْدوز *kandūz* **beef**, بِتِلّو *bitíllu* **veal**, ضاني *dˤāni* **lamb**, and جملي *gámali* **camel**. The word لحْمة *láħma* **meat** is generally understood to be beef unless specified otherwise. (Of course, you won't find لحْمِةْ خنْزير *láħmit xanzīr* **pork** in Egypt except at Christian butchers or as imported frozen meat in certain supermarkets that cater to foreign clientele.) Some butcher shops have a restaurant extension called a مسْمط *másmat̩* where traditional meat dishes and sandwiches are served. The other kind of butcher shop is the فرارْجي *farárgi,* which specializes in poultry and rabbits. Live birds are kept in cages next to the shop, so you can even pick out the chicken, etc. to be slaughtered and packaged. As with most neighborhood businesses, many butchers offer home delivery services. Large supermarkets also have their own butcher departments with both red meat and poultry. You can even find kebabs and seasoned meats ready to cook.

Buying meat

○ كيلو اللّحْمة المفْروم بِكام لَوْ سمحْت؟

◇ ١٢٠ جِنيْه.

○ طيِّب، اِوْزِنْلي نُصّ مِن اللّحْمة الحمْرا اللي هِناك دي و اُفْرُمْهالي.

◇ مِن عينيّا.

○ How much is one kilo of ground meat?

◇ 120 LE.

○ Okay, weigh half a kilo from the red meat over there and grind it for me, please.

◇ My pleasure!

○ *kīlu -lláђma -lmafrūm bi-kām, law samáђt?*

◇ *míyya w 3išrīn ginēh.*

○ *ţáyyib, iwzínli nuşş^ə min illáђma -lђámra -lli hināk di w ufrumhāli.*

◇ *min 3ináyya.*

In supermarkets, you can usually find three types of meat:

1. مُجمّد *mugámmad* **frozen**, which, especially when domestic, is the cheapest and lowest in quality.
2. سوداني *sudāni* **Sudanese** (imported from Sudan), generally a bit less expensive than domestic meat
3. بلدي *báladi* **domestic**, which is the freshest, of course, but also the most expensive.

2

Having a sheep slaughtered

○ كُنْت عايْزة أعْرف لَوْ حابّة أدْبح خروف بِيِبْقى أيْه النِّظام.

◇ بِتيجي تِشوفيه و تِنقّيه[1] و بعْديْن بدْبحْهولِك و أسْلُخْهولِك و أقطّع و أقسِّم و كُلّ حاجة[2].

○ طيِّب، أنا عايْزة في الآخِر كُلّ حاجة مِتْقسِّمة و مِتْقطّعة.

◇ ده اللي بيِحْصل بِالظّبْط و كُلُّه في أطْباق فِبْر و مِتْغلِّفة بِالبِلاسْتيك. مِش هتْشيلي همّ حاجة.

○ I wanted to know how it works if I want to have a sheep slaughtered.

◇ You come see and choose one, and then we slaughter it for you, skin, butcher, and divide it up—everything.

○ Okay, I want the end result to be everything butchered and divided.

◇ That's exactly what happens, and you receive them packed on disposable trays covered with plastic wrap. You won't have anything to worry about doing.

○ *kuntᵊ 3áyz- á3raf law ɧábba ádbaɧ xarūf biyíbʔa ʔē innizᶎām.*

◇ *bitīgi tšufī wi tnaʔʔī*[1] *wi ba3dēn badbaɧhūlik w asluxhūlik w aʔáṭṭa3 w aʔássim wi kullᵊ ɧāga*[2].

○ *ṭáyyib, ána 3áyza fi -lʔāxir kullᵊ ɧāga mitʔassíma wi mitʔaṭṭá3a.*

◇ *da -lli biyíɧṣal bi-ᶎᶎábṭ, wi kúllu f aṭbāʔ fibrᵊ wi mitɣallífa bi-lbilástik. miš hatšīli hammᵊ ɧāga.*

[1] = تِخْتاريه *tixtarī*

[2] = و أوَضّب كُلّ حاجة *w awáḍḍab kullᵊ ɧāga* **and I prepare everything**

Butchers also offer slaughtering services for those who are offering a sacrifice during عيد الأضْحى *3īd ilʔáḍɧa* **Eid Al-Adha** (the Feast of the Sacrifice). One can simply go to a butcher and make a deal regarding the whole sacrifice. The butcher will take care of the slaughter, butcher the meat, and package it up for you.

3

Buying chicken

○ عايْزة ٣ كيلو وِراك بسّ مِن فضْلك.

◇ طيِّب، فيه عِرْض[1] عَ الفِراخ الكّامْلة النّهارْده.

○ لا لا مِش بِنْحِبّ الصُّدور[2]. هاتْلي بسّ الوِراك.

◇ تمام حاجة تانْيَة؟

○ لا مُتْشكِّرة. بسّ اِبْعتْهُم بِسُرْعة عشان عنْدي عُزومة بِاللّيْل.

○ I want 3 kilos of chicken, legs, please.

◇ There is a special on whole chickens today.

○ No, we don't like the breast. Just bring me legs.

◇ Okay, anything else?

○ No, thanks. Just send them over quickly as I'm expecting company this evening.

○ *3áyza talāta kīlu wirāk bass^ə min fáḍlak.*

◇ *ṭáyyib, fī 3arḍ^ə [1] 3a -lfirāx ikkámla -nnahárda.*

○ *la? la?, miš binḫíbb iṣṣudūr[2]. hátli bass ilwirāk.*

◇ *tamām, ḫāga tánya?*

○ *la?, mutšakkíra. bass ib3áthum bi-súr3a 3ašān 3ándi 3uzūma bi-llēl.*

[1] = خصْم *xaṣm* **discount**

[2] = ملْناش في الصُّدور *ma-lnāš fi -ṣṣudūr*

4

CHOOSING ANIMALS TO SLAUGHTER

○ كُنْت عايِز ديك رومي حِلْو كِده.

◇ عنْدك يا باشا برّه. اِخْتار[1].

○ اِوْزِنْلي ده كِده و قولّي سِعْرُه كام[2]. و خُد الأرْنب ده كمان.

○ I'd like a really nice turkey.

◇ Here, they are outside. Choose one.

○ Okay, weigh this one for me, and tell me its price... and grab this rabbit, too.

○ *kunt*ᵊ *3āyiz dīk rūmi ɧilw*ᵊ *kída.*

◇ *3ándak ya bāša bárra. ixtār*[1].

○ *iwzínli, da kída wi ʔúlli sí3ru kām*[2]. *wi xud ilʔárnab da kamān.*

[1] نقّي اللي إنْتَ عايْزُه *ná22i -ll- ínta 3áyzu* **choose the one you want**

[2] = يِعْمِل كام *yímil kām*

Besides chicken and turkey, a فرارْجي *farárgi* **poultry butcher** also sells بطّ *baṯṯ* **duck**, وِزّ *wizz* **goose**, حمام *ɧamām* **pigeon**, and سِمّان *simmān* **quail**. Ducks and geese are sold by the kilo; pigeons and quails are sold by the piece. فرْد *fard* and فرْدة *fárda* mean piece (one whole animal), and جوْز *gōz* (lit. pair) means two. بِكام جوْز الحمام؟ *bi-kām gōz ilɧamām?* **How much for two pigeons? /** اِدّيني فرْدِة حمام. *iddīni fárdit ɧamām.* **Give me one pigeon.**

A delicious, popular Egyptian dish available in many restaurants is حمام محْشي *ɧamām máɧši* **stuffed pigeon**.

5

Having meat cut to specification

o مِن فضْلك قطّعْلي دوْل شرايِح رُفيّعة خالِص.

◇ تِحِبّي أخْليهالِك مِن الدِّهْن؟[1]

o لا سيبْها[2] عشان الشَّوْي[3] و قسِّمْهالي في طبقيْن مِن فضْلك.

o Please, slice these into really thin slices.

◇ Okay, you want me to remove the fat?

o No, leave it on for grilling, but split them onto two plates, please.

o *min fádlak ʔattá3li dōl šarāyiħ rufayyá3a xāliṣ.*

◇ *tiħíbbi axlihālik min iddíhn?*[1]

o *laʔ, síbha*[2] *3ašān iššáwy*[3] *wi ʔassimhāli f ṭabaʔēn, min fádlak.*

[1] = تِحِبّي اشيلّك الدِّهْن؟ *tiħíbbi ašíllik iddíhn?*

[2] = خلّيها *xallīha*

[3] هشْويها *hašwīha* **I will grill it**

Try to find a trustworthy butcher in your neighborhood. Ask neighbors for recommendations. When a butcher gets to know you as a زِبون طيّاري *zibūn ṭayyári* **regular customer**, he will be sure to give you قطْعِية كُويِّسة *ʔaṭ3íyya kwayyísa* **good cuts of meat**. Unfortunately, there are dishonest butchers out there, and occasionally there is news of a butcher caught selling لحْمِةْ حِمير *láħmit ħimīr* **donkey meat**.

6

Buying various meat products

o عايز نُصّ كيلو كباب و نُصّ كيلو فِلِتّو.

◇ مفيش فِلِتّو لِلْأسف.[1]

o خلاص تمام هات الكّباب بسّ و معاهُم نُصّ كيلو مُمْبار.

◇ تمام فيه برْضُه مَواسير لَوْ حابِب تِعْمِل عليْها مرقة.[2]

o هات نُصّ مَواسير كمان. مِش هَيْخسّر.

o I want half a kilo of kebab and half a kilo of tenderloin.

◇ I'm sorry but there isn't any tenderloin.

o That's okay. Just bring the kebab and half a kilo of stuffed intestines then.

◇ There is also bone with marrow if you'd like to make broth.

o Okay, bring me half a kilo of bones with marrow. They will come handy.

o *3āyiz nuṣṣᵊ kīlu kabāb wi nuṣṣᵊ kīlu filíttu.*

◇ *ma-fīš filíttu, li-lʔásaf.*[1]

o *xalāṣ tamām. hāt ikkabāb bassᵊ w ma3āhum nuṣṣᵊ kīlu mumbār.*

◇ *tamām, fī bárḍu mawasīr law ḥābib tí3mil 3alēha máraʔa*[2].

o *hāt nuṣṣᵊ mawasīr kamān. miš hayxássar.*

1 = الفِلِتّو خلْصان معْلِشّ *ilfilíttu xalṣān ma3líšš*

2 شورْبة *šúrba* **soup**

Extended Dialogue

AT THE BUTCHER'S COUNTER IN A SUPERMARKET

○ مِن فضْلك عايْزة شيش طاووك. بِكام الكّيلو؟

◇ المتِبِّل وَلّا العادي؟

○ أيْه ده فيه مِتبِّل؟ طب قوليّ سِعْرُه كام.

◇ فيه مِتبِّل بِالصّلْصة سِعْرُه ٧٥ الكّيلو و فيه مِتبِّل بِالزّبادي سِعْرُه ٧٠.

○ طب، هات طبقينْ نُصّ كيلو مِن ده و نُصّ كيلو مِن ده.

◇ مِن عينيّا. حاجة تانْيَة؟

○ آه عايْزة عِرْق حِلْو كِده أعْمِل بيه لحْمة بارْدة[1] بسّ مَيِبْقاش عجوز زيّ اللي جِبْتُه[2] مِنْكُم الأُسْبوع اللي فات.

◇ لا دبايِح النّهارْده كُلّها صُغيرّة، متِقْلقيش.

○ ماشي أمّا نْشوف. و عايْزة كمان كيلو لحْمة مفْرومة.

◇ مفيش لحْمة مفْرومة دِلْوَقْتي بسّ لَوْ تِحِبّي اِخْتاري و أفْرُمْلِك.

○ طيِّب، نقّيلي مِن الصّينية اللي هِناك دي كِده كيلو بسّ مَيْكونْش فيه دِهْن خالِص.

◇ تمام كِده؟

○ الله يِنوّر تِسْلم إيدك. آخِر حاجة بقى عايْزة كِبد فِراخ لَوْ فيه[3].

◇ كِبد بسّ وَلّا قَوانِص كمان؟

○ لَوْ فيه ميكْس و يِكون فيه قُلوب كمان ياريْت.

◇ هشوفْلِك حاضِر.

○ حضّرْلك الخيرْ[4]. و معلِشّ بِالمرّة لَوْ فيه رومي فيليْه؟

◇ آه فيه. أَوْزِنْلِك قدّ أيْه؟

○ اِوْزِنْلي نُصّ و قطّعْهولي رُفيّع.

◇ مِن عينيّا و هدُقُّهولِك برْضُه عشان يِبْقى جاهِز عَ التّتْبيل على طول.

o طيِّب، كِده الحِساب كُلُّه كام بقى متِعْرفْش؟

◇ كُلّ حاجة مكْتوب عليْها بِالظّبْط و هتِعْرفي عَ الكّاشير. و لَوْ مِش عايْزة حاجة سيبيها، مفيش مُشْكِلة.

o تمام تِسْلم إيدك.

o Excuse me, I'd like some chicken kebabs. How much is a kilo?

◇ Seasoned or regular?

o Seriously? You have seasoned? Tell me the price then.

◇ Seasoned with red sauce is 75 LE a kilo, and seasoned with yogurt sauce is 70 LE.

o Okay, bring two plates, a half kilo of both.

◇ My pleasure. Anything else?

o Yes, I want some round roast that is good for roast beef[1], but not too old [of an animal] like the one I bought from you last week.

◇ No, today's slaughters are all young. Don't worry.

o Okay, let's see... I also want one kilo of ground meat.

◇ There isn't any ground meat at the moment, but if you'd like, you can choose any cut and I can grind it up for you.

o Okay, pick some from that tray over there. One kilo but without any fat.

◇ Like this?

o Perfect, bless you. And the last thing I want is some chicken livers, if there are any.

◇ Just livers? Or giblets, too?

o If there are giblets with hearts, that would be great.

◇ I'll check for you.

o Bless you. And also, if there are any turkey fillets?

◇ Yes, there are. How much shall I weigh?

o Half a kilo, and slice it thin, please.

◇ My pleasure. I'll pound it for you, too, so that it is ready to be seasoned.

○ Okay, and how much does that come out to now?

◇ Everything has its exact price on it. You'll get the total at the check stand. If you want to leave anything behind, it's no problem.

○ Okay, thanks a lot.

○ *min fáḍlak, 3áyza šīš ṭāwūk. bi-kām ikkīlu?*

◇ *ilmitábbil wálla -l3ādi?*

○ *ʔē da, fī mitábbil? ṭab ʔúlli sí3ru kām.*

◇ *fī mtábbil bi-ṣṣálṣa sí3ru xámsa w sab3īn ikkīlu wi fī mtábbil bi-zzabādi sí3ru sab3īn.*

○ *ṭab, hāt ṭabaʔēn, nuṣṣᵊ kīlu min da wi nuṣṣᵊ kīlu min da.*

◇ *min 3ináyya. ḫāga tánya?*

○ *āh, 3áyza 3irʔᵊ ḫilwᵊ kída á3mil bī láḫma bárda*[1]*, bassᵊ ma-yibʔāš 3agūz zayy ílli gíbtu*[2] *mínkum ilʔusbū3 ílli fāt.*

◇ *lā, dabāyiḫ innahárda kulláha ṣuɣayyára, ma-tiʔlaʔīš.*

○ *māši, ámma nšūf. wi 3áyza kamān kīlu láḫma mafrūma.*

◇ *ma-fīš láḫma mafrūma dilwáʔti bassᵊ law tiḫíbbi, ixtāri w afrúmlik.*

○ *ṭáyyib, naʔʔīli min iṣṣiníyya ílli hināk di kída kīlu, bassᵊ ma-ykúnšᵊ fī dihnᵊ xāliṣ.*

◇ *tamām kída?*

○ *allāh yináwwar, tíslam īdak. āxir ḫāga báʔa 3áyza kíbad firāx law fī*[3]*.*

◇ *kíbad bassᵊ wálla ʔawāniṣ kamān?*

○ *law fī miks, wi ykūn fī ʔulūb kamān yarēt.*

◇ *hašúflik ḫāḍir.*

○ *ḫaḍḍárlak ilxēr*[4]*. wi ma3alíššᵊ bi-lmárra law fī rūmi filēh?*

◇ *āh, fī. awzínlik ʔaddᵊ ʔē?*

○ *iwzínli nuṣṣᵊ wi ʔaṭṭa3hūli rufáyya3.*

◇ *min 3ináyya wi haduʔʔuhūlik bárḍu 3ašān yíbʔa gāhiz 3a -ttatbīl 3ála ṭūl.*

○ *ṭáyyib, kída -lḫisāb kúllu kām báʔa ma-ti3ráfš?*

◇ *kullᵊ ḫāga maktūb 3alēha bi-ẓẓábṭᵊ w hati3ráfi 3a -kkašīr. wi law miš 3áyza ḫāga sibīha, ma-fīš muškíla.*

○ *tamām, tíslam īdak.*

[1] لَحْمة بارْدة *láḫma bárda* (lit. cold meat) is similar to roast beef, stuffed with garlic, sliced into very thin slices, and served cold.

[2] = أخدْتُه *axádtu*

[3] عنْدك كِبد فِراخ؟ *3ándak kíbad firāx?* **Do you have chicken livers?**

[4] حضّرْلك الخيْر *ḫaḍḍárlak ilxēr* (lit. may [God] prepare all good for you) is a common response to حاضِر *ḫāḍir*.

Vocabulary

butcher (of red meat)	*gazzār*	جزّار
butcher shop	*gizāra*	جِزارة
poultry butcher; poultry butcher shop	*farárgi*	فرارْجي
meat	*láḫma*	لحْمة
beef (adult cows and buffaloes more than one year old)	*(láḫma) kandūz* *láḫma (báʔari)* *báʔara*	(لحْمة) كنْدوز لحْمة (بقري) بقرة
buffalo	*gamūsa*	جاموسة
calf	*3igl*	عِجْل
veal (younger than two months)	*bitíllu*	بِتِلّو
tenderloin	*filíttu*	فِلِتّو
roast beef	*tiribiyánku*	تِرِبِيانْكو
steak	*buftēk*	بُفْتيْك
ground meat	*láḫma mafrūma*	لحْمة مفْرومة
round (of beef)	*fáxda*	فخْدة
shank, shin	*mōza*	موْزة
ribeye, sirloin	*antirikōt*	أنْترِكوْت

(Cairene) stuffed intestines	*mumbār*	مُمْبار
(Alexandrian) stuffed intestines	*3uṣbān*	عُصْبان
lamb	*ḍāni*	ضاني
sheep	*xarūf*	خروف
leg of lamb	*fáxda ḍāni*	فخْدة ضاني
lamb chops, cutlet, ribs	*ríyaš*	رِيَش
camel meat	*gámali*	جملي
chicken meat	*firāx*	فِراخ
a chicken	*fárxa (firāx)*	فرْخة (فِراخ)
a local chicken (small, brown feathers)	*fárxa báladi*	فرْخة بلدي
a white chicken (larger than local chickens)	*fárxa bēḍa*	فرْخة بيْضا
live chickens	*firāx ḥáyya*	فِراخ حيّة
whole chickens	*firāx kámla*	فِراخ كامْلة
chicken leg (thigh and drumstick)	*wirk (wirāk)*	وِرْك (وِراك)
chicken leg, drumstick	*dabbūsa (dababīs)*	دبّوسة (دبابيس)
chicken liver	*kíbda (kíbad)*	كِبْدة (كِبد)
(chicken) giblet	*ʔúnṣa (ʔawāniṣ)*	قُنْصة (قَوانِص)
(chicken) heart	*ʔalb (ʔulūb)*	قلْب (قُلوب)
(mixed) giblets	*mazalīka*	مزاليكا

breast	*ṣidr*	صِدْر
neck	*ráʔaba*	رقبة
wing	*gināɧ (agníɧa)*	جِناح (أجْنِحة)
turkey	*dīk rūmi*	ديك رومي
turkey fillet	*rūmi filēh*	رومي فيليْه
pigeons	*ɧamām*	حمام
quail	*simmān*	سِمّان
duck	*báṭṭa*	بطّة
local duck	*báṭṭa báladi*	بطّة بلدي
male duck	*dákar báṭṭ*	دكر بطّ
rabbit	*árnab*	أرْنب
shish tawouk, chicken kebab	*šīš ṭāwūk*	شيش طاووك
trotters, cow's feet	*kawāri3*	كَوارِع
brain	*muxx*	مُخّ
lungs	*físša*	فِشّة
liver	*kíbda*	كِبْدة
kidneys	*kalāwi*	كلاوي
tripe	*kírša*	كِرْشة
kebab	*kabāb*	كباب
meatballs	*kúfta*	كُفْتة
spiced	*mitábbil*	مِتبِّل
frozen	*mugámmad*	مُجمّد

locally slaughtered	*báladi*	بلدي
to slaughter	*dábaɧ*	دبح
slaughtered animal	*dibīɧa (dabāyiɧ)*	دِبيحة (دبايِح)
to grind up, mince	*fáram*	فرم
to skin, flay	*sálax*	سلخ

Expressions

○

I want two kilos of intestines, and clean them for me.	*3āyiz itnēn kīlu mumbār wi naḍḍafhúmli.*	عايِز اِتْنينْ كيلو مُمْبار و نضّفْهُمْلي.
I want two of those black rabbits.	*3āyiz arnabēn sūd min dōl.*	عايِز أرْنبينْ سود مِن دوْل.
I'd like the tripe I pre-ordered yesterday.	*min fáḍlak, 3āyiz ikkírša -lli kuntᵊ miwáṣṣi 3alēha min imbāriɧ.*	مِن فضْلك عايِز الكِّرْشة اللي كُنْت مِوَصّي عليْها مِن إمْبارِح.
There is an order of chicken and giblets that hasn't been delivered yet.	*kān fī ṭálab firāx wi kíbad wi ʔawāniṣ líssa ma-waṣálš.*	كان فيه طلب فِراخ و كِبد و قَوانِص لِسّه مَوَصلْش.
I want a part from the top of the round.	*3āyiz ɧítta min wišš ilfáxda.*	عايِز حِتّة مِن وِشّ الفخْدة.
Cut me a piece of roast beef.	*iʔṭá3li ɧíttit tiribiyánku.*	اِقْطعْلي حِتِّةْ تِريبيانْكو.

Tie this beef tenderloin, please.	*irbúṭli -l3irʔ, law samáħt.*	اِرْبُطْلي العِرْق لَوْ سمحْت.
Give me two hawawshi, one stuffed with meat and the other with sausage.	*ħaḍḍárli itnēn ħawáwši, wāħid láħma wi wāħid sugúʔʔ.*	حضّرْلي اِتْنينْ حَواوْشي واحِد لحْمة و واحِد سُجُقّ.
I want three kilos of sausages.	*3āyiz talāta kīlu sugúʔʔ.*	عايِز ٣ كيلو سُجُقّ.
Is this meat local or Sudanese, pleae?	*illáħma di báladi wálla sudāni, min fáḍlak?*	اللّحْمة دي بلدي وَلّا سوداني مِن فضْلك؟
Is this frozen meat?	*híyya -lláħma di mugammáda?*	هِيَّ اللّحْمة دي مُجمّدة؟

◇

This male duck weighs 2 kilos.	*dákar ilbáṭṭᵊ da biyí3mil itnēn kīlu.*	دكر البطّ ده بِيِعْمِل ٢ كيلو.
Anything else?	*ħāga tánya?*	حاجة تانْيَة؟

Shopping في المول

Retail therapy! A great way to escape from the noise and bustle outside is to duck into a nice محلّ *maħáll* **shop** or spend hours strolling around a large, air-conditioned مول *mōl* **shopping mall**. Shops in Egypt tend to open and stay open later than those in the U.S. Hours vary from shop to shop, but most open at 11 or 11:30 a.m. and close late in the evening, at 10 p.m. or even as late as midnight or 1 a.m. Most shops, especially brand-name stores in large malls, will take كْريدِت كارْد *krēdit kard* **credit cards**. The brand name Visa is commonly used by Egyptians to refer to credit cards and bank cards in general, so you can ask if a shop takes credit cards simply by asking فيه فيزا؟ *fī vīza?* **Do you accept credit/debit cards?** or مُمْكِن أدْفع بِالفيزا؟ *múmkin ádfa3 bi-lvīza?* **Can I pay by credit card?** If they don't take credit cards, you can easily find a "ATM مكنة" *mákana* [ATM] **ATM** in every mall. In some small, independent shops, you may be able to haggle a bit, especially if you are paying in cash, but in shopping malls and brand-name shops, prices are fixed.

GETTING HELP FROM A SALES CLERK

◇ بِتْدوّري على حاجة مُعيّنة؟

○ آه مِن فضْلِك. كُنْت بدوّر على[1] جيبة جينْز غامْقة.

◇ فيه تشْكيلة جِديدة لِسّه جايّة[2] هِناك.

◇ Are you looking for something in particular?

○ Yes, please. I'm looking for a dark jean skirt.

◇ There's a new collection that just came in over there.

◇ *bitdawwári 3ála ɧāga mu3ayyána?*

○ *āh, min fáḍlik. kuntᵊ badáwwar*[1] *3ála žība žīnz ɣámʔa.*

◇ *fī taškīla gdīda líssa gáyya*[2] *hinā̄k.*

[1] أنا مِحْتاجة *ána miɧtāga* **I need**

[2] = لِسّه نازْلة *líssa názla*

Most shopping malls in Egypt have food courts, cinemas, and sometimes play areas for kids, making them great places for friends and families to spend the day beating the heat–meet up, eat or drink something together, and maybe even doing some shopping.

2

BROWSING

◇ فيه حاجة مُعيّنة بِتْدوّر عليْها؟

○ لا أنا هلِفّ لِوَحْدي[1] و لَوْ حاجة عجبِتْني هَبْقى أسْألك عليْها.

◇ تمام، بِراحْتك يافنْدِم.

○ شُكْراً.

◇ Is there anything in particular that you're looking for?

○ No, I'll just have a look around and if I like something, I'll ask you about it.

◇ Sure, take your time, sir.

○ Thank you!

◇ *fī ɧāga mu3ayyána bitdáwwar 3alēha?*

○ *laʔ, ána halíffᵊ li-wáɧdi*[1] *wi law ɧāga 3agabítni hábʔa asʔálak 3alēha.*

◇ *tamām, bi-ráɧtak yafándim.*

○ *šúkran.*

[1] = هدوّر بِنفْسي *hadáwwar bi-náfsi* = هتْفرّج معَ نفْسي *hatfárrag má3a náfsi*

3

Asking about a sale

o هُمّا دوْل عليْهُم خِصْم[1] وَلّا لا؟

◇ لا دوْل برّه الخِصْم[2].

o طب، فيْن الحاجات اللي نازِل عليْها خُصومات[3]؟

◇ الصّفّ ده كُلُّه نازِل عليْه خُصومات عشان التّصْفِيّات[4].

o Are these on sale?

◇ No, they're not included in the sale.

o Where are the things on sale then?

◇ This whole row is on sale because they're on clearance.

o *húmma dōl 3alēhum xaṣmᵊ[1] wálla laʔ?*

◇ *laʔ, dōl bárra -lxáṣm[2].*

o *ṭab, fēn ilḥagāt ílli nāzil 3alēha xuṣumāt[3]?*

◇ *iṣṣáffᵊ da kúllu nāzil 3alē xuṣumāt 3ašān ittaṣfiyyāt[4].*

[1] = سيْل *sēl* = تخْفيض *taxfīḍ* = أوكازْيوْن *ukazyōn*

[2] = برّه السّيْل *bárra -ssēl*

[3] = اللي نازْلة في السّيل؟ *ílli názla fi -ssēl*

[4] تصْفِيّات آخِر الموسِم *taṣfiyyāt āxir ilmūsim* **end of season clearance**

الأوكازْيوْن الصّيْفي *ilʔukazyōn iṣṣēfi* **the summer sales** season starts in the second half of July; الأوكازْيوْن الشِّتْوي *ilʔukazyōn iššítwi* **the winter sales**

4

ASKING ABOUT SIZES

o فيه مِنْها مقاس أكْبر[1] لَوْ سمحْتي؟

◇ فيه الإكْس لارْج و الدّابل إكْس لارْج.

o مفيش لارْج طيِّب؟

◇ لا لِلْأسف مفيش.

o Does this come in a larger size?

◇ There is extra large and XXL.

o There's no large available?

◇ No, unfortunately, there isn't.

o *fī mínha maʔās ákbar*[1] *law samáħti?*

◇ *fī -lʔíksᵊ laržᵊ wi -ddābal iks larž.*

o *ma-fīš laržᵊ ṭáyyib?*

◇ *laʔ, li-lʔásaf ma-fīš.*

[1] = مفيش مِنْها أَوْسع مِن كِده؟ *ma-fīš mínha áwsa3 min kída?*

Returns and exchanges are not as easy as in the U.S. Some shops have a 14 or 30-day refund/exchange policy but only if the merchandise is like new, with the tag still on it, and with a receipt. However, the majority of shops will only give a refund if there is a manufacturing problem. Assume that all sales are final and be sure you double check for issues with the merchandise before making the purchase.

5

BUYING SHOES

o طب، فيه زيّ دي بِالظّبْط[1] بسّ تِكون فيرْنيْه؟

◇ لا فيه فيرْنيْه بسّ بِكعْب[2].

o لا أنا بدوّر على حاجة فْلات[3].

◇ طب، لازِم[4] فيرْنيْه؟ فيه شمْواه و شكْلها شيك أَوي.

o شكْلها حِلْو فِعْلاً.[5] فيه مقاس ٣٨؟

o Do you have a pair like these but in patent leather?
◇ No, there are patent leather ones but with high heels.
o No, I'm looking for flats.
◇ Do they have to be patent leather? We have them in suede and they look so stylish.
o They really look nice. Do you have them in size 38?

o *ṭab, fī zayyᵊ di bi-ẓẓábṭ*[1]*, bassᵊ tkūn virnē?*
◇ *laʔ, fī virnē bassᵊ b-ká3b*[2]*.*
o *laʔ, ána badáwwar 3ála ḫāga flāt*[3]*.*
◇ *ṭab, lāzim*[4] *virnē? fī šamwā wi šakláha šīk áwi.*
o *šakláha ḫilwᵊ fí3lan.*[5] *fī maʔās tamánya w talatīn?*

[1] = مفيش أُخْت دي *ma-fīš uxtᵊ di* / [2] كعْب ٥ سنْتي *ka3bᵊ xámsa sánti* **5-cm heels** / [3] = واطْيَة على الأرْض *wáṭya 3ála -lʔárḍ* / [4] = ضروري *ḍarūri* / [5] تِصدّق شكْلها حِلْو *tiṣádda?, šakláha ḫilw* **Know what? They do look nice!**

Women's Shoe Sizes

In Egypt, European sizes are used.

Euro	*US*	*UK*	*cm.*	*Euro*	*US*	*UK*	*cm.*
35	4	2	20.8	**38-39**	8	6	24.1
35	4.5	2.5	21.3	**39**	8.5	6.5	24.6
35-36	5	3	21.6	**39-40**	9	7	25.1
36	5.5	3.5	22.2	**40**	9.5	7.5	25.4
36-37	6	4	22.5	**40-41**	10	8	25.9
37	6.5	4.5	23	**41**	10.5	8.5	26.2
37-38	7	5	23.5	**41-42**	11	9	26.7
38	7.5	5.5	23.8	**42**	11.5	9.5	27.1

6

Asking about materials

o ده جِلْد طبيعي؟

◇ آه يافنْدِم.

o مصْري وَلّا مُسْتَوْرد؟

◇ لا يافنْدِم مصْري، اِنْتاج المصْنع بِتاعْنا في ٦ أُكْتوبر.

o طب، هاخُد الجّزْمة دي. و كُنْت عايِز حِزام نفْس الدّرجة لَوْ فيه.

o Are these genuine leather?

◇ Yes, sir.

o Egyptian or imported?

◇ Egyptian, sir, produced in our factory in 6th of October City.

o I'll take these shoes then, and I also want a belt with the same tone.

o *da gildᵊ ţabī3i?*

◇ *āh, yafándim.*

o *máşri wálla mustáwrad?*

◇ *la?, yafándim máşri, intāg ilmáşna3 bitá3na f sítta uktūbar.*

o *ţab, hāxud iggázma di. wi kuntᵊ 3āyiz ђizām nafs iddáraga law fī.*

Men's Shoe Sizes

In Egypt, European sizes are used.

Euro	*US*	*UK*	*cm.*	*Euro*	*US*	*UK*	*cm.*
39	6	5.5	23.5	**43**	10	9.5	27
39	6.5	6	24.1	**43-44**	10.5	10	27.3
40	7	6.5	24.4	**44**	11	10.5	27.9
40-41	7.5	7	24.8	**44-45**	11.5	11	28.3
41	8	7.5	25.4	**45**	12	11.5	28.6
41-42	8.5	8	25.7	**46**	13	12.5	29.4
42	9	8.5	26	**47**	14	13.5	30.2
42-43	9.5	9	26.7	**48**	15	14.5	31

◇ بِتْدوّري على حاجة مُعيّنة؟

○ لا مُتْشكِّرة. أنا باخُد فِكْرة[1] بسّ.

◇ تمام اِتْفضّلي.

○ هُوَّ السّيْل[2] بدأ وَلّا لِسّه؟

◇ بدأ بسّ مِش في كُلّ الحاجات.

○ طيِّب، فينْ الحاجات اللي نازِل عليْها خصْم[3]؟

◇ الجُزْء ده كُلُّه. اِشْترِي قطْعِتينْ تاخْدي التّالْتة مجّاناً.

○ مْمْم... حِلْو أوي! طيِّب مُمْكِن أقيس[4] البِلوزة دي؟

◇ أكيد يافنْدِم، تِقْدري تِقيسيها هِناك[5].

○ طب، هبُصّ بصّة كِده[6] و اِدْخُل مرّة واحْدة[7].

(comes out of changing room)

◇ أيْه الأخْبار؟

○ بُصّي هِيَّ دي طِلْعِت شكْلها مِش حِلْو[8] عليّا خالِص.

◇ تِحِبّي مقاس تاني؟

○ لا شكْلها مِش حِلْو عليّا أساساً[9] بسّ الشّميز ده مُمْكِن أشوف مِنُّه لَوْ فيه درجِة واحْدة بسّ أصْغر[10].

◇ آه فيه... اِتْفضّلي.

(comes out of changing room again)

◇ المقاس ظبط؟

○ آه المقاس ده أظْبط بِكْتير. خلاص، هاخُد الشّميز ده اللّوْن الأبْيَض و الإسْوِد و معاه البِلوزة دي.

◇ تمام يافنْدِم اِتْفضّلي على الكّاشير و أنا هحصّلِك[11].

(goes to cashier)

o فيه فيزا مِن فضْلك؟

◇ لا لِلْأسف مفيش.

o طب، معلِشّ اِحْجِزْلي الحاجات دي. هسْحب مِن أيّ مكنة برّه و أرْجع أحاسْبك.

◇ بِراحْتِك يافنْدِم.

◇ Are you looking for something in particular?

o No, thanks, I'm just browsing.

◇ Sure, come on in.

o Has the sale started yet?

◇ It has, but it doesn't include everything.

o Where is the stuff on sale then?

◇ All of this section. Buy two, get the third for free.

o Hmm... very nice! Okay, can I try on this blouse?

◇ Certainly, miss. You can try it on over there.

o All right. I'll look around some more [first], then go in there [just] once.

(comes out of changing room)

◇ How is it?

o Well, this doesn't look nice on me at all.

◇ Would you like another size?

o No, it doesn't look nice in the first place, but I can try the shirt in another size if there is one just one size smaller.

◇ Yes, there is. Here you are.

(comes out of changing room again)

◇ Does it fit?

o Yes, this size fits much better. I'll take this shirt then in black and in white and also this blouse.

◇ Sure, miss. You can go to the cashier and I'll follow you.

(goes to cashier)

○ Do you take credit cards?

◇ I'm sorry, no.

○ Okay, would you please hold onto these for me. I'll withdraw some cash from a nearby ATM and come back to you to pay for them.

◇ No hurry, miss.

◇ *bitdawwári 3ála ḥāga mu3ayyána?*

○ *laʔ, mutšakkíra. ána bāxud fíkra*[1] *bass.*

◇ *tamām, itfaḍḍáli.*

○ *húwwa -ssēl*[2] *bádaʔ wálla líssa?*

◇ *bádaʔ bassᵊ miš fi kull ilḥagāt.*

○ *ṭáyyib, fēn ilḥāgat ílli nāzil 3alēha xaṣm*[3]*?*

◇ *iggúzʔᵊ da kúllu. ištíri qaṭ3itēn táxdi -ttálta maggānan.*

○ *mmm... ḥilwᵊ áwi! ṭáyyib múmkin aʔīs*[4] *ilbilūza di?*

◇ *akīd yafándim, tiʔdári tʔisīha hinā*k[5].

○ *ṭab, habúṣṣᵊ báṣṣa kída*[6] *w ádxul márra wáḥda*[7].

(comes out of changing room)

◇ *ʔē -lʔaxbār?*

○ *búṣṣi híyya di ṭíl3it šakláha miš ḥilwᵊ*[8] *3aláyya xāliṣ.*

◇ *tiḥíbbi maʔās tāni?*

○ *laʔ, šakláha miš ḥilwᵊ 3aláyya asāsan*[9] *bass iššamīz da múmkin ašūf mínnu law fī dáraga wáḥda bass áṣɣar*[10].

◇ *āh, fī... itfaḍḍáli.*

(comes out of changing room again)

◇ *ilmaʔās ẓábaṭ?*

○ *āh, ilmaʔās da áẓbaṭ bi-ktīr. xalāṣ, hāxud iššamīz da, illōn ilʔábyaḍ wi -lʔíswid wi ma3ā -lbilūza di.*

◇ *tamām, yafándim itfaḍḍáli 3ála -kkašīr w ána haḥaṣṣálik*[11].

(goes to cashier)

○ *fī vīza, min fáḍlak?*

◇ *laʔ, li-lʔásaf ma-fīš.*

○ *ṭab, ma3alíšš iḥgízli -lḥagāt di. hásḥab min ayyᵊ mákana bárra w árga3 aḥásbak.*

◇ *bi-ráḥtik yafándim.*

[1] = بتْفرّج *batfárrag*

[2] = الأوكازْيوْن ilʔukazyōn

[3] النّازْلة في السّيل؟ innázla fi -ssēl

[4] = أجرّب agárrab

[5] = البرْوْفة هِناك ilbrōva hnāk **the fitting room is over there**

[6] = هلِفّ لفّة كِده halíffᵊ láffa kída

[7] = بِالمرّة bi-lmárra

[8] = وِحِش wíɧiš

[9] = أصْلاً áşlan

[10] = لَوْ فيه أصْغر نمْرة law fī aşɣar nímra

[11] = هاجي وَراكي hāgi warāki

Vocabulary

to buy	*ištára*	اِشْترَي
to go shopping (lit. to buy things)	*ištára ɧagāt*	اِشْترى حاجات
to pay	*dáfa3*	دفع
to sell	*bā3*	باع
cash	*kāš*	كاش
credit card	*krēdit kard*	كْريْدِت كارْد
price	*si3r (as3ār)*	سِعْر (أسْعار)
cheap	*rixīş*	رِخيص
expensive	*ɣāli*	غالي
sale, discount	*xaşm (xuşumāt)*	خصْم (خُصومات)
store, shop	*maɧáll*	محلّ

fitting room	*brōva*	بْروْفة
customer	*zubūn (zabāyin)*	زُبون (زبايِن)
shirt	*ʔamīṣ* *šimīz*	قميص شِميز
blouse	*bilūza*	بِلوزة
t-shirt	*tīširt*	تيشيرْت
pants	*banṭalōn*	بنْطلوْن
shorts	*šōrt*	شوْرْت
skirt	*žība*	جيبة
dress	*fustān*	فُسْتان
belt	*ḥizām*	حِزام
sweatshirt	*switšírt*	سْويتْشيرْت
thick sweater	*swītar*	سْويتر
thin, wool sweater	*bulōvar*	بُلوْفر
jacket	*žākit*	جاكيت
coat	*bálṭu*	بالْطو
shoes	*gázma*	جزْمة
sneakers, tennis shoes	*kútši*	كوتْشي
boots	*būt*	بوت
half boots	*hāf būt*	هاف بوت
sandal	*ṣándal*	صنْدل
ballerina flats	*balirīna*	بالِرينا

heel	*ka3b*	كعْب
shoelaces	*rubāṭ*	رُباط
wallet	*maḫfáẓa*	محْفظة
shawl, scarf	*šāl*	شال
headscarf	*ṭárḫa*	طرْحة
(natural) leather	*gildᵊ (ṭabīʒi)*	جِلْد (طبيعي)
suede	*šamwā*	شمْواه
glossy patent leather	*virnē*	فيرْنيْه
cotton	*ʔuṭn*	قُطْن
jean	*žīnz*	جينْز
linen	*kittān*	كِتّان
chiffon	*šifōn*	شيفوْن
synthetic	*ṣinā3i*	صِناعي
perfume	*barfān*	برْفان
glasses	*naḍḍāra*	نضّارة
watch	*sā3a*	ساعة
earring	*ḫálaʔ*	حلق
ring	*xātim*	خاتِم
bracelet (solid)	*ɣiwēša*	غِويْشة
bracelet (chain)	*ansiyāl*	أنْسِيال
necklace	*silsíla*	سِلْسِلة
pendant	*dallāya*	دلّايَة

silver	*fáḍḍa*	فضّة
gold	*dáhab*	دهب

Expressions

Is there a larger size, please?	*min fáḍlak, fī maʔās ákbar?*	مِن فضْلك، فيه مقاس أكْبر؟
I would like this color too, please.	*law samáћt, 3āyiz illōn da kamān.*	لَوْ سمحْت عايِز اللّوْن ده كمان.
This one has a small rip in it. Could I have another one?	*bassᵊ di fīha ʔáṭ3a ṣɣayyára. múmkin wáћda tánya?*	بسّ دي فيها قطْعة صْغيّره. مُمْكِن واحْدة تانْيَة؟
Can I try on both [pairs of shoes]?	*múmkin aʔīs ilʔitnēn má3a ba3ḍ?*	مُمْكِن أقيس الاِتْنيْن معَ بعْض؟
Is this Egyptian or Italian silver?	*di fáḍḍa máṣri wálla iṭāli?*	دي فضّة مصْري وَلّا إيطالي؟
How many karats is this gold?	*da dáhab 3iyār kām?*	ده دهب عِيار كام؟
Do these glasses have a warranty?	*innaḍḍāra di 3alēha ḍamān?*	النّضّارة دي عليْها ضمان؟
I bought this pair of shoes from here and they tore apart the second time I wore them.	*ána xádt iggázma di min 3andúkum wi -tʔáṭa3it min tāni márra.*	أنا خدْت الجّزْمة دي مِن عنْدُكُم و اِتْقطعِت مِن تاني مرّه.

Can I reserve this item until evening?	*ţáyyib, múmkin áħgiz di li-ħáddᵊ bi-llēl?*	طيِّب، مُمْكِن أحْجِز دي لِحدّ بِاللّيْل؟
Is there a smaller size at another branch?	*ţáyyib, fī maʔās áşɣar fi furū3 tánya ħátta?*	طيِّب، فيه مقاس أصْغر في فُروع تانْيَة حتّى؟
Wow! That's a real bargain!	*wāw! di fúrşa háyla! wāw! di şáfqa gámda!*	واو! دي فُرْصة هايْلة! واوْ! دي صفْقة جامْدة!
I have the right to return it. The 14 days aren't up yet.	*ána min ħáʔʔi araggá3u líssa -lʔarba3tāšar yōm ma-xilşūš yá3ni.*	أنا مِن حقّي أرجّعُه لِسّه الأرْبعْتاشر يوْم مخِلْصوش يَعْني.
I want to return this. Otherwise, I will file a complaint with the Consumer Protection Agency.	*ána 3āyiz arágga3 da, wa-ʔílla haʔáddim fīkum šákwa li-gihāz ħimāyit ilmustáhlik.*	أنا عايِز أرجّع ده، وَ إلّا هقدِّم فيكُم شكْوى لِجِهَاز حِمَايةْ المُسْتهْلِك.
	◇	
This credit card is not working.	*ilkártᵊ da miš šaɣɣāl.*	الكارْت ده مِش شغّال.
Refunds are within 30 days only with a receipt.	*ilʔistirgā3 xilāl talatīn yōm bi-šárţᵊ wugūd irrisīt.*	الاِسْترِْجاع خِلال ٣٠ يوْم بِشرْط وُجود الرّيسيت.
There are no returns, but you can exchange it within 14 days.	*ma-fīš istirgā3. múmkin tibáddil bassᵊ xilāl arba3tāšar yōm.*	مفيش اِسْترِْجاع. مُمْكِن تبِدِّل بسّ خِلال ١٤ يوْم.

At the Market — في السّوق

It goes without saying that أَسْواق *aswāʔ* **markets** are generally cheaper than shopping malls, and you can find local products and handicrafts that you won't find elsewhere. That said, some markets are popular with foreign tourists and tend to be more expensive. It is recommended to compare prices for the same item in a few different places to get a better idea of the going rate. بيّاعين *bayya3īn* **vendors/merchants** tend to quote high prices at first, and فِصال *fiṣāl* **haggling** is expected. But only start haggling if you're serious about buying the item in question if the price is right. If you make a counteroffer and the vendor agrees, it will not be well received if you then change your mind and walk away. Starting to walk away without making a counteroffer, on the other hand, is a popular strategy to elicit a lower price from the vendor. Of course, this doesn't always work, either. Another way to get a reasonable price is by buying several items from one vendor. Ask for a discount: طيِّب لَوْ هاخُد ده و ده، تِحْسِبْهُمْلي بِكام؟ *ṭáyyib law hāxud da wi da, tiḫsibhúmli b-kām?* **If I buy this, this, and this, how much?** or طب لَوْ هشْترِي خمْسة مِن دوْل، هَيِبْقوا بِكام؟ *haštíri xámsa min dōl, hayíbʔu b-kām?* **If I buy five of these, how much?** Haggling is an art form and takes practice. But it's also an excellent opportunity to practice your Arabic!

Buying a suitcase

○ لَوْ سمحْت كُنْت بدوّر على شُنط سفر[1] ٤ عجلات.

◇ فيه التّلات مقاسات دوْل و فيه قُماش و فيه بِلاسْتيك.

○ بِكام الصُّغيرّة البِلاسْتيك؟

◇ بِـ ٣٥٠ و وَزْنها خفيف و تِسْتحْمِل[2].

○ Excuse me, I was looking for a suitcase with four wheels.

◇ Here are the three sizes available, some of which are canvas while others are plastic.

○ How much is the small plastic one?

◇ 350 LE and it's light-weight and durable.

○ *law samáḥt, kuntᵊ badáwwar 3ála šúnaṭ sáfar*[1] *árba3 3agalāt.*

◇ *fī ittálat maʔasāt dōl wi fī ʔumāš wi fī bilástik.*

○ *bi-kām iṣṣuɣayyára -lbilástik?*

◇ *bi-tultumíyya w xamsīn wi waznáha xafīf wi tistáḥmil*[2].

[1] فيه شُنط سفر؟ *fī šúnaṭ sáfar?* **Do you have suitcases?**

[2] متين *matīn* **durable, strong, solid**

Carefully check the quality of the item you're considering purchasing. It may not be authentic or as valuable as the vendor would like you to think. In fact, some things are sold as if they are priceless when, in fact, they are worthless. Always be skeptical of a vendor's claims and remember: if it seems too good to be true, it probably is! مِنيْن تِعْرف الكِذْبة؟ مِن كُبْرْها. *minēn tí3raf ilkízba? min kubráha.* **How can you detect a lie? From its size.** (i.e. when it's too big to be believable)

2

Buying cloth

o مِن فضْلك، بِكام مِترْ القُماش مِن ده؟

◇ المِترْ عامِل ٧٥ جنيْه.

o طب، لَوْ عايْزة أعْمِل جيبة أجيب قدّ أيْه؟[1]

◇ هاتي مِترْ و نُصّ. هَيْفيض معاكي.[2]

o How much is a meter of this cloth?

◇ One meter is 75 LE.

o If I wanted to make a skirt, how much would I need?

◇ Get one and a half meters. That will be plenty for you.

o *min fáḏlak, bi-kām mitr ilʔumāš min da?*

◇ *ilmítrᵊ 3āmil xámsa w sab3īn ginēh.*

o *ṭab, law 3áyza á3mil žība, agīb ʔaddᵊ ʔē?*[1]

◇ *hāti mitrᵊ wi nuṣṣ. hayfīḏ ma3āki.*[2]

[1] = لَوْ هفصّل جيبة تِحْتاج قدّ أيْه؟ *law hafáṣṣal žība tiḥtāg ʔaddᵊ ʔē?*

[2] هَيْكفّي و زِيادة. *haykáffi w ziyāda.* **It'll be enough and then some.**

Markets can be a bit overwhelming. If you're still inexperienced with haggling, are not confident of your skills in Arabic, or need to make a large or important purchase, consider bringing an Egyptian friend along to help you get a fair price and avoid miscommunications.

Street markets are usually crowded and are a favorite hangout for نشّالين *naššalīn* **pickpockets**. They have clever ways to distract you while stealing your money. Wear a crossbody bag that you can keep in front of you (rather than a backpack or simple handbag) and always keep an eye on your belongings.

3

Haggling

o بِكامِ الصّينية دي و خامِتْها أيْه؟

◇ دي نِحاس يا سِتّ الكُلّ[1] و بِـ ٧٠٠ جِنيْهْ.

o لا أسْعارِك غالْيَة أوي.[2] أنا شُفْتها في محلّ تاني بِـ ٤٥٠، سلامِ عليْكم.

◇ طب، اِسْتنّي بسّ. ٥٠٠ يمِشي معاكي طيِّب؟[3]

o How much is this tray? And what is it made from?

◇ This is copper, miss. And it's 700 LE.

o No way! Your prices are too high. I've seen it in another shop for 450 LE. Goodbye!

◇ All right, hold on! How about if you take it for 500 LE?

o *bi-kām iṣṣiníyya di wi xamítha ʔē?*

◇ *di nħās ya sitt ikkúll*[1], *wi b-sub3umíyya ginēh.*

o *laʔ, as3ārak ɣálya áwi.*[2] *ána šuftáha fi maħáll*^{ə} *tāni b-rub3umíyya w xamsīn, salām 3alēkam.*

◇ *ṭab, istánni bass. xumsumíyya yímši ma3āki ṭáyyib?*[3]

[1] سِتّ الكُلّ *sitt ikkúll* (lit. lady of all) is a flattering form of address. A more common alternative is simply يافنْدِم *yafándim.*

[2] لا كِتير أَوي عليْها. *laʔ, kitīr áwi 3alēha.* **Oh no, that's too much for this.**

[3] هدّيهالِك بِـ ٥٠٠ طيِّب؟ *haddihālik bi-xumsumíyya, ṭáyyib?* **I'll give it to you for 500 (LE), okay?;** خُديها بِـ ٥٠٠، قُلْتي أيْه؟ *xudīha b-xumsumíyya, ʔúlti ʔē?* **Take it for 500. What do you say?**

See also the dialogue on p. 225 for more ways to deal with a market vendor who is trying to overcharge you.

4

Haggling

○ بسّ دي سِعْرها عالي أَوي.[1] آخِرْها كام طيِّب؟[2]

◇ عشان خاطْرِك[3] والله هدّيهالِك بِـ ٧ جِنيْهْ الواحْدة.

○ خلاص، هاخُد سبْعة بِـ ٥٠ جِنيْهْ.

◇ ماشي مبْروك عليْكي. تِحِبّي الِفُّهُمْلِك؟[4]

○ آه لِفّهالي لفّة حِلْوَة كِده.

○ But this is really expensive. What's the least I get it for?

◇ Just for you, I will give you it to you for 7 LE a piece.

○ Okay, I'll take 7 for 50 LE then.

◇ Okay, congratulations! Would you like me to wrap them for you?

○ Yes, wrap them up nicely for me.

○ *bassᵊ di si3ráha 3āli áwi.*[1] *axírha kām ṭáyyib?*[2]

◇ *3ašān xáṭrik*[3] *wallāhi haddihālik bi-sáb3a gnēh ilwáħda.*

○ *xalāṣ, hāxud sáb3a bi-xamasīn ginēh.*

◇ *māši mabrūk 3alēki. tiħíbbi aliffuhúmlik?*[4]

○ *āh, liffahāli láffa ħílwa kída.*

[1] = بسّ دي غالْيَة أوْفر. *bassᵊ di ɣálya ōvar.*

[2] آخِر كلام فيها كام؟ *āxir kalām fīha kām?* = بِكام آخِر كلام؟ *bi-kām āxir kalam?* **What's your final price?**

[3] = عشانِك إنْتي بسّ *3ašānik ínti bass*

[4] = عايْزة تِلفّيهُم؟ *3áyza tliffīhum?*

When you start haggling, some sellers will say خلّي عنّك خالِص *xálli 3ánnak xāliṣ* **Just take it for free then.** They are trying to embarrass you to stop you from haggling, but go ahead and continue the فِصال *fiṣāl* **haggling.**

5

Turning Down a Salesperson

◇ اِتْفضّل معانا شوف الميدالْيات و التُّحف.

o شُكْراً مِش عايِز.

◇ طب، خُد فِكْرة عن أسْعاري. مِش هتْلاقي زيّها.

o مِش عايِز أشْترِي أساساً[1] ، مُتْشكِّر.

◇ Come on and have a look at the antiques and medals we've got.

o Thank you, I don't want any.

◇ Just take a look. At prices like these, you won't find any [anywhere else].

o I don't want to buy anything anyway. Thanks!

◇ *itfáḍḍal ma3āna šūf ilmidalyāt wi -ttúḫaf.*

o *šúkran miš 3āyiz.*

◇ *ṭab, xud fíkra 3an as3āri. miš hatlāʔi zayyáha.*

o *miš 3āyiz aštíri asāsan*[1]*, mutšákkir.*

[1] = مِش جايّ أشْترِي *miš gayy aštíri*; هبْقى أجيلك مخْصوص بعْديْن. *hábʔa -gīlak maxṣūṣ ba3dēn.* **I'll come back [to take a look] later.**

When you start looking at merchandise, and the prices are higher than you expected, and you want to leave the shop but the seller is trying to persuade you to buy something, you can just say طيِّب هلِفّ لفّة و أرْجعْلك. *ṭáyyib halíff láffa w argá3lak.* **I'll just take a look around and come back later.**

See also the dialogue on p. 224 for more ways to be firm with a persistent and annoying market or street vendor.

When buying edible products, always check the expiration date or try out a sample first to make sure it is fresh. Also, keep in mind what may or may not be allowed through customs if you are bringing something back to your home country.

6

Paying

o طيِّب، كِده الحِساب كُلُّه كام؟
◇ كِده كُلُّه هَيِعْمِل ٧٥ جِنيْه.
o طيِّب، معاك بقيةْ مية؟
◇ معاك ٥ طيِّب و أدّيك ٣٠؟
o خلاص، شيل الخمْسة دي يا سيدي[1].
◇ ماشي[2] يا باشا، كُلّ سنة و إنْتَ طيِّب[3].

o Okay, so how much do I owe you?
◇ Altogether, that will be 75 LE.
o Do you have change for 100 LE?
◇ Well, do you have 5 LE and I'll give you 30 LE?
o Come on, just waive the 5, bro!
◇ Okay, boss. Enjoy!

o *ṭáyyib, kída -lḫisāb kúllu kām?*
◇ *kída kúllu hayí3mil xámsa w sab3īn ginēh.*
o *ṭáyyib, ma3āk baʔīt míyya?*
◇ *ma3āk xámsa ṭáyyib w addīk talatīn?*
o *xalāṣ, šīl ilxámsa di ya sīdi*[1].
◇ *māši*[2] *ya bāša, kullᵊ sána w ínta ṭáyyib*[3].

[1] يا سيدي *ya sīdi* literally means 'my master,' but in everyday speech, it's used as a friendly form of address for men, as is يا عمّ *ya 3amm*. For women, it's يا سِتّي *ya sítti* (lit. my lady).

[2] اللي إنْتَ عايْزُه *ill- ínta 3áyzu* **as you wish**

[3] كُلّ سنة و إنْتَ طيِّب *kullᵊ sána w ínta ṭáyyib* is a common set expression used in several contexts. It literally means 'may you be well every year' and is used for various annual occasions to say 'happy birthday', 'happy holiday', 'happy feast', 'merry Christmas', etc. It can also be used by service people to hint for a tip. Here, it's just used as a closure to the conversation.

○ عايْزة أجيب هِدية حِلْوَة كِده لِمامْتي مِن مصْر.

◇ فيه عنْدي حاجات كِتير: شباشِب جِلْد و مشْغولات و خُداديّات.

○ بُصّ هِيَّ بِتْحِبّ أوي[1] مشْغولات القُماش فا كُنْت بدوّر على حاجة حِلْوَة تِتْعلّق على الحيْطة.

◇ طب، أيْه رأيِك في دي؟

○ دي قِصّة دي وَلّا أيْه؟[2]

◇ آه قِصِّةْ جُحا و الحُمار مِتْطرّزة بِالقُماش عليْها.

○ ألْوانْها حِلْوَة أوي بسّ أيْه القِصّة دي؟[3]

◇ دي قِصّة مِ التُّراث الشّعْبي عن اللي يِمْشي وَرا كلام النّاس.[4]

○ آه افْتكرْتها. طب حِلْو أوي. دي هتِعْجِبْها خالِص. بسّ فيه ألْوان تانْيَة؟[5]

◇ فيه اللي خلْفيتْها كِتّان و فيه خلْفيتْها قُماش عادي ألْوان.

○ لا الكِّتّان أحْلى[6]. سِعْرها كام طيِّب؟[7]

◇ الكِّتّان بِـ ٤٠٠ و القُماش العادي بِـ ٣٥٠.

○ طب، بُصّ بقى، أنا هاخُد اِتْنيْن كِتّان بِـ ٧٠٠.

◇ صدّقيني، مِش هتْظبْط[8].

○ أنا في كُلّ أجازة مُمْكِن أجيلك تاني و هقول لِصُحابي عليْك[9] فا ظبّطْني في السِّعْر بقى.

◇ هدّيكي الاِتْنين بِـ ٧٥٠ و دي بِجدّ آخِرْها.

○ تمام خلاص، لِفُّهْلي لفّة حِلْوَة.

◇ مِن عينيّا.

[6] أشْيَك *ášyak* **more chic** (from شيك *šīk* **chic, stylish**)

[7] هتِدّيهالي بِكام؟ *hatiddihāli bi-kām?* **How much will you give it to me for?**

[8] = مِش هَيِنْفع *miš hayínfa3*; هتُقف عليّا بِخِسارة. *hatúʔaf 3aláyya bi-xsāra.* **It will be at a loss for me.**

[9] = هعْمِلّك دعايا عنْد أصْحابي *ha3míllik da3āya 3and aṣħābi.*

Vocabulary

market	*sūʔ (aswāʔ)*	سوق (أسْواق)
price	*si3r (as3ār)*	سِعْر (أسْعار)
haggling	*fiṣāl*	فِصال
wrapping	*láffa*	لفّة
plastic bag	*kīs*	كيس
fabric, cloth	*ʔumāš*	قُماش
cotton	*ʔuṭn*	قُطْن
wool	*ṣūf*	صوف
synthetic, polyester	*ṣinā3i*	صِناعي
linen	*kittān*	كِتّان
silk	*ħarīr*	حرير
dress	*fustān*	فُسْتان
galabeya (a long, loose traditional garment)	*gallabiya (galalīb)*	جلّابية (جلاليب)
fez	*ṭarbūš*	طرْبوش
flip-flops	*šíbšib (šabāšib)*	شِبْشِب (شباشِب)

headscarf	*ṭárḫa*	طرْحة
scarf	*skarf*	سْكارْف
shawl	*šāl*	شال
(natural) leather	*gildᵊ (ṭabī3i)*	جِلْد (طبيعي)
decorative object, nick-nack; antique	*túḫfa (túḫaf)*	تُحْفة (تُحف)
marble	*ruxām*	رُخام
carnelian, agate stone	*3aqīq*	عقيق
pearl	*lūli*	لولي
copper	*naḫās*	نحاس
silver	*fáḍḍa*	فضّة
gold	*dáhab*	دهب
tray	*ṣiníyya*	صينية
medal, keychain	*midálya*	ميدالْيَة
glass, cup	*kubbāya*	كُبّايَة
plate	*ṭábaʔ*	طبق
cushion	*xudadíyya*	خُدادية
beads	*xáraz*	خرز
thread	*xēṭ*	خيْط
doll	*3arūsa*	عروسة
camel	*gámal*	جمل
pyramid	*háram*	هرم

lantern	*fanūs*	فانوس
hibiscus	*karkadēh*	كرْكديْه
alum (stone/powder)	*šábba*	شبّة
loofah	*līfa*	ليفة
Aleppo Soap (a kind of natural soap)	*ṣabūn ḥálabi*	صابون حلبي
ambergris (a natural perfume substance)	*3ánbar*	عنْبر
musk	*misk*	مِسْك
papyrus	*bárdi*	برْدي
dried molokheyya	*muluxíyya nášfa*	مُلوخية ناشْفة
mint	*ni3nā3*	نِعْناع
edible seeds (sunflower, pumpkin, etc.)	*libb*	لِبّ
olive oil	*zēt zatūn*	زيْت زتون
date syrup	*dibs tamr*	دِبْس تمْر

Expressions

	○	
What is this, please?	*ʔē da min fáḍlak?*	أيْه ده مِن فضْلك؟
How much is this?	*bi-kām da?*	بِكام ده؟
Was this made in China or is it Egyptian?	*di maṣnū3a fi -ṣṣīn wálla máṣri?*	دي مصْنوعة في الصّين وَلّا مصْري؟

Please, tell me the total of these separately from those.	*buṣṣ íḫsib dōl li-waḫdúhum wi dōl li-waḫdúhum.*	بُصّ اِحْسِب دوْل لِوَحْدُهُم و دوْل لِوَحْدُهُم.
Well, if I buy 10, how much will it cost me?	*ṭáyyib, law xadtᵊ 3ášara hatḫasíbni 3ála kām?*	طيِّب، لَوْ خدْت عشرة هتْحاسِبْني على كام؟
(haggling) Make me a good discount in the total then.	*wággib ma3āya báʔa fi -lḫisāb.*	وَجِّب معايا بقى في الحِساب.
Weigh out three separate half-kilos of mountain mint for me.	*iwzínli tálat inṣāṣ ni3nā3 gábali.*	اِوْزِنْلي ٣ اِنْصاص نِعْناع جبلي.
Cut two meters of this cloth for me, please.	*iʔṭá3li mitrēn mi -lʔumāš da law samáḫt.*	اِقْطعْلي مِترْيْن مِ القُماش ده لَوْ سمحْت.
Can you please wrap each separately?	*min fáḍlak, múmkin tiliffíli kullᵊ wáḫda li-waḫdáha.*	مِن فضْلك، مُمْكِن تِلِفِّلي كُلّ واحْدة لِوَحْدها.
(looking for a stall's vendor) Is there anyone here?	*ma-fīš ḫaddᵊ wāʔif hína?*	مفيش حدّ واقِف هِنا؟

◇

This type of cloth's width is one-sided [not double-sided] and one meter costs 120 LE.	*ilʔumāš da 3arḍᵊ wāḫid wi -lmítrᵊ bi-míyya w 3išrīn.*	القُماش ده عرْض واحِد و المِترْ بِـ١٢٠.

No haggling. That's the final price.	*ma-fīš fiṣāl. da áxir si3r.* *ilfiṣāl mamnū3. issí3rᵊ nhāʔi.*	مفيش فِصال، ده آخِر سِعْر. الفِصال ممْنوع، السِّعْر نِهائي.
(in response to haggling) I won't be earning anything off that.	*kída miš hatgīb máksab, ṣaddaʔīni.*	كِده مِش هتْجيب مكْسب، صدّقيني.
(neighboring vendor:) Just wait a second and the merchant there will be back.	*sawāni hayīgi -lli wāʔif hína.*	ثَواني هَييجي اللي واقِف هِنا.

At a Hotel في الفُنْدُق

Unless you already have a حجْز *ħagz* **reservation** at a فُنْدُق *fúndu?* **hotel**, you'll have to ask if there are any أُوَض مُتاحة *úwaḍ mutāħa* **vacancies** at the رِسِبْشِن *risíbšin* **front desk**. You'll have better luck finding something—and maybe even negotiating a discount—during the low season, which is the summer for most of Egypt, when the oppressive heat keeps more tourists away. However, summer is the high season for the Mediterranean coast, when school is out, and Egyptians head for the seaside resorts between إِسْكِنْدِرِية *iskindiríyya* **Alexandria** and مرْسى مطْروح *mársa maṭrūħ* **Marsa Matruh**. Hotel staff does expect بقْشيش *ba?šīš* **tips**. Be sure to tip a porter who brings up your luggage, your waiter or waitress, as well as for room service, and housekeeping.

Asking about Vacancy

- ○ مِن فضْلك، أنا لِسّه واصِل مِن المطار و كُنْت عايِز أعْرف لَوْ فيه أُوَض فاضْيَة[1]؟[2]
- ◇ حمْدِ الله على سلامْتك[3] يافنْدِم. ثَواني أشوف لِحضْرِتك.
- ○ يا ريْت، أنا مِحْتاج بسّ ليلْتينْ لِحدّ ما أظبّط أُموري.
- ◇ تمام يافنْدِم، فيه أوْضة مُتَوَفِّرة بـ٥٠٠ جِنيْه في اللّيْلة فِطار بسّ.
- ○ مفيش مُشْكِلة.[4] اِحْجِزْهالي ليلْتينْ مِن فضْلك.

- ○ Excuse me, I just arrived from the airport, and I was wondering if there are any rooms available?
- ◇ Welcome, sir! Just a moment. I'll take a look for you.
- ○ Yes, please. I only need two nights, until I get everything settled.
- ◇ Okay, sir, there is a room available for 500 LE a night and includes breakfast only.
- ○ No problem. Book me it for two nights, please.

- ○ *min fáḍlak, ána líssa wāṣil min ilmaṭār wi kuntᵊ 3āyiz á3raf law fī úwaḍ fáḍya[1]?[2]*
- ◇ *ḫamdílla 3ála salámtak[3] yafándim. sawāni ašūf li-ḫaḍrítak.*
- ○ *ya rēt, ána miḫtāg bassᵊ liltēn li-ḫáddᵊ ma -ẓábbaṭ umūri.*
- ◇ *tamām, yafándim, fī ōḍa mutawaffíra b-xumsumīt ginēh fi -llēla, fiṭār bass.*
- ○ *ma-fīš muškíla.[4] iḫgizhāli liltēn min fáḍlak.*

[1] فاضْيَة *fáḍya* = مُتاحة *mutāḫa*

[2] يا ترى عنْدُكُم أماكِن مُتَوَفِّرة؟ *yatára 3andúkum amākin mutawáffira?* **Do you happen to have any vacancies?**

[3] حمْدِ الله على سلامْتك *ḫamdílla 3ála salámtak* and حمْدِ الله عَ السّلامة *ḫamdílla 3a -ssalāma* **Thank God you arrived safely!** is a formulaic greeting to someone who has arrived from a long trip.

[4] = مَيِجْراش حاجة *ma-yigrāš ḫāga*

2

Checking in

○ لَوْ سمحْتي، كُنْت حاجِز غُرْفة بِإِسْمِ يوسُف أبو المجْد.

◇ ثَواني أتْأكِّد لِحضْرِتك... آه مظْبوط، حضْرِتك كُنْت حاجِز أوْضة سينْجِل فِطار و عشا.

○ بِالظّبْط[1] كِده و كُنْت حاجِزْها بِبلكوْنة، مِن فضْلِك.

◇ مظْبوط. طيِّب، حضْرِتك تِحِبّ أوْضة بِتْطُلّ[2] على البحْر وَلّا الميدان؟

○ لا ياريْت البلكوْنة تِكون بِتْطُلّ على البحْر، مِن فضْلِك.

◇ تمام يافنْدِم، أسْتأْذِن حضْرِتك في الباسْبوْر[3] و الكْريْدِت كارْد.

○ Excuse me, I have a room booked under the name Yusuf Abou-l Magd.

◇ Just a moment. I'll double check... Yes, that's correct. You've booked a single room with half board.

○ Exactly. And I booked one with a balcony, please.

◇ Correct. All right, would you prefer the room overlook the sea or the square?

○ I'd rather have the balcony overlook the sea, please.

◇ All right, sir. Could I have your passport and credit card, please?

○ *law samáḫti, kuntᵊ ḫāgiz ɣúrfa bi-smᵊ yūsuf ábu -lmagd.*

◇ *sawāni atʔákkid li-ḫaḍrítak... āh, maẓbūṭ, ḫaḍrítak kuntᵊ ḫāgiz ōḍa síngil fiṭār wi 3áša.*

○ *bi-ẓẓábṭᵊ*[1] *kída wi kuntᵊ ḫagízha b-balakōna, min fáḍlik.*

◇ *maẓbūṭ. ṭáyyib, ḫaḍrítak tiḫíbbᵊ ōḍa bitṭúllᵊ*[2] *3ála -lbaḫrᵊ wálla -lmidān?*

○ *laʔ, yarēt ilbalakōna tkūn bitṭúllᵊ 3ála -lbaḫr, min fáḍlik.*

◇ *tamām, yafándim, astáʔzin ḫaḍrítak fi -lpaspōr*[3] *wi -lkrēdit kard.*

[1] مظْبوط *maẓbūṭ* / [2] بِتْبُصّ *bitbúṣṣ* / [3] مُمْكِن الباسْبوْر؟ *múmkin ilpaspōr?* **Can I have your passport?**

3

ARRIVING IN YOUR ROOM

○ مُمْكِن تِحُطِّلي الشُّنط جمْب الدّولاب؟[1]

◇ تحْت أمْرك يافنْدِم... الشُّنط جمْب الدّولاب. اِتْفضّل مُفْتاح الأوْضة.

○ تمام مُتْشكِّر جِدّاً... مُمْكِن بسّ تِقوليّ رقم الرِّسِبْشِن كام؟

◇ حضْرِتك دوس صِفْر[2] هتِتْحوِّل لِلرِّسِبْشِن و هُمّا هَيرُدّوا عليْك لَوْ حضْرِتك اِحْتاجْت[3] أيّ حاجة.

○ Could you put the luggage next to the wardrobe?

◇ Yes, sir... The luggage is beside the wardrobe. Here's the room key.

○ Okay, thank you very much. Would you please tell me the number for the front desk?

◇ You press zero and you'll be connected to front desk. They will respond to you if you need anything.

○ *múmkin tiḫuṭṭíli -ššúánaṭ gamb iddulāb?*[1]

◇ *taḫtᵊ ámrak yafándim... iššúánaṭ gamb iddulāb. itfáḍḍal muftāḫ ilʔōḍa.*

○ *tamām, mutšákkir gíddan... múmkin bassᵊ tʔúlli ráqam irrisíbšin kām?*

◇ *ḫaḍrítak dūs ṣifr*[2]*, hatitḫáwwil li-rrisíbšin wi húmma hayrúddu 3alēk law ḫaḍrítak iḫtágt*[3] *ayyᵊ ḫāga.*

[1] مِن فضْلك، حُطّ الشُّنط جمْب الدّولاب. *min fáḍlak, ḫuṭṭ iššúnaṭ gambᵊ -ddulāb.*
Please, put the suitcases by the wardrobe.

[2] = اِضْغط صِفْر *íḍɣaṭ ṣifr* = اِتّصِل بِصِفْر *ittíṣil bi-ṣifr*

[3] = عُزْت *3uzt*

Unmarried couples can share the same room as long as both have Western passports. However, it is strictly illegal for an Egyptian to stay in the same room with someone of the opposite sex unless a marriage certificate is presented (or unless they are close relatives).

Calling the Front Desk

○ لَوْ سمحْتي، كُنْت عايِز بشْكير عشان البحْر و مفيش في الحمّام.

◇ البشاكير بِتْكون على الشّاطِئ[1] يافنْدِم. بِتِقْدر تاخُد واحِد بِنفْس كارْت الأوْضة.

○ آها... طيِّب، معلِشّ مُمْكِن برْضُه بشْكير زِيادة في الأوْضة عنْدي؟

◇ تحْت أمْرك يافنْدِم. خمس دقايِق بِالظّبْط و هَيْكون عنْدك.

○ تمام مُتْشكِّر جِدّاً و ياريْت تِحَوِّليني[2] بِأوْضة رقم ١٥.

○ I'd like a towel for the beach, please, but there aren't any in the bathroom.

◇ Towels can be found at the beach. You can take one using the same room card.

○ Aha... okay. I need an extra one in my room, please.

◇ Yes, sir. You'll have one in just five minutes.

○ All right, thanks a lot. Also, please, connect me to room 15.

○ *law samáђti, kuntᵊ 3āyiz baškīr 3ašān ilbáђr, wi ma-fīš fi -lђammām.*

◇ *ilbašakīr bitkūn 3ála -ššāṭiʔ*[1] *yafándim. bitíʔdar tāxud wāђid bi-náfsᵊ kart ilʔōḍa.*

○ *ahā... ṭáyyib, ma3alíšš, múmkin bárḍu baškīr ziyāda fi -lʔōḍa 3ándi?*

◇ *taђtᵊ ámrak yafándim. xámas daʔāyiʔ bi-ẓẓábṭ, wi haykūn 3ándak.*

○ *tamām, mutšákkir gíddan wi yarēt tiђawwlīni*[2] *b-ōḍa ráqam xamastāšar.*

[1] = بِلاج *bilāž*

[2] = تِوَصّليني بِـ *tiwaSSalīni bi-*; معلِشّ حَوِّليني لِـ... *ma3alíšš ђawwilīni li-...* **please, connect me to...**

5

ASKING TO CHANGE ROOMS

o مِن فضْلك، كُنْت عايْزة أغيرّ[1] الأوْضة بِتاعْتي.[2]

◇ أكيد يافنْدِم، بسّ أقْدر أعْرف أيْه السّبب؟

o المفْروض الأوْضة على البحْر بسّ مِش شايْفة حاجة مِ المباني.

◇ تمام يافنْدِم، مُمْكِن نِنْقِل حضْرِتِك لِأوْضة في دوْر أعْلى.

o يا ريْت فِعْلاً، مُتْشكِّرة جِدّاً.

o I'd like to change rooms, please.

◇ Certainly, miss. May I know the reason?

o It's supposed to be a room overlooking the sea, but I cannot see anything because of the buildings.

◇ Okay, miss. We can move you to a room on an upper floor.

o Yes, please. Thanks so much!

o *min fáḍlak, kuntᵊ 3áyza -ɣáyyar ilʔōḍa bitá3ti.*[1]

◇ *akīd yafándim, bassᵊ áʔdar á3raf ʔē issábab?*

o *ilmafrūḍ ilʔōḍa 3ála -lbaħr, bassᵊ miš šāyfa ħāga mi -lmabāni.*

◇ *tamām, yafándim, múmkin nínʔil ħaḍrítik li-ōḍa f dōr á3la.*

o *ya rēt fí3lan, mutšakkíra gíddan.*

[1] = أبدِّل *abáddil*

[2] كُنْت عايْزة أنْقِل أوْضة تانْية. *kuntᵊ 3áyz- ánʔil ōḍa tánya.* **I'd like to move to another room.**

Hotels' quoted room rates often don't include taxes and service charges, which, all together, can add as much as 25% to the bill.

Asking about breakfast

o مُمْكِن أعْرف مَواعيد الفِطار؟[1]

◇ الفِطار في المطْعم مِن ٨ لِـ ١٠ الصُّبْح، أوْبِن بوفيْه[2].

o طيِّب، هل فيه اِمْكانية إنُّه يِجيلي في الأوْضة؟[3]

◇ مفيش مُشْكِلة يافنْدِم، بسّ بلّغْنا[4] قبْلها بِنُصّ ساعة بِالظّبْط.

o Can I find out the times for breakfast?

◇ Breakfast is in the restaurant from 8 until 10 a.m. It's an open buffet.

o All right. Is it possible to have it delivered to my room?

◇ No problem, sir. Just notify us 30 minutes in advance.

o *múmkin á3raf mawa3īd ilfiṭār?*[1]

◇ *ilfiṭār fi -lmáṭ3am min tamánya l-3ášara -ṣṣúbḫ,* [open buffet][2].

o *ṭáyyib, hal fī imkaníyya ínnu ygīli fi -lʔōḍa?*[3]

◇ *ma-fīš muškíla yafándim, bass*^{ə} *balláɣna*[4] *ʔabláha binúṣṣ*^{ə} *sā3a bi-ẓẓábṭ.*

[1] الفطار مَواعيدُه أيْه؟ *ilfiṭār mawa3īdu ʔē?*, الفِطار إمْتى؟ *ilfiṭār ímta?*, الفِطار مِن (السّاعة) كام لِكام؟ *ilfiṭār min (issā3a) kām li-kām?* **When is breakfast (available)?**

[2] = بوفيْه مفْتوح *būfēh maftūḫ*

[3] مُمْكِن ييجيلي الأوْضة؟ *múmkin yigīli -lʔōḍa?* **Can it be brought up to my room for me?**

[4] = قولِّنا *ʔullína*

Extended Dialogue

- ○ مِن فضْلِك، كُنْت عايِز أحْجِز أوْضة سينْجِل لِمُدّةْ ٣ لَيالي.
- ◇ هِل فيه حجْز سابِق بِإسْمِ حضْرِتك؟[1]
- ○ لِلأسف. أنا حجزْت أوْنْلايْن[2] بسّ فيه مُشْكِلة. مِش عارِف حجز فِعْلاً وَلّا لأ.
- ◇ طيِّب، خلّيني أتْأكِّد لِحضْرِتك. مُمْكِن الباسْبوْر؟
- ○ اِتْفضّلي. كُنْت حاجِز مِن حَوالي أُسْبوعيْن[3]، بسّ دخلْت النّهارْده على الموْقع ملقتْش أيّ تفاصيل.
- ◇ هُوَّ لِلأسف الحجْز متْأكِّدْش، بسّ خلّيني أشوف لِحضْرِتك لَوْ فيه أوْضة بِنفْس المُواصفات مُتَوَفِّرة.
- ○ يا ريْت ضروري فِعْلاً. أنا مِحْتاجْها ضروري، ٣ لَيالي بسّ.
- ◇ طيِّب، هُوَّ فيه أوْضة مُتَوَفِّرة، بسّ مِش بِتْطُلّ مُباشرة على النّيل.
- ○ طيِّب، فيها بلكوْنة؟
- ◇ هِيَّ الأوْضة جانِبية و فيها بلكوْنة بسّ بِتْطُلّ على الميدان و جُزْء مِن النّيل.
- ○ تمام، مفيش مُشْكِلة. اِحْجِزيهالي، مِن فضْلِك.
- ◇ تمام، اِتْفضّل حضْرِتك المُفْتاح و اِنْتِظِر[4] الشُّنط فوْق.
- ○ طيِّب... معلِشّ كُنْت مِحْتاج خريطة لِلْمدينة أقْدر اتْحرّك بيها، لَوْ يِنْفع[5].
- ◇ أكيد يافنْدِم. اِتْفضّل. دي خريطة فيها أهمّ المعالِم و خُطوط المُواصْلات.
- ○ طيِّب، رقم السِّويتْش[6] كام مِن فضْلِك؟
- ◇ لَوْ حضْرِتك اِحْتاجْت أيّ حاجة مُمْكِن تِتّصِل بِرقم الرِّسِبْشِن •• (صِفْريْن).

o طيِّب، و باسْوورْد الإنْترْنِت[7] معلِشّ؟

◇ حضْرِتك هتْلاقيه مكْتوب جمْب التِّليفوْن في الأوْضة.

o تمام شُكْراً جزيلاً.

◇ العفْو يافنْدِم و حمْدِ الله عَ السّلامة.

o I need to book a single room for three nights, please.

◇ Did you book in advance under your name?

o Unfortunately, I made the reservation online, but there was some problem and I'm not sure if it really got booked or not.

◇ Okay, let me check for you. Could I have your passport?

o Here you are. I booked it about two weeks ago, but today I checked the website and couldn't find any details.

◇ Unfortunately, the reservation was not confirmed, but let me check for you if there are any available rooms with the same preferences.

o Yes, please, it's urgent. I need it urgently just for three nights.

◇ All right, there is a room available, but it doesn't overlook the Nile directly.

o Is there a balcony?

◇ It's a side room with a balcony overlooking the square and a part of the Nile.

o Okay, no problem. Book it for me, please.

◇ Okay, here are the keys, and wait for the luggage upstairs.

o All right. And I needed a city map for getting around, if possible.

◇ Certainly, sir. Here's a map with the important sights and transportation lines.

o Okay. And what is the number for the front desk, please?

◇ If you need anything, just dial 00 for the reception.

- Okay, and how about the wifi password?
- ◇ You will find it written down next to the telephone in your room.
- All right, thanks a lot!
- ◇ You're welcome, sir. Have a pleasant stay!

- *min fáḍlik, kuntᵊ 3āyiz áɧgiz ōḍa síngil li-múddit tálat layāli.*
- ◇ *hal fī ɧagzᵊ sābiʔ bi-ʔísmᵊ ɧaḍrítak?*[1]
- *li-lʔásaf. ána ɧagázt ōnlāyn*[2]*, bassᵊ fī muškíla. miš 3ārif ɧágaz fí3lan wálla laʔ.*
- ◇ *ţáyyib, xallīni atʔákkid li-ɧaḍrítak. múmkin ilpaspōr?*
- *itfaḍḍáli. kuntᵊ ɧāgiz min ɧawāli usbu3ēn*[3]*, bassᵊ daxált innahárda 3ála -lmáwqi3, ma-laʔítš ayyᵊ tafaşīl.*
- ◇ *húwwa li-lʔásaf ilɧágzᵊ ma-tʔakkídš, bassᵊ xallīni ašūf li-ɧaḍrítak law fī ōḍa bi-náfs ilmuwaşafāt mutawaffíra.*
- *ya rēt ḍarūri fí3lan. ána miɧtágha ḍarūri, tálat layāli bass.*
- ◇ *ţáyyib, húwwa fī ōḍa mutawaffíra, bassᵊ miš bitţúllᵊ mubašáratan 3ála -nnīl.*
- *ţáyyib, fīha balakōna?*
- ◇ *híyya -lʔōḍa ganibíyya wi fīha balakōna, bassᵊ bitţúllᵊ 3ála -lmidān wi guzʔᵊ mn innīl.*
- *tamām, ma-fīš muškíla. iɧgizihāli, min fáḍlik.*
- ◇ *tamām, itfáḍḍal ɧaḍrítak ilmuftāɧ wi -nţíẓir*[4] *iššúnaţ fōʔ.*
- *ţáyyib... ma3alíššᵊ kuntᵊ miɧtāg xarīţa li-lmadīna áʔdar atɧárrak bīha, law yínfa3*[5]*.*
- ◇ *akīd yafándim. itfáḍḍal. di xarīţa fīha ahámm ilma3ālim wi xuţūţ ilmuwaşlāt.*
- *ţáyyib, ráqam issiwítšᵊ*[6] *kām min fáḍlik?*
- ◇ *law ɧaḍrítak iɧtágt ayyᵊ ɧāga múmkin tittíşil bi-ráqam irrisíbšin şifrēn.*
- *ţáyyib, wi páswurd ilʔíntarnat*[7] *ma3alíšš?*
- ◇ *ɧaḍrítak hatlaʔī maktūb gamb ittilifōn fi -lʔōḍa.*
- *tamām, šúkran gazīlan.*
- ◇ *il3áfwᵊ yafándim wi ɧamdílla 3a -ssalāma.*

[1] حضْرِتك حاجِز قبْل كِده؟ *ɧaḍrítak ɧāgiz ʔablᵊ kída?* **Have you made a reservation?**

[2] على الإنْترْنت *3ála -lʔíntarnat* **on the internet**, على المَوْقع *3ála -lmáwqi3* **on the website**

[3] = تقْريباً مِن أُسْبوعين *taʔrīban min usbu3ēn*

[4] = اِسْتنّى *istánna*

[5] = لَوْ مُمْكِن *law múmkin*

[6] (lit. switchboard)

[7] = باسْوورْد الوايْفاي *páswurd ilwāyfay* **the wifi password**

Vocabulary

hotel	*fúnduʔ (fanādiʔ)*	فُنْدُق (فنادِق)
lobby	*lōbi*	لوْبي
front desk, reception	*risíbšin* *istiʔbāl*	رِسِبْشِن اِسْتِقْبال
reservation, booking	*ɦagz*	حجْز
confirmation	*taʔkīd ɦagz*	تأْكيد حجْز
credit card	*krēdit kard*	كْريْدِت كارْد
cash	*kāš*	كاش
room key	*muftāɦ ilʔōḍa*	مُفْتاح الأوْضة
room card	*kart ilʔōḍa*	كارْت الأوْضة
single room	*ōḍa síngil*	أوْضة سينْجِل
double room	*ōḍa dābil*	أوْضة دابِل
suite	*swīt*	سْويت
half board, with breakfast and dinner	*fiṭār wi 3áša*	فِطار و عشا
full board, with three meals a day	*fiṭār wi ɣáda wi 3áša, fūl bōrd*	فِطار و غدا و عشا

		فول بوْرْد
balcony	*balakōna*	بلكوْنة
a room facing the sea/Nile	*ōḑa baɧríyya*	أوْضة بحْرية
a room with a partial view	*ōḑa ganibíyya*	أوْضة جانِبية
bathroom	*ɧammām*	حمّام
room with a private bathroom	*ōḑa bi-ɧammām*	أوْضة بِحمّام
common/ shared bathroom	*ɧammām muštárak*	حمّام مُشْترك
shower	*dušš*	دُشّ
bath towel	*fōţa (fúwaţ)*	فوطة (فُوَط)
shampoo	*šámbu*	شامْبو
hair dryer	*sišwār*	سِشْوار
swimming pool	*ɧammām sibāɧa*	حمّام سِباحة
beach	*bilāž* *šāţiʔ*	بِلاج شاطِئ
beach towel	*baškīr (bašakīr)*	بشْكير (بشاكير)
sauna	*sáwna*	ساوْنا
gym	*žīm*	جيم
massage	*masāž*	مساج
iron	*mákwa*	مكْوَة
dry cleaning	*drāy klīn*	دْراي كْلين
beverages	*mašrubāt*	مشْروبات
internet	*íntarnat*	إنْترِنْت

tissues	*manadīl*	مناديل
safe, lock box	*xázna*	خزْنة
bed	*sirīr (sarāyir)*	سِرير (سرايِر)
pillow	*mixádda*	مِخدّة
covers, bedspread	*kuvírta*	كوفِرْتة
blanket	*baṭṭaníyya*	بطّانية
transportation map	*xarīṭit ilmuwaṣlāt*	خريطِةْ المُواصْلات
subway map	*xarīṭit ilmítru*	خريطِةْ المِترْو
city map	*xarīṭit ilmadīna*	خريطِةْ المدينة
emergency numbers	*arqām iṭṭawāriʔ*	أرْقام الطَّوارِئ

Expressions

	○	
I need an iron.	*miḫtāg mákwa.*	مِحْتاج مكْوَة.
I want to get this suit ironed.	*kuntᵊ 3āyiz ákwi -ṭṭaʔmᵊ da.*	كُنْت عايِز أكْوي الطّقْم ده.
Is there a hairdryer in the room?	*fī siśwār fi -lʔōḍa?*	فيه سِشْوار في الأوْضة؟
I want to know the gym location and schedule.	*kuntᵊ 3āyiz á3raf makān ižžīmm wi mawa3īdu.*	كُنْت عايِز أعْرف مكان الجّيمّ و مَواعيدُه.

I want to have these laundered/dry-cleaned.	*3āyiz áb3at ilhudūm di li-lmaɣsála /li-ddrāy klīn.*	عايِز أبْعت الهُدوم دي لِلْمغْسلة /لِلدّْراي كْلين.
Can you give me a wake-up call at 6 a.m.?	*múmkin tiṣaḫḫūni 3ála -ssā3a sítta -lfágr?*	مُمْكِن تِصحّوني على السّاعة ٦ الفجْر؟
I have a safari tomorrow morning.	*3ándi safāri búkra -ṣṣúbḫ.*	عنْدي سفاري بُكْره الصُّبْح.
May I have the breakfast to go?	*múmkin ilfiṭār* [take away]?	مُمْكِن الفِطار تيْك أَواي؟
May I have the dinner delivered to my room?	*múmkin il3áša ygīli -lʔōḍa?*	مُمْكِن العشا يِيجيلي الأوْضة؟
I want extra tissues, please.	*3āyiz manadīl ziyāda, law samáḫt.*	عايِز مناديل زِيادة لَوْ سمحْت.
I don't want my room cleaned today.	*múmkin irrūm sarvīs ma-y3iddīš innahárda.*	مُمْكِن الرّوم سرْفيس مَيْعِدّيش النّهارْده.
Is tomorrow an official holiday?	*húwwa búkra agāza rasmíyya?*	هُوَّ بُكْرا أجازة رسْمية؟
Will the museum be open?	*(hal) ilmátḫaf haykūn maftūḫ?*	(هل) المتْحف هَيْكون مفْتوح؟

Renting an Apartment تأجير شقّة

Of course, you can find apartments for rent in online ads, Facebook groups, etc. You can also visit a real estate agency—just be prepared to pay the سِمْسار *simsār* **broker** up to one month's rent in سمْسرة *samsára* **commission**. But the best way to find an apartment in Egypt is by asking around. And who better to ask than a بوّاب *bawwāb* **doorman**, who will undoubtedly know about availability in his عِمارة *3imāra* **building** and will likely know about nearby apartment buildings, as well. Of course, if you do end up renting an apartment thanks to a doorman pointing you in the right direction, be sure to give him a modest finder's fee. If صاحِب الشّقّة *ṣāħib iššá??a* the **landlord** or صاحْبِة الشّقّة *ṣáħbit iššá??a* the **landlady** has rented to foreigners before—some prefer this and rent exclusively to foreigners—they will make the contract in English. You will likely have to pay a تأْمين *ta?mīn* **deposit** and first (or first and last) month's rent before you move in.

1

LOOKING FOR AN APARTMENT

○ متِعْرفْش طريق شقّة لِلْإيجار قُريِّب؟[1]

◇ فاضي[2] وَلّا مفْروش؟

○ لا مفْروش.

◇ فيه اِتْنينْ. واحْدة في العِمارة دي أوضْتينْ، و واحْدة أوِّل الشّارِع ٣ أُوَض.

○ طيِّب، وَرّيني[3] اللي عنْدك في العِمارة لَوْ معاك مُفْتاحْها.

○ Do you know a way [I can find] a nearby apartment for rent?

◇ Furnished or unfurnished?

○ Unfurnished.

◇ There are two. One is in this building with two bedrooms. The other is down the street and has three bedrooms.

○ Okay. Show me the one you have [in your building] if you have its key.

○ *ma-ti3ráfšᵊ ṭarīʔ šáʔʔa li-lʔigār ʔuráyyib?*[1]

◇ *fāḍi*[2] *wálla mafrūš?*

○ *laʔ, mafrūš.*

◇ *fī itnēn. wáħda fi -l3imāra di uḍtēn, wi wáħda áwwil iššāri3 tálat úwaḍ.*

○ *ṭáyyib, warrīni*[3] *-lli 3ándak fi -l3imāra law ma3āk muftáħha.*

[1] مفيش شقّة للإيجار قُريِّب؟ *ma-fīš šáʔʔa li-lʔigār ʔuráyyib?* **Is there an apartment for rent around here?**; أنا عايِز شقّة إيجار تِكون قُريِّبة. *ána 3āyiz šáʔʔa igār tikūn ʔurayyíba.* **I want an apartment to rent nearby.**

[2] قانون جِديد *qanūn gidīd* (lit. new law) is synonymous with مِش مفْروش *miš mafrūš* **unfurnished**. The 'new law' stipulates that an apartment be rented out unfurnished; however, furniture and appliances can be added as an addendum.

[3] = فرّجْني *farrágni*

2

ASKING ABOUT DETAILS

o طيِّب، الشّقّة كام أوْضة و الرِّسِبْشِن و كِده؟

◇ هِيَّ أوضْتينْ و صالة قطْعِتينْ و حمّام و مطبْخ.

o و الصّالة[1] حِلْوَة؟ تِشيل قطْعِتينْ مِسْترِيّح يَعْني؟

◇ آه حَوالي تلاتين مِتر. تِشيل[2]، متِقْلقْش.

o How many rooms are there in the apartment? And what about the living room?

◇ It has two bedrooms, a two-section living room, a kitchen, and a bathroom.

o Is the living room nice? Will it hold two living room sets?

◇ Yeah, it's about 30 square meters. It will fit. Don't worry.

o *ṭáyyib, iššáʔʔa kām ōḍa wi -rrisíbšin wi kída?*

◇ *híyya uḍtēn wi ṣāla qaṭ3itēn wi ħammām wi máṭbax.*

o *wi -ṣṣāla[1] ħílwa? tišīl qaṭ3itēn mistiráyyaħ yá3ni?*

◇ *āh, ħawāli talatīn mitr. tišīl[2], ma-tiʔláʔš.*

[1] = الرِّسِبْشِن *irrisíbšin*

[2] = تاخُد *tāxud*; تِكفّي *tikáffi* **it's enough**

Usually, rental contracts for extended periods will specify an annual 10% increase. Otherwise, the landlord has the right to set a new rent rate at the beginning of each year. Some others make a long term contract with an exact amount of money stated for each year.

3

Asking about rent

o طيِّب... و دي ايجارْها كام في الشّهْر؟

◇ دي ايجارْها اِتْنينْ و نُصّ[1].

o طيِّب، ده شامِل[2] المايّة و النّور و كِده وَلّا دوْل بدْفعْهُم؟[3]

◇ لا دوْل المُسْتأْجِر بِيِدْفعْهُم[4] برْضُه.

o How much is the monthly rent then?
◇ This one's rent is 2.5 [thousand].
o Does it include water, electricity bills, et cetera, or do I have to pay them myself?
◇ The tenant pays them, too.

o *ṭáyyib... wi di igárha kām fi -ššahr?*
◇ *di igárha -tnēn wi nuṣṣ*[1].
o *ṭáyyib, da šāmil*[2] *ilmáyya wi -nnūr wi kída wálla dōl badfá3hum?*[3]
◇ *laʔ, dōl ilmustáʔgir biyidfá3hum*[4] *bárḍu.*

[1] = ألْفينْ و نُصّ *alfēn wi nuṣṣ* **two and a half thousand;** = ألْفينْ و خُمْسُمية *alfēn wi xumsumíyya* **two thousand five hundred**

[2] = بِما فيه *bi-ma fī;* مِن ضِمْنُهُم *min ḍimnúhum* **including**

[3] = وَلّا دوْل عليّا أنا؟ *wálla dōl 3aláyya ána?*

[4] بِيِتْحمِّلْهُم *biyitḫammílhum*

If you leave before the end of the contract, you may be responsible for the rent until the end of the contract or have to forfeit your deposit. Read the terms of the contract carefully. You may also be able to negotiate with your landlord to pay a smaller fine or help them find a new tenant to replace you.

4

Asking about Utilities

○ طيِّب، الشّقّة هِنا فيها خطّ تِليفوْن؟

◇ آه فيها و معاه نِت، بسّ شوف لَوْ عايِز النِّت وَلّا ألْغيه[1].

○ لا خلّيه[2]. أنا هحْتاجُه. طب، البوّاب و النّضافة[3]؟ ليها فِلوس بِتِتْدِفع شهْري؟

◇ آه بِتِدْفع ٥٠ جِنيْه لِلْبوّاب قُصاد[4] لمّ الزِّبالة و تنْضيف[5] السِّلِّم.

○ Well, does this apartment have a landline?

◇ Yes, and internet, too. But check if you need internet, or shall I cancel it?

○ No, leave it. I'll be needing it. How about the doorman and the cleaning service[2]? Is there a monthly charge?

◇ Yeah, you just pay 50 LE to the doorman for collecting the garbage and sweeping the stairs.

○ *ṭáyyib, iššá??a hína fīha xaṭṭᵊ tilifōn?*

◇ *āh, fīha wi ma3ā nit, bassᵊ šūf law 3āyiz innít wálla alɣī[1].*

○ *lā, xallī[2]. ána haḥtāgu. ṭab, ilbawwāb wi -nnaḍāfa[3]? līha flūs bititdífi3 šáhri?*

◇ *āh, bitídfa3 xamsīn ginēh li-lbawwāb ?uṣād[4] lamm izzibāla wi tanḍīf[5] issíllim.*

[1] = أشيلُه *ašīlu*

[2] = سيبيه *sibī*

[3] النّضافة *innaḍāfa* **cleaning** refers to the doorman picking up garbage set out by each apartment, cleaning the building's stairwell, etc.

[4] = عشان *3ašān*

[5] = مسْح *masḥ*

When you receive your first utility bills, check the billing period against your move-in date before paying them. They may be the responsibility of the owner to pay.

5

Asking about utilities

o طب، الشّقّة فيها عدّاد كهْربا و مايّة؟

◇ آه يا مدام، فيها عدّادات قديمة كمان[1].

o طب، و الغاز؟

◇ هَيرِكْب أوِّل الشّهْر و فيه أنْبوبة لِحدّ ما يِرْكب.

o حِلْو أَوي. و النِّت و التِّليفوْن؟

◇ لا مفيهاش. حضْرِتِك مُمْكِن تِدخّلي[2] لَوْ عايْزة.

o Does the apartment have meters for water and electricity?

◇ Yes, miss. It even has the old meters[1].

o What about natural gas?

◇ It will be installed on the first of the month. There is a gas pipe until the natural gas system is installed.

o Great. What about phone and internet?

◇ No, it doesn't have either. You can have them installed if you wish.

o *ţab, iššáʔʔa fīha 3addād kahrába wi máyya?*

◇ *āh, ya madām, fīha 3addadāt ʔadīma kamān*[1].

o *ţab, wi -lɣāz?*

◇ *hayírkab áwwil iššáhr wi fī anbūba l-ɧaddᵊ ma yírkab.*

o *ɧilw áwi. w innít wi -ttilifōn?*

◇ *laʔ, ma-fihāš. ɧaɖrítik múmkin tidaxxáli*[2] *law 3áyza.*

[1] 'Old meters' refers to water and/or electricity meters which the utility companies check monthly and bill you for. The 'new meters' are operate by prepaid cards that insert into them. In this dialogue, the landlord mentions the old meters as a selling point, as they come out less expensive than paying by prepaid cards.

[2] = تِقدِّمي *tiʔaddími* = تِشْترِكي *tištiríki*

6

SIGNING THE CONTRACT

o طيِّب، نمْضي العقْد بُكْره إن شاء الله؟

◇ آه بإِذْن الله. بسّ هيِبْقى فيه شهْريْن تأْمين و شهْر مُقدّم.

o تمام، هبْعتْلك صورِةْ الباسْبوْر.

◇ مفيش مُشْكِلة و هنِمْضي على قايْمِة[1] بِالحاجات اللي في الشّقّة برْضُه.

o Shall we sign the contract tomorrow then?

◇ Yes, God willing, but there will be a two-month deposit and one month paid in advance.

o Okay, I'll send you a copy of my passport then.

◇ No problem. And we will also sign a list of the items included in the apartment.

o *ṭáyyib, nímḍi -l3aʔdᵊ búkra in šāʔ allāh?*

◇ *āh, b-izn allāh. bassᵊ hayíbʔa fī šahrēn taʔmīn wi šahrᵊ muʔáddam.*

o *tamām, hab3átlak ṣurt ilpaspōr.*

◇ *ma-fīš muškíla wi hanímḍi 3ála ʔáyma[1] bi-lḫagāt ílli fi -ššáʔʔa bárḍu.*

[1] = لِسْتة *lísta*

When renting an apartment, always check carefully before you sign a contract whether any utilities are included in the monthly rent and which you will need to take care of yourself. The doorman can go pay bills for you. Just give him the bill, money, and a tip.

Extended Dialogue

○ طيِّب، الشّقّة دي كام مِترْ تقْريباً؟[1]

◇ ميةْ مِترْ صافي.

○ و أوضْتينْ، مِش كِده؟

◇ آه اِتْفضّلي حضْرِتك شوفي[2].

○ و الأجْهِزة كُلّها شغّالة؟

◇ آه التّلاجة و الغسّالة و البوتاجاز كُلُّه شغّال.

○ فيها سخّان غاز وَلّا كهْربا؟

◇ لا سخّان غاز و فيه تِليفوْن و راوْتر كمان.

○ طب، و فيها غسّالِةْ أطْباق؟

◇ لا مفيهاش بسّ السّخّان مِتْوَصّل بِحنفيةْ المطْبخ و فيه كُلّ حاجة مُمْكِن تِحْتاجيها في المطْبقية.

○ حِلْو جِدّاً! خلاص أنا حابّة أجّرْها.

◇ يِبْقى كِده الإيجار هَيِبْقى ٥٠٠٠ جِنيْهْ في الشّهْر شامِل الخدمات.

○ نِقْدر نِمْضي العقْد إمْتى؟

◇ مِن النّهارْده لَوْ حبّيْتي بسّ أسْتأْذِنِك في الباسْبوْر[3].

○ و العقْد هَيِبْقى بِالعربي وَلّا بِالإنْجِليزي؟

◇ زيّ ما تِحِبّي. أنا دايْماً بأجّر لِأجانِب فا ده مَوْجود و ده مَوْجود.

○ خلّي العقْد بِالإنْجِليزي أحْسن. فيه أيّ حاجة بِتِتْدِفع تاني[4] أحضّرْها؟

◇ آه شهْريْن تأْمين بِتاخْديهُم[5] آخِر المدّة و شهْر مُقدّم.

○ يَعْني ١٥٠٠٠. تمام، نِتْقابِل النّهارْده بِاللّيْل إن شاء الله.

◇ تمام، السّاعة ٨ هكون عنْد حضْرِتِك. مبْروك مُقدّماً.

○ Well, how many square meters is this apartment?
◇ 100 square meters net.

- o Two bedrooms, right?
- ◇ Yes, go ahead and have a look for yourself.
- o Do all the appliances work?
- ◇ Yes, the refrigerator, washing machine, and stove all work.
- o Is the heater gas or electric?
- ◇ It's a gas one, and there is also a telephone and a router.
- o Does it have a dishwasher?
- ◇ No, but the water heater is connected to the kitchen tap. And you have everything you need in the plate rack.
- o Very nice! All right then, I'd like to rent it.
- ◇ The rent will be 5,000 LE a month including services.
- o When can we sign the contract?
- ◇ Today if you would like to, but I need your passport, please.
- o Will the contract be in Arabic or English?
- ◇ Whatever you wish. I always rent to foreigners so I have both versions.
- o Let's make the contract in English. That would be better. Is there anything else that needs to be paid that I should prepare?
- ◇ Yes, two months' deposit and one month's [rent] in advance.
- o So that will be 15,000. All right, we'll meet tonight then, God willing.
- ◇ Okay, at 8 p.m., I'll be at your place. Congratulations in advance!

- o *ţáyyib, iššáʔʔa di kām mitrᵊ taʔrīban?*[1]
- ◇ *mīt mitrᵊ şāfi.*
- o *wi uḑtēn, miš kída?*
- ◇ *āh, itfaḑḑáli ḫaḑrítik šūfi*[2].
- o *w ilʔaghíza kulláha šaɣɣāla?*
- ◇ *āh, ittalāga wi -lɣassāla wi -lbutagāz kúllu šaɣɣāl.*
- o *fīha saxxān ɣāz wálla kahrába?*
- ◇ *lā, saxxān ɣāz wi fī tilifōn wi ráwtar kamān.*

○ ṭab, wi fīha ɣassālit aṭbāʔ?
◇ laʔ, ma-fihāš bass issaxxān mitwáṣṣal bi-ḥanafīt ilmáṭbax wi fī kullᵊ ḥāga múmkin tiḥtagīha fi -lmaṭbaʔíyya.
○ ḥilwᵊ gíddan! xalāṣ ána ḥábba -ʔaggárha.
◇ yíbʔa kída ilʔigār hayíbʔa xamastalāf ginēh fi -ššahr, šāmil ilxadamāt.
○ níʔdar nímḍi -l3aʔdᵊ ímta?
◇ min innahárda law ḥabbēti, bass astaʔzínik fi -lpaspōr[3].
○ w il3áʔdᵊ hayíbʔa bi-l3árabi wálla bi-lʔingilīzi?
◇ zayyᵊ ma tḥíbbi. ána dáyman baʔággar li-ʔagānib, fa da mawgūd wi da mawgūd.
○ xálli -l3aʔdᵊ bi-lʔingilīzi áḥsan. fī ayyᵊ ḥāga bititdífi3 tāni[4] aḥaḍḍárha?
◇ āh, šahrēn taʔmīn biṭaxdīhum[5] áxir ilmúdda wi šahrᵊ muʔáddam.
○ yá3ni xamastāšar alf. tamām, nitʔābil innahárda bi-llēl in šāʔ allāh.
◇ tamām, issā3a tamánya hakūn 3andᵊ ḥaḍrítik. mabrūk muʔaddáman.

1 مِساحِتْها قدّ أيْه؟ *misaḥítha ʔaddᵊ ʔē?* **What is its area?** (i.e., **How many square meters is it?**)

2 = اِتْفرّجي *itfarrági*

3 = مُمْكِن الباسْبوْر؟ *múmkin ilpaspōr?*

4 فيه أيّ مصاريف تانْيَة *fī ayyᵊ maṣarīf tánya*

5 = بيِرْجعولِك *biyirga3ūlik* = بِتِسْترِدّيهُم *bitistariddīhum*

Vocabulary

apartment	*šáʔʔa*	شقّة
(bed)room	*ōḍa (úwaḍ)*	أوْضة (أُوَض)
two rooms	*uḍtēn*	أوضْتيْن
three rooms	*tálat úwaḍ*	تلات أُوَض
floor, story	*dōr*	دوْر

apartment building	*3imāra* *3umāra*	عِمارة عُمارة
doorman	*bawwāb*	بوّاب
security guard	*ɧāris*	حارِس
maintenance fees	*ištirāk*	اِشْتِراك
housekeeper, cleaning lady	*šaɣɣāla*	شغّالة
to rent	*ʔággar*	أجّر
rent	*igār*	إيجار
real estate agent, rental agent	*simsār*	سِمْسار
brokerage fees, commission	*samsara* *3umūla*	سمْسرة عُمولة
landlord, owner	*ṣāɧib šáʔʔa* *mālik*	صاحِب شقّة مالِك
contract	*3aʔd*	عقْد
furnished	*mafrūš*	مفْروش
non-furnished	*fāḍi* *qanūn gidīd*	فاضي قانون جِديد
kitchen	*máṭbax*	مطْبخ
bathroom	*ɧammām*	حمّام
balcony	*balakōna*	بلكوْنة
stairs	*síllim*	سِلِّم
(utility) meter	*3addād*	عدّاد

electricity	*kahrába*	كهْربا
water	*máyya*	مايّة
(natural) gas	*ɣāz*	غاز
telephone	*tilifōn*	تِليفوْن
internet	*nit* *íntarnat*	نِت إنْترِنْت
washing machine	*ɣassāla*	غسّالة
stove	*butagāz*	بوتاجاز
refrigerator	*talāga*	تلاجة
heater	*saxxān*	سخّان
light shaft, skylight	*mánwar*	منْوَر
security deposit	*taʔmīn*	تأْمين
fees, charges	*ištirāk*	اِشْترِاك
(itemized) list	*ʔáyma (ʔawāyim)*	قايْمة (قَوايِم)

Expressions

○		
Can I rent it by the day?	*múmkin aʔaggárha bi-lyōm?*	مُمْكِن أجّرْها بِاليوْم؟
We only need the apartment for two months.	*íḫna miḫtagīn iššáʔʔa di šahrēn bass.*	إحْنا مِحْتاجين الشّقّة دي شهْريْن بسّ.

Can I put a screen on this window?	*ţáyyib, yínfa3 arákkib silk[ə] 3ála -ššibbāk da?*	طيِّب، ينْفع أركِّب سِلْك على الشِّبّاك ده؟
Can I paint the walls?	*yínfa3 aɣáyyar lōn ilђēţa?*	ينْفع أغيرّ لوْن الحيْطة؟
Do you know a cleaning lady who can come clean the apartment once a week?	*ma-ti3ráfš wáђda tīgi tinaɖɖáfli -ššá??a kull[ə] usbū3?*	متِعْرفْش واحْدة تيجي تِنضّفْلي الشّقّة كُلّ أُسْبوع؟
Isn't there a gardener who can take care of the plants?	*ma-fīš ganáyni biyīgi yirā3i -zzar3?*	مفيش جنايْني بِييجي يِراعي الزّرْع؟

◇

You have received the apartment as it is and with these items included.	*ђaɖrítak istalamtáha kída bi-lђagāt di.*	حضْرِتك اِسْتلمْتها كِده بِالحاجات دي.
You have to return it in the same condition you received it in.	*lāzim tisallímha bi-náfs ilђāla -lli istalamtáha bīha.*	لازِم تِسلِّمْها بِنفْس الحالة اللي اِسْتلمْتها بيها.
The monthly maintenance fees for building are 100 LE.	*ištirāk il3imāra mīt ginēh fi -ššahr.*	اِشْتِراك العِمارة ١٠٠ جِنيْه في الشّهْر.
If you would like to change anything, that's fine, but you have to return it as it was before you move out.	*law ђābib tiɣáyyar ђāga tamām, bass[ə] ʔabl[ə] ma tímši rágga3 ilʔadīm bitá3ha.*	لَوْ حابِب تِغيرّ حاجة تمام بسّ قبْل ما تمْشي رجّع القديم بِتاعْها.

You can change the door's lock, but please return the old one before moving out.	*múmkin tiɣáyyar ţáblit ilbāb wi tíbʔa tiraggá3li -lʔadīma w ínta māši.*	مُمْكِن تِغيرّ طبْلِةْ الباب و تِبْقى ترِجّعْلي القديمة و إنْتَ ماشي.
There are fees for cleaning the water tank (on the roof) and elevator maintenance.	*fī filūs li-tanḑīf xazzān ilmáyya wi şiyānit ilʔasansīr.*	فيه فِلوس لِتنْضيف خزّان المايّة و صِيانِةْ الأسانْسير.
You should give the doorman a finder's fee for telling you about the apartment.	*lāzim tirāḑi -lbawwāb bi-ayyᵊ ђāga bárḑu ţālama húwwa -lli ʔállak 3ála -ššáʔʔa.*	لازِم تِراضي البوّاب بِأيّ حاجة برْضُه طالما هُوَّ اللي قالّك على الشّقّة.
Brokerage fees are usually a month's rent, but they could just be half a month.	*issamsára bitkūn šahrᵊ bassᵊ múmkin tínzil li-nuşşᵊ šahr.*	السّمْسرة بِتْكون شهْر بسّ مُمْكِن تِنْزِل لِنُصّ شهْر.
The doorman's wife can come up and clean for you, if you'd like.	*mirāt ilbawwāb múmkin tíţla3 tinaḑḑáflak law 3āyiz.*	مِرات البوّاب مُمْكِن تِطْلع تِنضّفْلك لَوْ عايِز.

Dealing with the Doorman

كلام معَ البوّاب

Most apartment buildings in Egypt employ a بوّاب *bawwāb* **doorman**, whose many responsibilities go beyond just providing security for the عِمارة *3imāra* **building** to include cleaning the stairs, collecting the garbage from each apartment, repairs (handling minor repairs inside apartments and organizing and supervising professional repairmen when needed), running errands for tenants (paying bills, buying items from local shops, etc.), and basically just assisting tenants in various ways (carrying things upstairs, receiving deliveries, etc.). The doorman will also take it upon himself to be the 'morality police,' and may not allow you to have visitors of the opposite sex, which is frowned upon in Egyptian society. Whatever you do, don't get on your doorman's bad side, as you would suddenly find life much more unpleasant and difficult. The doorman receives his salary from the building's tenants. Ask your neighbors (not the doorman) how much they give each month. (See p. 91 for more on tipping your doorman.)

Meeting the Doorman

◇ أهْلاً وَ سهْلاً يا باشا. حضْرِتك لِسّه مِأجّر جِديد[1] مِش كِده؟

○ آه لِسّه إمْبارِح. مِأجِّر الشّقّة المفْروش اللي في العاشِر.

◇ مبْروك عليْك يا باشا بسّ بما إنّ حضْرِتك أجْنبي قُلْت أقولّك[2] برْضُه على نِظام العِمارة.

○ آه ياريْت اِتْفضّل.

◇ أوّلاً[3] مَيِنْفعْش حضْرِتك تِسْتقْبِل سِتّات في الشّقّة... و اِشْتِراك العِمارة ١٠٠ جِنيْه في الشّهْر و البوّابة بِتِقْفِل السّاعة ١١.

○ تمام طب بِالمرّة بقى اِعْمِلّي نُسْخة مِن [مُفْتاح] البوّابة عشان ساعات بتْأخّر[4].

◇ Welcome, sir! You've just started renting here, right?

○ Yeah, I just rented the furnished one on the tenth floor yesterday.

◇ Congratulations, sir. But since you're a foreigner, I'd like to inform you of the building system.

○ Yes, please go ahead.

◇ First of all, you cannot invite women over to the apartment. And the monthly service fees for the building are 100 LE, and the gate closes at 11 p.m.

○ Okay. Speaking of which, make me a copy of the gate key, as I get back late sometimes.

◇ *áhlan wa sáhlan ya bāša. ḫadrítak líssa miʔággar gidīd[1] miš kída?*

○ *āh, líssa -mbāriḫ. miʔággir iššáʔʔa ilmafrūš ílli fi -l3āšir.*

◇ *mabrūk 3alēk ya bāša, bassᵊ bí-ma innᵊ ḫadrítak agnábi ʔult aʔúllak[2] bárdu 3ála niẓām il3imāra.*

○ *āh, yarēt, itfáddal.*

◇ *awwálan[3] ma-yinfá3šᵊ ḫadrítak tistáʔbil sittāt fi -ššáʔʔa... wi -štirāk il3imāra mīt ginēh fi -ššahrᵊ wi -lbawwāba btíʔfil issā3a ḫidāšar.*

○ *tamām, ṭab bi-lmárra báʔa, i3mílli núsxa min muftāḫ ilbawwāba 3ašān sa3āt batʔáxxar*[4].

[1] حضرتك السّاكِن الجِّديد *ḫaḍrítak issākin iggidīd*

[2] = خلّيني أقولّك *xallīni aʔúllak*

[3] = أوِّل حاجة *áwwil ḫāga*

[4] ساعات *sa3āt* = أوْقات *awʔāt* = أحْياناً *aḫyānan* **sometimes;** عشان لمّا أتْأخّر *3ašān lámma -tʔáxxar* **for when I'm late**

When should you tip the doorman? It is customary to give the doorman a monthly tip to cover all of his services in advance, or every now and again... but not every single time he helps you carry something or hands you your mail. However, extra tips are expected for running errands (going to pay bills, etc.) and making deliveries (from a local shop, etc.), even if it's just letting him keep the change. For example, if the total is 52.50 LE, you could give him 55 LE... unless he's lugged something quite heavy upstairs to you, in which case you should tip him an extra 5 or 10 pounds, according to your estimation of the effort exerted.

Most doormen are migrant workers from rural areas, especially Upper Egypt (i.e., the south)–so you may notice your doorman's accent (dialect) is a bit different than the locals. A doorman might work for many years in the city, living alone in a small room on the ground floor of the building he works in, and only making a trip home to visit his family once or twice a year.

If a doorman's wife lives with him (and not back in their home village), she will likely offer housekeeping services. Otherwise, you can ask your neighbors to recommend a شغّالة *šaɣɣāla* **housekeeper** to come over to clean once or twice a week.

Doormen sometimes work as unofficial brokers, receiving a finder's fee both from a landlord and the tenant when they find someone to rent an available apartment. (See **Renting an Apartment** on p. 75.)

2

INFORMING THE DOORMAN OF A PROBLEM

○ بقولّك يا عمّ شعْبان. هُوَّ الأسانْسير الفرْدي مِش شغّال ليْه؟

◇ لا شغّال عادي بسّ تِلاقي حدّ مقفلْش الباب كُوَيِّس.

○ طيِّب، شوف كِده عشان أنا فِضِلْت مِسْتنّية و بعْديْن نِزِلْت في الزَّوْجي.

◇ لا هطْلع أشوفُه حاضِر.

○ Hey, Shaban, why is the elevator for odd floors not working?

◇ No, it's working normally, but someone probably hasn't shut the door properly.

○ Then check it, because I kept waiting and then had to take the one for even floors.

◇ Okay, I'll go up and check it right away.

○ *baʔúllak ya 3ammᵊ ša3bān. húwwa -lʔasansīr ilfárdi miš šaɣɣāl lē?*

◇ *lā, šaɣɣāl 3ādi, bassᵊ tlāʔi ɧaddᵊ ma-ʔafálš ilbāb kuwáyyis.*

○ *ţáyyib, šūf kída, 3ašān ána fḍíltᵊ mistanníyya wi ba3dēn nizíltᵊ fi -zzáwgi.*

◇ *lā, háţla3 ašūfu ɧāḍir.*

In some larger, high-rise buildings, there are two elevators–one which stops on even-numbered floors, and one for odd floors.

In every building, there is supposed to be a person who is in charge of the building's finances and (legal) matters, the مسْئول العِمارة *masʔūl il3imāra* **building manager**. This person is also the doorman's boss–and can hire or fire a doorman (supposedly, after consulting the rest of tenants/landlords). The doorman acts as the communication liaison between all tenants and the building manager, handling negotiations and issues that may arise.

3

Asking about garbage collection

o هِيَّ الزِّبالة بِتِتْلمّ إمْتَي[1] يا أبو عبْد الله؟

◇ بعدّي ألِمّها عَ المغْرِب يا مدام.

o آه عشان كِده بِتاعِة إمْبارِح لِسّه متْلمِّتْش. طيِّب بِالمرّة اِبْقى نضّف السِّلِّم.

◇ لا السِّلِّم بِيِتْنضّف[2] مرّة كُلّ أُسْبوعينْ.

o When is garbage collected, Abu Abdallah?

◇ I come around to collect it around sunset, ma'am.

o Ah, this is why yesterday's bags haven't been collected yet. Okay, you'd better clean the stairs while you're at it.

◇ No, the stairs are cleaned once every two weeks.

o *híyya -zzibāla btitlámmᵊ ímta*[1] *ya ábu 3abdálla?*

◇ *ba3áddi alimmáha 3a -lmáɣrib ya madām.*

o *āh, 3ašān kída btā3it imbāriḫ líssa ma-tlammítš. ṭáyyib bi-lmárra íbʔa náḍḍaf issíllim.*

◇ *laʔ, issíllim biyitnáḍḍaf*[2] *márra kull usbu3ēn.*

[1] = أيْه معاد لمّ الزِّبالة *ʔē ma3ād lamm izzibāla*

[2] بنضف السِّلِّم *banáḍḍaf issíllim* **I clean the stairs**

Some smaller (3-6 story) buildings don't employ a doorman at all, and instead have an agreement with someone to clean the stairwells once in a while and with a زبّال *zabbāl* **trash collector** to come around and collect the garbage every day. (Beware of scams. Do not give money to anyone who comes to your door unless you are sure he is the garbage collector.) Such buildings may also place an intercom outside the gate and even add electronic locks (and even security cameras) to the gate, so you can buzz people in. It varies from one building to another.

4

RECEIVING DELIVERIES

○ بقولّك فيه طلبات جايّالي عَ السّاعة ١٢ و أنا جالي[1] مِشْوار ضروري.

◇ مفيش مُشْكِلة. حضْرِتك اِنْزِلي و أنا هسْتِلِمْهومْلك. أحاسِب وَلّا حاجة؟[2]

○ لا مدْفوع حِسابْها. اِسْتِلِمْها بسّ لِحدّ ما أرْجع و اِبْقى أخُدْهُم مِنّك.

◇ تحْت أمْرِك.

○ Hey, I have some deliveries arriving around 12, and something came up.

◇ No problem. Just go ahead, and I will receive them on your behalf. Will I have to pay or something?

○ No, they're already paid for. Just hold onto them until I get back, and I'll get them from you.

◇ As you wish.

○ *baʔúllak, fī ṭalabāt gayyāli 3a -ssā3a -tnāšar, w ána gāli*[1] *mišwār ḍarūri.*

◇ *ma-fīš muškíla. ḫaḍrítik inzíli w ána hastilimhúmlik. aḫāsib wálla ḫāga?*[2]

○ *laʔ, madfū3 ḫisábha. istilímha bassᵊ l-ḫaddᵊ m- árga3 w ábʔa axúdhum mínnak.*

◇ *taḫtᵊ ámrik.*

1 = و طِلِعْلي *wi ṭilí3li*

2 = حِسابُه مدْفوع؟ *ḫisābu madfū3*

In smaller buildings without a parking garage, you can make a monthly deal with the doorman to wash your car and assist you with parking (guiding you into a tight spot, leaving a tire in your parking spot when you pull out, finding the driver of a car that is blocking yours, etc.). But in larger buildings, there will be designated parking spaces and a سايِس *sāyis* **garage attendant** to take care of your car.

5

DEALING WITH A COMPLAINT AGAINST YOU

◇ الشّقّة اللي تحْت حضْرتك بِيِشْتِكوا مِن مايّةْ التّكْييف.

o أنا لِسّه مِأجِّر الشّقّة جِديد فا معْرفْش الوَضْع أيْه.

◇ أَيْوَه ما هُوَّ صاحِب الشّقّة كان المفْروض يمِدّ خرْطوم مايّة لِحدّ تحْت[1].

o طيِّب، خلّيني أرْجعْله و أشوف أيْه القِصّة دي.

◇ The apartment below you is complaining about water dripping from your air conditioner.

o I just started renting the apartment, so I don't know what's up with that.

◇ Yeah, the owner should have extended a drain line all the way down.

o Okay, let me get back to him and see about this.

◇ *iššáʔʔa -lli taḫtᵊ ḫaḍrítak biyištíku min máyyit ittakyīf.*

o *ána líssa mʔággir iššáʔʔa gdīd fa ma-3ráfš ilwáḍ3 ʔē.*

◇ *áywa, ma húwwa ṣāḫib iššáʔʔa kān ilmafrūḍ yimíddᵊ xarṭūm máyya l-ḫaddᵊ taḫt*[1].

o *ṭáyyib, xallīni argá3lu w ašūf ʔē ilqíṣṣa di.*

[1] خرْطوم التّكْييف لِحدّ الأرْضي *xarṭūm ittakyīf li-ḫádd ilʔárḍi* **the air-conditioner's drain line all the way to the ground floor**

Some buildings have a فرْد أمْن *fardᵊ amn* **security guard** instead of a doorman. Security guards don't live in the building but instead sit at a desk, working in shifts, at the entrance of the building. In that case, their primary duty is to guard the building and thus cannot be asked for the same services that can be requested from a doorman.

6

Having the doorman run an errand

- ○ بقولّك يا مْحمّد، أنْبوبِةْ الغاز خِلْصِت[1].
- ◇ طيِّب، اِدّيني عشر دقايِق أجيبْلِك غيرْها و أغيّرْهالِك.
- ○ تِسْلم ربِّنا يِكْرِمك. بسّ بِسُرْعة عشان مِش عارْفة أطْبُخ.
- ◇ متُؤْمُريش بِحاجة تانْيَة؟[2]
- ○ لَوْ تِعْرف تِشْترِيلي[3] كبْريت بِالمرّة ياريْت.
- ◇ مِن عينيّا.

- ○ Hey, Mohamed, my [propane] tank is out of gas.
- ◇ Okay, just give me 10 minutes to get you another one and replace it for you.
- ○ Thank you. God bless you, but quickly, please, as I cannot cook.
- ◇ Would you like anything else?
- ○ If you can buy me some matches while you're at it, that would be great.
- ◇ My pleasure!

- ○ *baʔúllak ya mḫámmad, anbúbt ilɣāz xílṣit*[1].
- ◇ *ṭáyyib, iddīni 3ášar daʔāyiʔ agíblik ɣírha w aɣayyarhālik.*
- ○ *tíslam rabbína yikrímak. bassᵊ bi-súr3a 3ašān miš 3árfa áṭbux.*
- ◇ *ma-tuʔmurīš bi-ḫāga tánya?*[2]
- ○ *law tí3raf, tištirīli*[3] *kabrīt bi-lmárra yarēt.*
- ◇ *min 3ináyya.*

[1] الأنْبوبة عايْزة تِتْغيرّ *ilʔanbūba 3áyza titɣáyyar* **the tank needs to be replaced**

[2] = عايْزة أيّ حاجة تاني؟ *3áyza ayyᵊ ḫāga tāni?* = مِحْتاجة حاجة تاني؟ *miḫtāga ḫāga tāni?*

[3] = تِجيبْلي *tigíbli*

If you don't have natural gas lines, which are metered (whether prepaid or billed), you will have a propane gas tank in the kitchen for the stove and hot water. Just let your doorman know when it's empty, and he'll bring you a replacement. As with other errands, be sure to give him enough money, and let him keep some of the change as a tip.

If you do not have a doorman in your building and you need a propane tank, there are propane tank vendors who walk up and down the streets. You'll hear them as they knock loudly on the tanks to make noise or shout أنابيب! *anabīb!* **[Propane] tanks!** You can call one from your window by shouting يا بِتاع الأنابيب! *ya bitā3 ilʔanabīb!* **Hey, [propane] tank seller!** He will come up to your apartment and replace your tank with a full one for you.

Extended Dialogue

○ سلامُ عليْكُم يا عمّ مُصْطفى.

◇ و عليْكُم السّلام يا خَواجِة[1].

○ بقولّك هُوَّ أيْه الخبْط[2] اللي بسْمعُه في الشّقّة اللي فوْقي دي؟

◇ أصْلُهُم بِيْغيرّوا الأرْضِيّات و شغّالين في الشّقّة[3].

○ طيِّب، و هَيْطوِّلوا وَلّا أيْه؟[4] أنا مِش عارِف أنام خالِص.

◇ هِيَّ دِيِّتْها[5] أُسْبوع وَلّا حاجة متِقْلقْش.

○ طيِّب، مفيش حاجة جاتْلي عَ العِمارة؟

◇ أيْوَه فيه واحِد سابْلك الكّيس ده و قالّي أوَصّلْهولك.

○ آه تمام و مفيش حاجة جت على صنْدوق البوسْطة؟

◇ لا ما هُوَّ البوسْطجي ساب كُلّ الجَّوابات عَ الكُّرْسي اللي في دخْلِةْ العِمارة. فا أنا سِبْت بِتوع حضْرِتك على جمْب[6].

○ طيِّب، هاتْهُم بِالمرّة بقى.

◇ اِتْفضّل أهُه يا باشا جَوابيْن، واحِد مِن برّه و التّاني مِن البنْك.

○ ماشي يا أبو نِسْمة[7]، بُصّ أنا مِسافِر تلات أسابيع فا هسيبْلك إنْتَ أيّ فِلوس تِتْدِفع.

◇ طيِّب، هُوَّ بِتاع المايّة عدى إمْبارِح و بِتاع الكّهْربا هَييجي على أوِّل الشّهْر.

o خلاص أنا هسيبْلك فِلوس بزِيادة لِلْمايّة و الكّهْربا و الغاز و اِشْتِراك العِمارة كمان و اِبْقى شيل الوُصولات معاك لِحدّ ما أرْجع.

◇ تحْت أمْرك يا باشا، تِروح و تِرْجع بِالسّلامة[8].

o الله يِسلِّمك.

o Hello, Moustafa!

◇ Hello, Khawaga[1]!

o I was wondering what this hammering sound I hear coming from the apartment above me is.

◇ They're changing out the flooring and doing some work in the apartment.

o Will it take long? I cannot sleep at all.

◇ It's a matter of a week or something, don't worry.

o Okay. And did anything come for me?

◇ Yes, someone came and left you this plastic bag and asked me to get it to you.

o All right, and did I receive anything in my mailbox?

◇ The mail carrier came and left all the mail on the chair at the entrance of the building, so I put yours aside.

o Okay, bring them over, too.

◇ Here you are, Pasha. Two letters: one from abroad and the other from the bank.

o Okay, Abu Nesma. Look, I'll be traveling for three weeks, so I'll leave you money so you can pay [bills].

◇ Okay, the water service guy came by yesterday, and someone from the electricity [company] will come by at the beginning of the month.

o Okay, I'll leave you extra money for water, electricity, gas, and the building's maintenance fees, too. Keep the receipts until I come back.

◇ Whatever you command, Pasha. Have a good trip!

○ Thank you!

○ *salāmu 3alēkum ya 3amm[ə] muṣṭáfa.*
◇ *wi 3alēkum issalām ya xawāga*[1].
○ *baʔúllak, húwwa ʔē ilxábṭ*[2] *ílli basmá3u fi -ššáʔʔa ílli fōʔi di?*
◇ *aṣlúhum biyɣayyáru -lʔarḍiyyāt wi šaɣɣalīn fi -ššáʔʔa*[3].
○ *ṭáyyib, wi hayṭawwílu wálla ʔē?*[4] *ána miš 3ārif anām xāliṣ.*
◇ *híyya diyyítha*[5] *usbū3 wálla ḥāga, ma-tiʔláʔš.*
○ *ṭáyyib, ma-fīš ḥāga gátli 3a -l3imāra?*
◇ *áywa, fī wāḥid sáblak ikkīs da wi ʔálli awaṣṣalhūlak.*
○ *āh, tamām wi ma-fīš ḥāga gat 3ála sandūʔ ilbúsṭa?*
◇ *lā, ma húwwa -lbusṭági sāb kull iggawabāt 3a -kkúrsi ílli f dáxlit il3imāra. f- ána sibt[ə] btū3 ḥaḍrítak 3ála gamb*[6].
○ *ṭáyyib, háthum bi-lmárra báʔa.*
◇ *itfáḍḍal ahú ya bāša, gawabēn: wāḥid min bárra wi -ttāni min ilbánk.*
○ *māši y- ábu nísma*[7], *buṣṣ, ána msāfir tálat asabī3, fa hasíblak ínta ayy[ə] filūs titdífi3.*
◇ *ṭáyyib, húwwa btā3 ilmáyya 3ádda imbāriḥ wi bitā3 ikkahrába hayīgi 3ála áwwil iššáhr.*
○ *xalāṣ ána hasíblak filūs bi-ziyāda li-lmáyya wi -kkahrába wi -lɣāz wi -štirāk il3imāra kamān w íbaʔa šīl ilwuṣulāt ma3āk li-ḥádd[ə] m- árga3.*
◇ *taḥt[ə] ámrak ya bāša, tirūḥ wi tírga3 bi-ssalāma*[8].
○ *allāh yisallímak.*

[1] خَواجة *xawāga* is a respectful title for a foreign man. A foreign woman is خَواجايَة *xawagāya.*

[2] = الدقّ *iddáʔʔ*

[3] بِيْوَضّبوا الشّقّة *biywaḍḍábu -ššáʔʔa* **they're doing repairs in the apartment**; بِيْجدِّدوا الشّقّة *biygaddídu -ššáʔʔa* **they're renovating the apartment**

[4] هَيْخلّصوا إمْتى؟ *hayxalláṣu ímta?* **when will they finish?**

[5] دِيّتْها *diyyítha* **its worst case scenario, at the very most**

[6] = ركنْت جَوابات حضْرِتك لِوَحْدُهُم *rakánt[ə] gawabāt ḥaḍrítak li-waḥdúhum*

[7] أبو نِسْمة *ábu nísma* is what is known as a كُنْيَة *kúnya* **teknonym**, a friendly, informal form of address using the name of one's first-born son–and if there are no sons, one's eldest daughter, as must be the case with the doorman in this dialogue. His teknonym is literally 'Father of Nesma.' His wife's teknonym would be أُمّ نِسْمة *umm*ᵊ *nísma* 'Mother of Nesma.'

[8] = ربِّنا يِجيبك بِالسّلامة *rabbína ygībak bi-ssalāma*

Who you gonna call? The doorman! Call the doorman if:

- the elevator is not working.
- there is a problem with a utility (electricity, gas, water, sewage).
- you suspect something dangerous.
- you are expecting a guest and want to make sure they find their way.
- you are not sure who to go to. The doorman will either help you himself, talk to the building manager on your behalf, or point you in the right direction.

Vocabulary

apartment building	*3imāra* *3umāra*	عِمارة عُمارة
apartment	*šáʔʔa (šúʔaʔ)*	شقّة (شُقق)
floor, story	*dōr*	دوْر
entrance, entryway	*mádxal*	مدْخل
stairs	*síllim*	سِلِّم
landing (of the stairs)	*básṭit issíllim*	بسْطِةْ السِّلِّم
mailbox	*sandūʔ búsṭa* *(sanadīʔ búsṭa)*	صنْدوق بوسْطة (صناديق بوسْطة)
gate	*bawwāba*	بوّابة
intercom	*íntirkum*	إنْترِكُم
elevator	*asansīr*	أسانْسير
garbage	*zibāla*	زِبالة
garage	*garāž*	جراج
doorman, bawaab	*bawwāb* *ḥāris (il3imāra)*	بوّاب حارِس (العِمارة)
the doorman's wife	*mirāt ilbawwāb*	مِرات البوّاب
the doorman's kids	*wilād ilbawwāb*	وِلاد البوّاب
the building's monthly maintenance fees	*ištirāk il3imāra*	اِشْتِراك العِمارة
electricity	*kahrába*	كهْربا

water	*máyya*	مايّة
gas	*ɣāz*	غاز
deliveries	*ṭalabāt*	طلبات
cleaning	*tanḍīf*	تنْضيف
(gas) tank	*anbūba (anbūbit ɣāz)*	أنْبوبة (أنْبوبِة غاز)
groceries	*xaḍār*	خضار
fruit	*fákha*	فاكْهة
(plastic) bag	*kīs (akyās)*	كيس (أكْياس)
luggage, bags	*šúnaṭ*	شُنط
security	*ilʔámn* *sikyūriti*	الأمْن سِكْيوريتي
security guard	*fardᵊ amn (afrād amn)* *(sikyūriti) gard*	فرْد أمْن (أفْراد أمْن) (سِكْيوريتي) جارْد
garage attendant	*sāyis*	سايِس
camera	*kāmira*	كاميرا
roof	*saṭḥ* *rūf*	سطْح روف
basement	*badrōm*	بدْروْم
light shaft, skylight	*mánwar*	منْوَر
(water/sewage) pipes	*mawasīr*	مَواسير

Expressions

	○	
Hey, could you please clean the landing on the tenth floor?	*íbʔa náḍḍaf básṭit issíllim fi -ddōr il3āšir.*	اِبْقى نضّف بسْطِةْ السِّلِّم في الدّوْر العاشِر.
Do you know why the water pressure is so low?	*ma-ti3ráfš ilmáyya ḍa3īfa lē?*	متِعْرفْش المايّة ضعيفة ليْه؟
Buzz me on the intercom before you come up.	*iḍrábli/rinníli 3ála -lʔíntirkum ʔabl^{ə} ma tíṭla3.*	اِضْربْلي/رنِّلي على الإنْترِكُم قبْل ما تِطْلع.
Could you please bring those suitcases (bags) upstairs?	*ma3alíšš, múmkin tiṭálla3 iššúnaṭ 3ála fōʔ?*	معلِشّ مُمْكِن تِطلّع الشُّنط على فوْق؟
I need urgent medication and there is no delivery service available from the pharmacy.	*miḫtāg adwíyya ḍarūri wi -ṣṣaydalíyya ma-fihāš tawṣīl.*	مِحْتاج أدْوية ضروري و الصَّيْدلية مفيهاش توْصيل.
Where is the card for the elevator?	*fēn ikkárt^{ə} bitā3*[1] *ilʔasansīr?*	فيْن الكّارْت بِتاع[1] الأسانْسير؟
I have some guests coming this afternoon. Please, bring them upstairs.	*3ándi ḍuyūf gayyínli 3ála -l3aṣr, ṭallá3hum.*	عنْدي ضُيوف جايّينْلي على العصْر، طلّعْهُم.
There is a power outage on my floor.	*fī ʔáflit kahrába fi -ddōr 3ándi.*	فيه قفْلِةْ كهْربا في الدّوْر عنْدي.

The elevator is stuck between the third and fourth floors.	*il?asansīr mi3álla? bēn ittālit wi -rrābi3.*	الأسانْسير مِعلّق بينْ التّالِت و الرّابِع.
There is a thief on the stairs!	*fī ђarāmi 3ála -ssíllim!*	فيه حرامي على السِّلّم!
I need a plumber. The faucet is leaking.	*ána miђtāg sabbāk 3ašān ilђanafíyya bitná??aţ.*	أنا مِحْتاج سبّاك عشان الحنفية بِتْنقّط.
The light on our floor has burned out. Please replace it.	*lámbit iddōr bitá3na ithára?it, yarēt títla3 tiɣayyárha.*	لمْبِةْ الدّوْر بِتاعْنا اِتْحرقِت، يا ريْت تِطْلع تِغيرّها.

[1] = الشّفْرة بِتاعِةْ... *iššáfra bitā3it...*

Getting Laundry Done عنْد المكْوَجي

Laundromats (i.e., self-service laundry shops) are extremely uncommon in Egypt. Most furnished apartments have a غسّالة *ɣassāla* **washing machine**–but not a مُجفِّف *mugáffif* **clothes dryer**, which is also rare, as the norm is to hang up clothes to dry on a منْشر *mánšar* **drying rack** or حِبال الغسيل *ḫibāl ilɣasīl* **clothesline**. But while washing and drying a load of غسيل *ɣasīl* **laundry** is easy enough, ironing clothes can be a tedious, time-consuming affair. Fortunately, there should be a مكْوَجي *makwági* **ironing shop** a stone's throw from your apartment. For a very reasonable charge, they will gladly iron your laundered items and can even deliver them to you. Some such shops also offer laundry service. Just ask: يا ترى بِتِغْسِلوا هُدوم؟ *yatára, bitiɣsílu hudūm?* **Do you wash clothing?**[1] Other services commonly offered are repairs, alterations, dying, steam cleaning, carpet and drape cleaning, and sometimes suit tailoring. Again, just ask what services are available, as it varies from shop to shop.

[1] = فيه غسيل لَوْ سمحْت؟ *fī ɣasīl, law samáḫt?*; مكْوَة بسّ وَلّا مُمْكِن غسيل كمان؟ *mákwa bass? wálla múmkin ɣasīl kamān?* **Do you only do ironing? Or laundry, too?**

Getting clothes ironed

o كُنْت عايْزك تِكْويلي البنْطلوْن ده.[1]

◇ تمام تحْت أمْرك. فينْ العِنْوان؟

o العِمارة اللي في وِشّك[2] بِالظّبْط الدّوْر العاشِر شقّة ١٢.[3]

◇ تمام النّهارْده بِاللّيْل يِكون عنْدك إن شاء الله.[4]

o I'd like to get this pair of pants ironed.

◇ Sure, whatever you wish. What is the address?

o The building right across [the street] from you, 10th floor, apartment number 12.

◇ Okay, it will be at your place this evening, God willing.

o *kuntᵊ 3áyzak tikwīli -lbanṭalōn da.*[1]

◇ *tamām, taḥtᵊ ámrak. fēn il3inwān?*

o *il3imāra ílli f wíššak*[2] *bi-ẓẓábṭ, iddōr il3āšir šáʔʔa -tnāšar.*[3]

◇ *tamām, innahárda bi-llēl yikūn 3ándak in šāʔ allāh.*[4]

[1] = عايِز أكْوي البنْطلوْن ده *3āyiz ákwi -lbanṭalōn da*

[2] = اللي قُدّامك *ílli ʔuddāmak*

[3] لا هقف على إيدك و أخْدُه معايا. *laʔ, háʔaf 3ála īdak w áxdu ma3āya* **I'll just wait for you and take it.**

[4] تمام خمس دقايِق و يِكون جاهِز. *tamām, xámas daʔāyiʔ wi ykūn gāhiz.* **Okay, five minutes and it'll be ready.;** هعْمِلْهولك و إنْتَ واقِف. *ha3milhūlak w ínta wāʔif.* **I'll iron it for you immediately.**

2

GETTING CLOTHES WASHED AND IRONED

o بقولّك أيْه، خُد القُمْصان دي و قولُّه عايِزْهُم[1] قبْل يوْم الخميس.

◇ تحْت أمْرك يا باشا، أيّ حاجة تانْيَة؟

o آه ياريْت تِجيبْهُم مِتْعلّقين[2] مِش مِتْطبّقين عشان الكّسْرة بِتِبْقى بايْنة[3].

◇ مِن عينيّا.

o Hey, just take these shirts, and tell him I need them before Thursday.

◇ As you wish, Pasha. Anything else?

o Yes, please, bring them hanging, not folded because the creases [from folding] would be visible.

◇ My pleasure!

o *baʔúllak ʔē, xud ilʔumṣān di wi ʔúllu 3ayízhum[1] ʔablᵊ yōm ilxamīs.*

◇ *taḫtᵊ ámrak ya bāša. ayyᵊ ḫāga tánya?*

o *āh, yarēt tigíbhum mit3allaʔīn[2] miš mittabbaʔīn 3ašān ikkásra bitíbʔa báyna[3].*

◇ *min 3ináyya.*

[1] = مِحْتاجْهُم *miḫtághum*

[2] هاتْهُم على شمّاعات *háthum 3ála šamma3āt* **bring them on (coat) hangers**

[3] بيِتْكسّروا مكان التّطْبيقة *biyitkassáru makān ittaṭbīʔa* **they'll crease at the folds**

3

Getting clothing altered

○ بقولّك لَوْ سمحْت كُنْت عايْزة أقصّر الفُسْتان ده.

◇ تمام أشيل مِنُّه قدّ أيْه؟

○ أنا مِعلِّمالك بِالدّبابيس بسّ عايْزة أتْأكِّد بسّ إنيّ مِش هحْتاج أغْسِلُه.

◇ متِقْلقيش. إحْنا عنْدِنا غسيل برْضُه. هقصّرُه و بعْديْن أغْسِلُه و أكْويه كمان.

○ ألْف شُكْر.

○ Hey there, I'd like to have this dress shortened, please.

◇ Okay, how much should I shorten it?

○ I've marked the length with some pins, but I need to make sure I won't need to wash it.

◇ Don't worry we have laundry, too. I'll shorten it and then wash and iron it.

○ Thanks a million!

○ *baʔúllak law samáħt, kuntᵊ 3áyza -ʔáṣṣar ilfustān da.*

◇ *tamām, ašīl mínnu ʔaddᵊ ʔē?*

○ *ána mi3allimālak bi-ddababīs bassᵊ 3áyza -tʔákkid bass ínni miš haħtāg aɣsílu.*

◇ *ma-tiʔlaʔīš. íħna 3andína ɣasīl bárḍu. haʔaṣṣáru wi ba3dēn aɣsíllu w akwī kamān.*

○ *alfᵊ šukr.*

While many مكْوَجي *makwági* / دْراي كْلين *dray klīn* do clothing alterations, find an أتيليْه *atilēh* or محلّ خِياطة *maħáll xiyāṭa* **tailoring shop** if you want لِبْس تفْصيل *libsᵊ tafṣīl* **custom-made clothing** made to measure, especially formal wear.

4

GETTING CLOTHING ALTERED

○ عنْدي بِلوزة مِحْتاجة أصغّرْها[1].

◇ عنْدِك بِلوزة مقاسْها مظْبوط طيِّب؟[2]

○ آه أجيبْلك الاِتْنين يَعْني؟[3]

◇ آه هاتيهومْلي بسّ و أنا هقولِّك لَوْ هَيِنْفع تِتْصغّر وَلّا لا.

○ I want to take in this blouse.

◇ Do you have another blouse in the size you want?

○ Yes, should I bring them both?

◇ Yes, just bring both of them, and I'll let you know if it can be taken in or not.

○ *3ándi bilūza miħtāga aṣaɣɣárha*[1].

◇ *3ándik bilūza maʔásha maẓbūṭ ṭáyyib?*[2]

○ *āh, agíblak ilʔitnēn yá3ni?*[3]

◇ *āh, hatihúmli bassᵊ w ána haʔúllik law hayínfa3 titṣáɣɣar wálla laʔ.*

1 = أضيّقْها *aḍayyáʔha*

2 ثَواني أجيب المازورة آخُد المقاسات. *sawāni, agīb ilmazūra, āxud ilmaʔasāt.* **Hold on, let me bring the measuring tape to take your measurements.**

3 خُد البِلوزة دي قيس على مقاساتْها بِالظّبْط. *xud ilbilūza di, ʔīs 3ála maʔasátha bi-ẓẓábṭ.* **Take this blouse to measure against for the exact size.**

This is a useful tip for having alterations done. Just bring in a similar article of clothing that fits you well, which the tailor can use as a model.

5

Having a suit cleaned

○ بقولّك أيْه عنْدي فرح بعْد بُكْره، و عايز تِعْمِلّي البدْلة دي درْاي كْلين.

◇ معنْديش درْاي كْلين بسّ هغْسِلْهالك و أكْويهالك متِقْلقْش.

○ تمام بسّ خلّي بالك عليْها عشان خامِتْها لازِم تِتْغِسِل عَ البارِد.

◇ متِقْلقْش. هظبّطْهالك.

○ I want to dry clean this suit as I have a wedding [to attend] tomorrow.

◇ I don't have dry cleaning, but I'll clean and iron it for you. Don't worry.

○ Okay, but please be careful with it as the material must be washed in cold water.

◇ Don't worry. I'll take care of it.

○ *baʔúllak ʔē, 3ándi fáraḫ ba3dᵊ búkra, wi 3āyiz ti3mílli -lbádla di drāy klīn.*

◇ *ma-3andīšᵊ drāy klīn, bassᵊ haɣsilhālak w akwihālak ma-tiʔláʔš.*

○ *tamām, bassᵊ xálli bālak 3alēha 3ašān xamítha lāzim tiɣísil 3a -lbārid.*

◇ *ma-tiʔláʔš. haẓabbaṭhālak.*

There are also shops that call themselves درْاي كْلين *drāy klīn* "Dry Clean" but may not offer actual drycleaning services. Check when in doubt.

6

Getting a stain removed

◇ البُقْعة دي صعْب تِطْلع.

○ ليْه بسّ؟

◇ عشان ده كُلوْر وِقِع عليْها[1] و خد مِن اللّوْن الأصْلي.

○ طب، يِنْفع نِصْبُغْها؟

◇ آه بسّ هَيِبْقى لوْن أغْمق.

◇ This stain is difficult to get out.

○ How come?

◇ Because it's chlorine, and it already ate away the original color.

○ Well, can we dye it?

◇ Yes, but it will be a darker color.

◇ *ilbúʔ3a di ṣa3bᵊ títla3.*

○ *lē bass?*

◇ *3ašān da kulōr wíʔi3 3alēha*[1] *wi xad min illōn ilʔáṣli.*

○ *ṭab, yínfa3 nisbúɣha?*

◇ *āh, bassᵊ hayíbʔa lōn áɣmaʔ.*

[1] = اِتْدلق عليْها *itdála? 3alēha*

Extended Dialogue

○ كان عنْدي كام حاجة كِده مِحْتاجة أظبّطْها.

◇ اِتْفضّلي حضْرِتِك، تحْت أمْرِك.

○ إنْتو عنْدُكو رفّا وَلّا لا؟

◇ على حسب القطْعة و نوْع القُماش.

○ طيِّب، شوف السِّويتر ده كِده. شبك في مُسْمار و اِتْقطع القطْعة دي.

◇ هُوَّ صعْب يِتِعْمِلُه رفّا عشان خامْتُه نايْلوْن بسّ مُمْكِن نِلْزق عليْه بادْج أَوْ نِعْمِل حركة فيه.[1]

○ طب، إزّاي؟[2]

◇ مُمْكِن آخُد جُزْء مِن الجّيْب الدّاخِلي و أخيّطْلِك بيه جيْب صُغيّر يِداري القطْعة.

○ فِكْرة برْضُه تمام! طيِّب و الجّيبة دي كُنْت عايْزة أقصّرْها و أغيرّ السّوسْتة بِتاعِتْها.

◇ تمام مفيش مُشْكِلة. اللي بعْدُه؟[3]

○ آخِر حاجة بقى الجّاكيت ده عليْه البُقْعة دي و مِش عارْفة أطلّعْها[4] خالِص.

◇ دي بُقْعِةْ زيْت دي وَلّا أيْه؟

○ معْرفْش. حاوِلْت بِكُلّ الطُّرُق[5] و مطِلْعِتْش.

◇ طيِّب، خلّيني أحاوِلْك فيها و نْشوف بسّ مُمْكِن متِطْلعْش.

○ طيِّب، لَوْ صبغْناه مثلاً تِتْدارى[6]؟

◇ مُمْكِن تِفْضل بايْنة[7] برْضُه.

○ طيِّب، عُموماً شوف دوْل كِده و قوليّ أيْه النِّظام.

◇ خلاص سيبيلي رقم التِّليفوْن و هقولِّك قبْل ما أصْبُغ.

o خُد وَقْتك[8] في دوْل، مِش مِسْتعْجِلة بسّ أهمّ حاجة الطّقْم ده مِحْتاجاه دْراي كْلين و مكْوَة.

◇ تمام لَوْ بعْد بُكْره الصُّبْح يِمْشي معاكي؟[9]

o لا ياريْت بُكْره بِاللّيْل بِالكِّتير.

◇ تمام خلاص، مِن عينيّا.

o I have a couple of things that need to be mended.

◇ Certainly, miss. I'm at your service.

o Do you guys do patches?

◇ Depending on the type of the tear/hole and the fabric.

o Okay, can you check this sweater? It got snagged on a pin and has this rip.

◇ It's hard to be darned because it's nylon, but we can stick a patch over it, or we can sew around it.

o All right, how's that done?

◇ I can take a part from the internal pocket and sew an little external decorative pocket to hide the rip.

o That's a good idea! All right. And I wanted to shorten this skirt and replace its zipper.

◇ Okay, no problem. What else?

o One last thing: this jacket has this stain on it, and I have no idea how to get it out.

◇ Is it an oil stain or what?

o I have no idea. I tried all sorts of things and it won't come out.

◇ Let me try and see, but there's a good chance it might not come out.

o If we dyed it, would it be concealed?

◇ It might be still visible.

o Well, just check these things and let me know what we'll do.

◇ Okay, give me your phone number, and I'll let you know before I dye it.

○ Take your time on these; they're not urgent. But more urgently, I need this outfit to be dry cleaned and ironed.
◇ Okay, if we deliver it the day after tomorrow in the morning, will that be okay?
○ No, tomorrow night at the latest, please.
◇ Okay then. Whatever you wish.

○ *kān 3ándi kām ђāga kída miђtāga -ʐabbáţha.*
◇ *itfaɖɖáli ђaɖrítik, taђtᵊ ámrik.*
○ *íntu 3andúku ráffa wálla laʔ?*
◇ *3ála ђásab ilʔáţ3a wi nō3 ilʔumāš.*
○ *ţáyyib, šūf issiwītar da kída. šábak fi musmār wi -tʔáţa3 ilʔáţ3a di.*
◇ *húwwa ʂa3bᵊ yiti3mílu ráffa 3ašān xámtu naylōn bassᵊ múmkin nílzaʔ 3alē badž aw ní3mil ђáraka fī*[1]*.*
○ *ţab, izzāy?*[2]
◇ *múmkin āxud guzʔᵊ min iggēb iddaxíli w axayyáţlik bī gēb ʂuɣáyyar yidāri -lʔáţ3a.*
○ *fíkra bárɖu, tamām! ţáyyib wi -žžība di kuntᵊ 3áyza -ʔaʂʂárha w aɣáyyar issústa bta3ítha.*
◇ *tamām, ma-fīš muškíla. ílli bá3du?*[3]
○ *āxir ђāga báʔa, ižžākit da 3alē ilbúʔ3a di wi miš 3árʃa -ţallá3ha*[4] *xāliʂ.*
◇ *di búʔ3it zēt di wálla ʔē?*
○ *ma-3ráfš. ђāwiltᵊ bi-kúll iţţúruʔ*[5] *wi ma-ţil3ítš.*
◇ *ţáyyib, xallīni aђawíllik fīha wi nšūf, bassᵊ múmkin ma-tiţlá3š.*
○ *ţáyyib, law sabaɣnā másalan, titdāra*[6]*?*
◇ *múmkin tífɖal báyna*[7] *bárɖu.*
○ *ţáyyib, 3umūman šūf dōl kída wi ʔúlli ʔē inniʐām.*
◇ *xalāʂ sibīli ráqam ittilifōn wi haʔúllik ʔablᵊ m- ásbuɣ.*
○ *xud wáʔtak*[8] *fi dōl, miš mista3gíla. bass ahámmᵊ ђāga, iţţáʔmᵊ da miђtagā drāy klīn wi mákwa.*
◇ *tamām, law ba3dᵊ búkra iʂʂúbђᵊ yímši ma3āki?*[9]
○ *laʔ, yarēt búkra bi-llēl bi-kkitīr.*
◇ *tamām xalāʂ. min 3ináyya.*

1 نداريه بحركة *nidarī bi-ђáraka* **we'll conceal it by sewing**

2 حركة ازّاي؟ *ђáraka -zzāy?* **Sew it how?**

[3] = أيْه تاني؟ *ʔē tāni?* = و أيْه كمان؟ *wi ʔē kamān?*

[4] = و مِش عايْزة تِطْلع *wi miš 3áyza tíṭla3*

[5] = جرّبْت كُلّ حاجة *garrábt kull^{ə} ḥāga*

[6] = تِخْتِفي *tixtífi*

[7] = ظاهْرة *ẓáhra*

[8] = على مهْلك *3ála máhlak*

[9] = يِناسْبِك؟ *yinásbik?*

Vocabulary

laundry, washing	*ɣasīl*	غسيل
to iron, press	*káwa*	كَوى
ironing	*mákwa*	مكْوَة
ironer; ironing shop	*makwági*	مكْوَجي
laundry shop	*maɣsála*	مغْسلة
dry cleaning	*drāy klīn* *tanḍīf gāff*	دْراي كْلين تنْضيف جافّ
steam cleaning	*kayy bi-lbuxār*	كيّ بِالبُخار
carpet cleaning	*tanḍīf siggād*	تنْضيف سِجّاد
tailor, dressmaker	*tárzi* *xayyāṭ*	ترْزي خيّاط
seamstress	*xayyāṭa*	خيّاطة
tailoring	*tafṣīl*	تفْصيل
to tailor; to have (clothes) made	*fáṣṣal*	فصّل

custom-made clothing	*libsᵊ tafṣīl*	لِبْس تفْصيل
ready-to-wear clothing	*libsᵊ gāhiz*	لِبْس جاهِز
to sew	*xáyyaṭ*	خيّط
darning, mending; patch	*ráffa*	رفّة/رفّا
tear, rip, cut	*ʔáṭ3a*	قطْعة
spot, stain	*búʔ3a*	بُقْعة
stitching, sewing	*xiyāṭa*	خِياطة
button	*zurār (zarāyir)*	زُرار (زرايِر)
zipper	*sústa (súsat)*	سوسْتة (سوست)
shortening	*taʔṣīr*	تقْصير
to take in (make smaller)	*ḍáyyaʔ* *ṣáɣɣar*	ضيّق صغّر
to let out (make larger)	*wássa3*	وَسّع
lengthen	*ṭáwwil*	طوِّل
shorten	*ʔáṣṣar*	قصّر
buttonhole	*3írwa (3arāwi)*	عِرْوَة (عراوي)
skirt	*žība (žíyab)*	جيبة (جِيَب)
pants	*banṭalōn (-āt, banaṭīl)*	بنْطلوْن (ـات، بناطيل)
shorts	*šurt*	شوْرْت
shirt	*ʔamīṣ (ʔumṣān)*	قميص (قُمْصان)
blouse	*bilūza*	بِلوزة

dress	*fustān (fasatīn)*	فُسْتان (فساتين)
suit	*bádla (bídal)*	بدْلة (بِدل)
women's suit (dress suit, pantsuit)	*tayyīr*	تايّير
suit jacket	*bilēzar*	بِليْزر
jeans	*žīnz*	جينْز
linen	*kittān*	كِتّان
chiffon	*šifōn*	شيفوْن
satin	*satān*	ساتان
velvet	*ʔaṭīfa*	قطيفة
headscarf	*ṭárḥa* *išárb*	طرْحة إيشارْب
t-shirt	*tīširt*	تيشيرْت
sweatshirt	*switšírt*	سْويتْشيرْت
thick sweater	*swītar*	سْويتر
thin, wool sweater	*bulōvar*	بُلوْفر
jacket	*žākit*	جاكيت
coat	*bálṭu*	بالْطو
dye, dying	*sábɣa*	صبْغة
to dye	*sábaɣ*	صبغ
steam	*buxār*	بُخار
to straighten	*fárad*	فرد
to shrink	*kašš*	كشّ

tape measure	*mazūra*	مازورة
coat hanger	*šammā3a*	شمّاعة
clothespin	*mášbak (mašābik)*	مشْبك (مشابِك)
to hang up (to dry)	*nášar*	نشر
to bring in the laundry (from drying)	*lamm ilɣasīl*	لمّ الغسيل
to rinse	*šáṭaf*	شطف
laundry detergent	*masḫūʔ*	مسْحوق
fabric softener	*munáʒʒim malābis*	مُنعِّم ملابِس
to fade	*báhat*	بهت
to cut	*ʔaṣṣ*	قصّ
scissors	*maʔáṣṣ*	مقصّ
needle	*íbra*	إبْرة
to fold	*ṭábbaʔ*	طبّق

Expressions

○		
There's still extra fabric inside, so we have room to take it out a bit.	*fī xiyāṭa min gúwwa múmkin niwassá3u šuwáyya.*	فيه خِياطة مِن جُوّه مُمْكِن نِوَسّعُه شْوَيّة.
Iron this pair of pants without a crease.	*ikwīli -lbanṭalōn min ɣēr issēf.*	اِكْويلي البنْطلوْن مِن غيرْ السّيْف.

Don't push too hard while ironing the [shirt's] cuffs because the buttons get loose this way.	*ma-tdúsš[ə] gāmid 3ála -lʔaswíra w ínta bitíkwi 3ašān izzarāyir bititfákk.*	متْدوسْش جامِد على الأسْوِرة و إنْتَ بتِكْوي عشان الزّرايِر بتِتْفكّ.
I need to have this dress hemmed.	*miђtāga -lfustān da yit3imíllu sarfála.*	محْتاجة الفُسْتان ده يتْعِمِلُه سرْفلة.
I want you to go over the stitching on this embroidered patch because it's starting to fall off.	*3āyiz ti3ídli 3ála -ttaṭrīz da 3ašān ibtáda yifúkk.*	عايِز تِعيدْلي على التّطْريز ده عشان اِبْتدى يِفُكّ.
I need this tear mended.	*miђtāg ilʔáṭ3a di yit3imílha ráffa.*	محْتاج القطْعة دي يتْعِمِلْها رفّا.
I need these ironed right away as I'm going out in an hour.	*3āyiz ilmákwah di ḍarūri 3ála ṭūl 3ašān 3ándi mišwār kamān sā3a.*	عايِز المكْوَة دي ضروري على طول عشان عنْدي مِشْوار كمان ساعة.
The shirt got burned while you were ironing it.	*ilʔamīṣ itlása3 mínnak w ínta bitikwī.*	القميص اِتْلسع مِنّك و إنْتَ بتِكْويه.

At the Post Office في البوسْطة

In nearly every district, you can find a بوسْطة *búsṭa* **post office**, where you can easily send letters and parcels domestically or internationally. You can also find outgoing صناديق بريد *sanadīʔ barīd* **mailboxes** on the street in the postal service's signature green and yellow colors. It can take up to three weeks for a regular دَوْلي *dáwli* **international** delivery, while domestic خِدْمِةْ البريد السّريع *xídmit ilbarīd issarī3* **EMS (express mail)** is considerably faster. Always send anything of value مُسجّل *musággal* **by registered mail**. It may take longer, but at least, each step of the journey is recorded. If you bring a طرْد *ṭard* **parcel** to the post office, be sure it is unsealed so that the contents can be inspected for security and customs. They usually have boxes and tape on hand, but not always, so bring packing supplies with you, just in case. Incoming parcels are subject to inspection, and valuables will be charged customs duties. The post office also offers financial services. You can send and receive money, as well as pay bills.

SENDING A PACKAGE

○ مِن فضْلك، كُنْت عايِز أبْعت شُحْنة لِفرنسا. بِتِوْصل خِلال قدّ أيْه؟[1]

◇ هِيَّ عِبارة عن أيْه؟ كامِ كيلو يَعْني؟[2]

○ لا هِيَّ كذا حاجة. تِعْمِلّها حَوالي ٣ كيلو.[3]

◇ لَوْ عادي مِش سريع تِوْصل خِلال ٢٠ يوْم و تِتْكلِّف ٤٦٠ جِنيْه.

○ Excuse me, I would like to send a package to France. How long will it take?

◇ What is it exactly? How many kilos?

○ It's a couple of things actually, but altogether it's around 3 kilos.

◇ By standard shipment, it will arrive within 20 days and will cost 460 LE.

○ *min fáḍlak, kuntᵊ 3āyiz áb3at šúḫna l-fáránasa. bitíwṣal xilāl ʔaddᵊ ʔē?*[1]

◇ *híyya 3ibāra 3an ʔē? kām kīlu yá3ni?*[2]

○ *lā, híyya káza ḫāga. ti3milláha ḫawāli talāta kīlu.*[3]

◇ *law 3ādi miš sarī3 tíwṣal xilāl 3išrīn yōm wi titkállif rub3umíyya w sittīn ginēh.*

[1] = هتوْصل إمْتى؟ *hatíwṣal ímta?*

[2] = وَزْنها قدّ أيْه؟ *waznáha ʔaddᵊ ʔē?* (lit. how much is its weight?)

[3] وَزْنها ٣ كيلو. *waznáha talāta kīlu* **It weighs 3 kg.**

For money transfers, the post office takes 1% as a fee, which is capped at 250 LE. You can specify if you will pay the fee so that recipient receives the full amount or whether to deduct it from that amount at the recipient's end. The recipient can instantly collect the money from the post office where the money was sent. To transfer money, be sure you have the full name of the recipient (four names for Egyptians) and the post office address or branch name where the recipient will collect the money. If you are the recipient, you will need your passport as ID. (See the dialogue on the next page.)

2

Sending money

o كُنْت عايْزة أبْعت[1] مبْلغ لِمكْتب بريد سيدي جابِر في إسْكِنْدِرية.

◇ المبْلغ قدّ أيْه؟

o ١٢٠٠ جِنيْه.

◇ هتِدْفعي عليْهُم ١٢ جِنيْه رُسوم و هَيِقْدر يِصْرِفْهُم مِن النّهارْده لَوْ عايِز.[2]

o تمام أحِبّ أبْعتْهُم.

◇ إسْم المُسْتلِم و بلّغيه[3] إنُّه لازِم يِسْتِلِم بإثْبات شخْصية.

o I wanted to send an amount [of money] to Sidi Gaber Postal Office in Alexandria.

◇ What amount?

o 1200 LE.

◇ You will pay 12 LE in fees, and they can withdraw it today if they wish.[2]

o Okay, I'd like to send it.

◇ I need the recipient's name, and tell them they have to provide their ID.

o *kunt^a 3áyza áb3at[1] máblaɣ li-máktab barīd sīdi gābir f iskindiríyya.*

◇ *ilmáblaɣ ʔadd^a ʔē?*

o *alf^e w mitēn ginēh.*

◇ *hatidfá3i 3alēhum itnāšar ginēh rusūm wi hayíʔdar yiṣrífhum min innahárda law 3āyiz.[2]*

o *tamām, aɦíbb ab3áthum.*

◇ *ism ilmustálim wi ballaɣī[3] ínnu lāzim yistílim bi-isbāt šaxṣíyya.*

[1] = أحوِّل *aɦáwwil*

[2] In English, when speaking about a non-specific person, the pronoun 'they' (or 'he/she') is commonly used. In Arabic, the third-person masculine (هُوَّ *húwwa*) forms are used.

[3] = قوليلُه *ʔulīlu*

3

RENTING A POST OFFICE BOX

○ مِن فضْلك، عايِز أجّر صنْدوق بوسْطة. أيْه الإجْراءات المطْلوبة؟[1]

◇ ٩٠ جِنيْهْ في السّنة و صورة مِن إثْبات الشّخْصية و دمْغة.

○ طيِّب، أقْدر أسْتخْدِمُه بِدايَةً مِن إمْتى؟

◇ الأوِّل غيرّ عِنْوان المُراسْلات و مِن بعْدها تِقْدر تِسْتِلِم أيّ حاجة عليْه.

○ Excuse me, I want to rent a P.O. box. What is required?

◇ A 90-LE annual fee, a photocopy of your ID, and a stamp.

○ When can I start using it?

◇ First, change your mailing address to it and then you can receive anything there.

○ *min fáḍlak, 3āyiz aʔággar sandūʔ búsṭa. ʔē ilʔigraʔāt ilmaṭlūba?*[1]

◇ *tis3īn ginēh fi -ssána wi ṣūra min isbāt iššaxṣíyya wi dámɣa.*

○ *ṭáyyib, áʔdar astaxdímu bidāyatan min ímta?*

◇ *ilʔáwwil ɣáyyar 3inwān ilmuraslāt wi min ba3dáha tíʔdar tistílim ayyᵊ ḫāga 3alē.*

[1] أيْه المطْلوب؟ *ʔē -lmaṭlūb?*; أيْه الوَرق اللّازِم؟ *ʔē -lwáraʔ illāzim?*

Information about various services and costs can be found at Egypt Post's official website: **www.egyptpost.org**

٤

SENDING IMPORTANT DOCUMENTS

o لَوْ سمحْتي، مِحْتاج أبْعت الوَرق ده ضروري بريد مِسْتعْجِل.

◇ شِبّاك ١١ معَ مدام سامْية.

(goes to window 11)

o لَوْ سمحْتي، مِحْتاج أبْعت الوَرق ده مِسْتعْجِل لِلَنْدن.

◇ مُمْكِن يِتْشِحِن بُكْره الصُّبْح و يِوْصل خِلال ٥ أيّام عمل بسّ هَيِتْكلِّف ٤٧٥ جِنيْه.

o تمام، أنا مِحْتاجُه يِوْصل بِأسْرِع ما يِمْكِن[1].

o I would like to send these papers express, please.

◇ Window 11, with Mrs. Samia.

(goes to window 11)

o Excuse me, I need to send this to London express.

◇ It can be sent off tomorrow morning and will arrive within 5 business days, but it will cost 475 LE.

o That's fine. I need it to arrive as soon as possible.

o *law samáђti, miђtāg áb3at ilwára? da ḍarūri barīd mistá3gil.*

◇ *šibbāk ђidāšar má3a madām sámya.*

(goes to window 11)

o *law samáђti, miђtāg áb3at ilwára? da mistá3gil li-lándan.*

◇ *múmkin yitšíђin búkra -ṣṣúbђ, wi yíwṣal xilāl xámas ayyām 3ámal, bassᵊ hayitkállif rub3umíyya xámsa w sab3īn ginēh.*

o *tamām, ána miђtāgu yíwṣal bi-?ásra3 ma yúmkin*[1].

[1] في اسْرع وَقْت *fi ásra3 wa?t*

5

PICKING UP A PACKAGE

◇ الشُحْنة دي وَصَلِت بِإِسْم حضْرِتِك مِن مدْريد مظْبوط؟
o أَيْوَه تمام، أنا كُنْت مِسْتنِيّاها.
◇ تمام حضْرِتِك هتِدْفعي ٢٥٠ جِنيْه جمارِك قبْل ما تِسْتِلْميها.[1]

◇ You received a package from Madrid, right?
o Yes, that's me. I've been waiting for it.
◇ Okay, you will need to pay 250 LE for customs before receiving it.

◇ *ilšúħna di wáṣalit bi-smᵊ ħaḍrítik min madrīd maẓbūṭ?*
o *áywa, tamām. ána kuntᵊ mistaniyyāha.*
◇ *tamām, ħaḍrítik hatidfá3i mitēn w xamsīn ginēh gamārik ʔablᵊ ma tistilmīha.*[1]

[1] طيِّب، نِزِل عليْها جمارِك بِـ ٢٥٠ جِنيْه. *ṭáyyib, nízil 3alēha gamārik bi-mitēn wi xamsīn ginēh.*

6

Picking up a package

○ طيِّب، أنا الوَصْل اللي معايا بِيْقوليّ إنُّه وَصل المكْتب هِنا.

◇ مُمْكِن تِكون اِتْأخّرْت في اسْتِلامُه فا رِجِع عَ المكْتب الرّئيسي.

○ لا المفْروض يِكون وَصل إمْبارِح.[1]

◇ طيِّب، اِدّيني الوَصْل و إسْم حضْرِتك و نْشوف نِحاوِل نِحِلّها إزّاي.

○ Okay, the receipt I have tells me it has arrived at this post office.

◇ Maybe you came late, so it has already been shipped back to the central post office.

○ No, it supposedly arrived yesterday.

◇ Okay, just give me the receipt and your name, and let's see what can be done.

○ *ṭáyyib, ána -lwaṣl ílli ma3āya biyʔúlli -nnu wáṣal ilmáktab hína.*

◇ *múmkin tikūn itʔaxxártᵊ f istilāmu, fa rígi3 3a -lmáktab irraʔīsi.*

○ *lā, ilmafrūḍ yikūn wáṣal imbāriḥ.*[1]

◇ *ṭáyyib, iddīni -lwaṣlᵊ w ismᵊ ḥaḍrítak wi nšūf niḥāwil niḥilláha izzāy.*

[1] معاد وُصولُه إمْبارِح *ma3ād wuṣūlu -mbāriḥ* **its delivery date was yesterday**

Extended Dialogue

○ مِن فضْلك، كان فيه مبْلغ مِتْحوِّلّي على مكْتب البريد هِنا.[1]

◇ بإِسْم مين؟[2]

○ ماريا روبرْتْسون.

◇ طيِّب، أَسْتأْذِن حضْرِتِك في إِثْبات شخْصية.[3]

○ اِتْفضّل الباسْبوْر.

◇ آه يافنْدِم، وَصل. حضْرِتِك مُمْكِن تِسْتِلْميه مِن شِبّاك ٣.

(goes to window 3)

○ مِن فضْلك، فيه مبْلغ مِتْحوِّلّي هِنا و الأُسْتاذ قالّي أَسْتِلْمُه مِن الشِّبّاك ده.

◇ اِتْفضّلي يافنْدِم المبْلغ.

○ بسّ ده ناقِص. المفْروض يوْصلّي ٢٥٠٠.

◇ يِبْقى اللي بعت لِحضْرِتِك حمِّلِك إِنْتي رُسوم الخِدْمة.

○ مْمْم... طيِّب. لَوْ حابّة أنا أحوِّل[4] مبْلغ لِحدّ مُمْكِن ياخُد وَقْت قدّ أيْه؟[5]

◇ مِن يوْمْها[6] يِقْدر يِسْتِلْمُه يافنْدِم.

○ طيِّب، حاجة تانْيَة معلِشّ[7]. لَوْ عايْزة أبْعت وَرق مُهِمّ لِفْلوْريدا في أمْريكا. يوْصل خِلال قدّ أيْه؟[8]

◇ حضْرِتِك مُمْكِن تِتْأكِّدي مِن شِبّاك ١ أفْضل.

○ تمام، مُتْشكِّرة جِدّاً.

(goes to window 1)

○ لَوْ سمحْتي، مِحْتاجة أبْعت وَرق مِسْتعْجِل لِفْلوْريدا في أمْريكا. يوْصل خِلال قدّ أيْه؟

◇ ياخُد ٢١ يوْم لَوْ بريد عادي و تلاتّ إيّام لَوْ مِسْتعْجِل.

○ طَيِّب، دِه سِعْرُه كام و دِه سِعْرُه كام؟⁹

◇ الوَرق قَدّ أيْه و حَجْمُه أيْه؟¹⁰

○ لا دوْل ٤ وَرقات بِالظّبْط A4.

◇ هَيْكَلِّفِك حَوالي ٤٦٠ لَوْ عادي، لَوْ مِسْتَعْجِل ٤٩٠. مِش فارْقة كِتير¹¹.

○ لَوْ كِده يِبْقى المِسْتَعْجِل أحْسن. تَمام مُتْشَكِّرة أوي.

○ Excuse me, I am here to receive a money transfer to this postal office.
◇ What's your name?
○ Maria Robertson.
◇ Okay, your ID, please
○ Here's my passport.
◇ Okay, miss. It has arrived. You can pick it up at window 3.

(goes to window 3)

○ Excuse me, there's a money transfer for me here, and the gentleman over there told me I could receive it at this window.
◇ Here's your money, miss.
○ But I was supposed to receive 2500. This is less.
◇ The sender must have deferred the fees to you.
○ Hmm... I see, okay. What if I want to send some money to someone else? How long will it take?
◇ They can receive it on the same day, miss.
○ Okay. And one more question, please. If I need to send some important documents to Florida in the U.S., how long will it take?
◇ You had better ask at window 1.
○ All right. Thanks a lot.

(goes to window 1)

○ Excuse me, I need to send some urgent documents to Florida, USA. How much time will it take?
◇ It will take 21 days by standard delivery, and three days for express.

○ How much are those?
◇ How many sheets of paper and what size?
○ There are just 4 papers, A4.
◇ It will cost you around 460 for standard delivery and 490 for express. Not a big difference.
○ In that case, then express would be better. Okay, thank you.

○ *min fáḍlak, kān fī máblaɣ mitḥawwílli 3ála máktab ilbarīd hína.*[1]
◇ *bi-smᵊ mīn?*[2]
○ [Maria Robertson]
◇ *ṭáyyib, astáʔzin ḥaḍrítik fi isbāt šaxṣíyya.*[3]
○ *itfáḍḍal ilpaspōr.*
◇ *āh, yafándim, wáṣal. ḥaḍrítik múmkin tistilmī min šibbāk talāta.*

(goes to window 3)

○ *min fáḍlak, fī máblaɣ mitḥawwílli hína wi -lʔustāz ʔálli astílmu min iššibbāk da.*
◇ *itfaḍḍáli yafándim ilmáblaɣ.*
○ *bassᵊ da nāʔiṣ. ilmafrūḍ yiwṣálli alfēn w xumsumíyya.*
◇ *yíbʔa -lli báʕat li-ḥaḍrítik ḥammílik ínti rusūm ilxídma.*
○ *mmm... ṭáyyib. law ḥábba ána aḥáwwil*[4] *máblaɣ li-ḥádd, múmkin yāxud waʔtᵊ ʔaddᵊ ʔē?*[5]
◇ *min yúmḥa*[6] *yíʔdar yistílmu yafándim.*
○ *ṭáyyib, ḥāga tánya ma3alíšš*[7]*. law 3áyza áb3at wáraʔ muhímmᵊ li-flōrida f amrīka. yíwṣal xilāl ʔaddᵊ ʔē?*[8]
◇ *ḥaḍrítik múmkin titʔakkídi min šibbāk wāḥid áfḍal.*
○ *tamām, mutšakkíra gíddan.*

(goes to window 1)

○ *law samáḥti, miḥtāga áb3at wáraʔ mistá3gil li-flōrida f amrīka. yíwṣal xilāl ʔaddᵊ ʔē?*
◇ *yāxud wāḥid w 3išrīn yōm law barīd 3ādi wi tálat tiyyām law mistá3gil.*
○ *ṭáyyib, da síʕru kām wi da síʕru kām?*[9]
◇ *ilwáraʔ ʔaddᵊ ʔē wi ḥágmu ʔē?*[10]
○ *laʔ, dōl árba3 waraʔāt bi-ẓẓábṭ* [A4].
◇ *haykallífik ḥawāli rub3umíyya w sittīn law 3ādi, law mistá3gil rub3umíyya w tis3īn. miš fárʔa ktīr.*[11]
○ *law kída yíbʔa -lmistá3gil áḥsan. tamām mutšakkíra áwi.*

1 = جايّة أسْتِلِم مبْلغ مِتْحوِّلّي هِنا. gáyya -stílim máblaɣ mitɦawwílli hina.

2 إسْم حضْرِتِك؟ ismᵊ ɦaḑrítik? **Your name?**

3 مُمْكِن بِطاقة أَوْ باسْبور؟ múmkin biţāʔa aw paspōr? **Can I have your ID card or passport?**

4 لَوْ حبّيْت أبْعت... law ɦabbēt áb3at... **if I wanted to send...**

5 = بِيوْصل خِلال قدّ أيْه؟ biyíwşal xilāl ʔaddᵊ ʔē?

6 بعْدها على طول ba3dáha 3ála ţūl **right afterward;** في ساعِتْها fi sa3ítha **instantly**

7 = معلِشّ سُؤال كمان ma3alíšš suʔāl kamān

8 = يوْصل إمْتى؟ yíwşal ímta?

9 = طيِّب و الأسْعار أيْه لِلاِتْنيْن؟ ţáyyib wi -lʔas3ār ʔē li-lʔitnēn? = بِكام ده و بِكام ده؟ bi-kām da wi b-kām da?

10 على حسب مقاس الوَرق و حجْمُه. 3ála ɦásab maʔās ilwáraʔ wi ɦágmu. **It depends on the size of the paper and its weight.**

11 = الفرْق بسيط ilfárʔᵊ basīţ

Vocabulary

post office	búsţa máktab (makātib) barīd	بوسْطة مكْتب (مكاتِب) بريد
mail carrier	busţági	بوسْطجي
mail	búsţa barīd	بوسْطة بريد
mail box; P.O. box	sandūʔ barīd sandūʔ búsţa	صنْدوق بريد صنْدوق بوسْطة
letter	gawāb	جَواب
registered letter (that needs to be	gawāb musággal	جَواب مُسجّل

picked up at the post office)		
address	*3inwān (3anawīn)*	عِنْوان (عناوين)
to send	*bá3at*	بعت
sender	*múrsil* *rāsil*	مُرْسِل راسِل
recipient, addressee	*mustálim* *múrsal ilē*	مُسْتلِم مُرْسل إليْه
post card	*kart (kurūt)*	كارْت (كُروت)
window	*šibbāk*	شِبّاك
stamp	*ţābi3 (ţawābi3)*	طابِع (طَوابِع)
to stamp (with a postmark)	*xátam*	ختم
fiscal stamp (to show payment)	*dámɣa*	دمْغة
envelope	*ẓarf (aẓruf)*	ظرْف (أظْرُف)
shipping	*šaɧn*	شحْن
shipment	*šúɧna*	شُحْنة
urgent, express	*mistá3gil*	مِسْتعْجِل
parcel, package	*ţard (ţurūd)*	طرْد (طُرود)
amount (of money)	*máblaɣ*	مبْلغ
fees	*rusūm*	رُسوم
receiving	*istilām*	اِسْتِلام
ID card	*biţāʔa*	بِطاقة

proof of identity (any ID)	*isbāt šaxṣíyya*	إثْبات شخْصية
passport	*paspōr*	باسْبوْر

Expressions

○		
Customs shouldn't be applied to this.	*bassᵊ di miš ilmafrūḍ titgámrak.*	بسّ دي مِش المفْروض تِتْجمْرك.
This is a gift for me.	*di hidíyya gayyāli.*	دي هِدية جايّالي.
I need to send this contract registered and express.	*miḥtāg áb3at il3áʔdᵊ da f gawāb musággal mistá3gil.*	مِحْتاج أبْعت العقْد ده في جَواب مُسجّل مِسْتعْجِل.

◇		
You see, this shipment was sent back to the main office.	*buṣṣ, iššúḥna di ríg3it 3a -lmáktab irraʔīsi.*	بُصّ الشُّحْنة دي رِجْعِت عَ المكْتب الرّئيسي.
The address is incorrect.	*il3inwān maktūb ɣálaṭ.*	العِنْوان مكْتوب غلط.
Double-check the address.	*itʔákkid min il3inwān.*	اِتْأكِّد مِن العِنْوان.
You can pick it up at window 5.	*ilʔistilām min šibbāk xámsa.*	الاِسْتِلام مِن شِبّاك ٥.
We have to unwrap this parcel.	*ṭáyyib, iṭṭárdᵊ da lāzim yitfákk ilɣilāf ílli 3alē.*	طيِّب، الطّرْد ده لازِم يِتْفكّ الغِلاف اللي عليْه.

At the Bank في البنْك

Egypt is home to many local بُنوك *bunūk* banks, as well as some international branches from other countries. All banks are subject to adjustments as instructed by البنْك المرْكزي المصْري *ilbánk ilmarkázi -lmáṣri* **the Central Bank of Egypt (CBE)**. بُنوك إسْلامية *bunūk islamíyya* **Islamic banks** do not give interest but instead share revenues from investments the bank makes with its holdings, and they offer alternatives to loans that comply with sharia law. To open an account, foreigners are generally required to present a passport as ID, and in some cases, proof of income, such an HR letter. Banks may have different names for the kinds of accounts they offer, but they basically fall under two types: جاري *gāri* **checking** and تَوْفير *tawfīr* **savings**. Many banks also offer accounts in major foreign currencies. Exchange rates are generally a bit better at banks than at currency exchange offices.

3

Opening a dollar account

○ لَوْ سمحْت كُنْت عايْزة أفْتح حِساب عنْدُكُم بِالدّوْلار.

◇ تِقْدري يافنْدِم تِفْتحي حِساب بِحدّ أدْنى ١٠٠٠ دوْلار.

○ طيِّب، و هل ده بيِنْزِلُّه أرْباح[1]؟

◇ بِتِتْراوِح مِن ١ لِـ ١.٥ ٪. بِتِنْزِل في آخِر السّنة.

○ Excuse me, I'd like to open a dollar account at your bank.

◇ You can open an account with a minimum deposit of 1,000 dollars.

○ Does it pay interest?

◇ Yes, it ranges from 1 to 1.5 percent, which is paid out at the end of the year.

○ *law samáḫt, kuntᵊ 3áyza áftaḫ ḫisāb 3andúkum bi-ddōlar.*

◇ *ti?dári yafándim tiftáḫi ḫisāb bi-ḫádd ádna alfᵊ dōlar.*

○ *ţáyyib, wi hal da biyinzíllu arbāḫ[1]?*

◇ *bititrāwiḫ min wāḫid li-wāḫid wi nuşşᵊ fi -lmíyya. bitínzil fi āxir issána.*

[1] = فَوايِد *fawāyid*

٤

MAKING A TRANSFER

o مِن فضْلك، عايْزة أحوِّل المبْلغ ده لِلْحِساب ده[1].

◇ طيِّب، التّحْويل هَياخُد يومينْ يافنْدِم لِحدّ ما يِسمّع[2].

o طيِّب، مفيش طريقة تانْيَة أسْرع؟

◇ مُمْكِن نِعْمِل سحْب و إيداع طالما إنْتو الاِتْنينْ في نفْس البنْك.

o Excuse me, I'd like to transfer this amount to this bank account.

◇ It will take around two days to be reflected.

o Isn't there any other quicker way?

◇ We can do a withdrawal then deposit as long as they're both with the same bank.

o *min fáɖlak, 3áyza -ɧáwwil ilmáblaɣ da li-lɧisāb da*[1].

◇ *ʈáyyib, ittaɧwīl hayāxud yumēn yafándim li-ɧádd*ᵊ *ma yisámma3*[2].

o *ʈáyyib, ma-fīš ʈarīʔa tánya ásra3?*

◇ *múmkin ní3mil saɧb*ᵊ *w idā3, ʈālama -ntu -lʔitnēn fi nafs ilbánk.*

[1] لِحِساب رقم __ *li-ɧisāb ráqam* __ **to account number __**

[2] المبْلغ بِيوْصل خِلال يومينْ. *ilmáblaɣ biyíwṣal xilāl yumēn.* **The money will arrive within two days.**

If you're sending money to someone else in Egypt, you may find using the money transfer service at the post office a better option. There are also popular phone apps by major telecommunication companies and banks that make transferring money convenient.

5

Reporting a Faulty Bank Card

o لَوْ سمحْت الكّارْت بِتاعي مِش شغّال[1].

◇ ثَواني يافنْدِم أجرّبْه لِحضْرِتك.

o أنا جرّبْتُه في كذا مكنة ATM و برْضُه مِش بيِسْحب خالِص وَلا بيِعْمِل أيّ حاجة[2].

◇ مظْبوط... هُوَّ فِعْلاً كِده باظ. طيِّب إحْنا كِده نِقدِّم على واحِد تاني. و حضْرِتك تِقْدر تِسْتِلْمُه خِلال أُسْبوعيْن.

o و ده هَيْكون بمِصاريف زِيادة؟

◇ لا يافنْدِم مفيش أيّ مصاريف زِيادة.

o Excuse me, my card is not working.

◇ One moment, sir. I'll test it for you.

o I have already tried it in more than one ATM, but it still won't let me make withdraws or do anything.

◇ True... It's been damaged. We can request a new one be issued. You should receive it within two weeks.

o Will there be additional fees for that?

◇ No sir, there are no additional fees.

o *law samáɦt ikkártᵊ btā3i miš šaɣɣāl*[1].

◇ *sawāni yafándim agarrábu li-ɦaḍrítak.*

o *ána garrábtu fi káza mákana* [ATM] *wi bárḍu miš biyísɦab xāliṣ wála biyí3mil ayyᵊ ɦāga*[2].

◇ *maẓbūṭ... húwwa fí3lan kída bāẓ. ṭáyyib íɦna kída nʔáddim 3ála wāɦid tāni. wi ɦaḍrítak tíʔdar tistílmu xilāl usbu3ēn.*

o *wi da haykūn bi-maṣarīf ziyāda?*

◇ *lā, yafándim ma-fīš ayyᵊ maṣarīf ziyāda.*

[1] فيه حاجة غلط. *fī ɦāga ɣálaṭ.* **There's something wrong.**; **فيه** مُشْكِلة في الكارْت بِتاعي *fī muškíla fi -kkartᵊ btā3i.* **There's a problem with my card.**

[2] = لا بيِسْحب وَلا بيِعْمِل أيّ حاجة. *la biyísɦab wála biyí3mil ayyᵊ ɦāga.*

6

Changing money

○ لَوْ سمْحتي كُنْت عايْزة أبدِّل الدّولارات دي[1].

◇ حابّة تْبدِّلي كام؟

○ معايا ٢٠٠ دوْلار. يِعْمِلوا كام جِنيْه؟

◇ حَوالي ٣٤٧٥ جِنيْه.

○ تمام اِتْفضّلي.

○ I would like to change some dollars, please.
◇ How much do you want to change?
○ I have 200 dollars. How many pounds would that make?
◇ Around 3475 LE.
○ Okay, here you are.

○ *law samáђti, kuntᵊ 3áyza -báddil iddularāt di*[1].
◇ *ђábba tbaddíli kām?*
○ *ma3āya mitēn dōlar. yi3mílu kām ginēh?*
◇ *ђawāli talatalāf rub3umíyya xámsa w sab3īn ginēh.*
○ *tamām, itfaddáli.*

[1] أغيّر فِلوس *aɣáyyar filūs* **(I) change some money**

If you bring your home currency into Egypt to exchange into Egyptian pounds, make sure the bills are crisp and unmarked. Many merchants and exchange services will turn away damaged bills, even if they have only small blemishes or tears. Keep this in mind also when buying dollars at a bank. They may try to give you a blemished bill on purpose.

Don't forget to let your bank in your home country know that you'll be in Egypt so that your card doesn't get flagged for suspicious activity.

Extended Dialogue

○ أنا كُنْت فتحْت حِساب عنْدُكُم الشّهْر اللي فات بسّ بسْحب مِش راضي[1].

◇ طيِّب، أسْتأْذِن حضْرتِك في الباسْبوْر.

○ اِتْفضّل و ده كارْت بِرقم الحِساب كمان.

◇ تمام يافنْدِم مظْبوط. هُوَّ حصل تجْميد مُؤقّت لِلْحِساب[2] لِحين اِسْتِكْمال الأَوْراق بسّ.

○ مُش[3] فاهِم. أوْراق أيْه اللي ناقْصة؟ ما أنا قدِّمْت الباسْبوْر.

◇ هنْضيف عليْه بسّ يافنْدِم HR letter مِن مكان عمل حضْرِتك عشان إثْبات مصْدر الدّخْل.

○ غريبة دي. محدِّش طلبْها مِنّي ساعِتْها ليْه يَعْني؟

◇ معلِشّ يافنْدِم. هِيَّ تعْليمات جِديدة.

○ طيِّب، و لَوْ جِبْتهالْكُم يِتْرِفع الحظْر[4] بعْد قدّ أيْه؟

◇ بعْدها بِيوْم بِالكِّتير[5] يافنْدِم.

○ تمام لَوْ كِده هجيبْلُكُم واحْدة بُكْره بسّ عايِز أقدِّم على دفْتر شيكات كمان.

◇ مفيش مُشْكِلة يافنْدِم. أنا هحضّر لِحضْرِتك الطّلب لِحدّ ما تِجيلي بُكْره.

○ و حاجة تانْيَة معلِشّ... أنا اِحْتِمال أسافِر كمان شهْر[6]. أقْدر أشْترِي دولارات مِ البنْك؟

◇ آه طبْعاً أكيد.

○ عظيم. خلاص بُكْره آجي إن شاء الله و نْخلّص القِصص دي.

◇ في اِنْتِظار حضْرِتك يافنْدِم.[7]

- ○ I opened an account with your bank last month, but when I try to make a withdrawal, it won't work.
- ◇ May I have your passport, please?
- ○ Here you are. And here's a card with the account number.
- ◇ Yes, sir, that is correct. A temporary freeze has been put on your account until all documents have been completed.
- ○ I don't understand. What documents are missing? I have already submitted my passport.
- ◇ We just need to add an HR letter from your workplace as proof of source of income.
- ○ That's strange. Why didn't anyone ask me for this at that time?
- ◇ We apologize, sir. These are some new instructions.
- ○ Okay, if I bring that, how long will it take for the hold to be lifted?
- ◇ By the next day at most, sir.
- ○ Okay, in that case, I'll bring you one tomorrow, but I'd also like to have a checkbook issued.
- ◇ No problem, sir. I'll prepare the request for you by the time you come to me again tomorrow.
- ○ And just one more thing... I might be traveling in a month. Can I buy dollars from the bank?
- ◇ Yes, certainly.
- ○ Great. Okay then, I'll come back tomorrow, God willing, and we'll get these done.
- ◇ I'll be waiting for you, sir.

- ○ *ána kuntᵊ fatáɧtᵊ ɧsāb 3andúkum iššáhr ílli fāt bassᵊ básɧab miš rāḍi*[1].
- ◇ *ţáyyib, astáʔzin ɧaḍrítak fi -lpaspōr.*
- ○ *itfáḍḍal wi da kartᵊ bi-ráqam ilɧisāb kamān.*
- ◇ *tamām, yafándim maẓbūţ. húwwa ɧáşal tagmīd muʔáqqat li-lɧisāb*[2] *li-ɧīn istikmāl ilʔawrāʔ bass.*
- ○ *muš*[3] *fāhim. awrāʔ ʔē ílli náʔşaʔ ma ána ʔaddímt ilpaspōr.*
- ◇ *handīf 3alē bassᵊ yafándim* [HR letter] *min makān 3ámal ɧaḍrítak 3ašān isbāt máşdar iddáxl.*

- ○ *ɣarība di. ma-ɧáddiš ţalábha mínni sa3ítha lē yá3ni?*
- ◇ *ma3alíšš[ə] yafándim. híyya ta3limāt gidīda.*
- ○ *ţáyyib, wi law gibtahálkum yitrífi3 ilɧáẓr[ə] [4] ba3d[ə] ʔadd[ə] ʔē?*
- ◇ *ba3dáha bi-yōm bi-kkitīr[5] yafándim.*
- ○ *tamām, law kída hagiblúkum wáɧda búkra, bass[ə] 3āyiz aʔáddim 3ála dáftar šikāt kamān.*
- ◇ *ma-fīš muškíla yafándim. ána haɧáḍḍar li-ɧaḍrítak iţţálab li-ɧádd[ə] ma tgīli búkra.*
- ○ *wi ɧāga tánya ma3alíšš... ána iɧtimāl asāfir kamān šahr[6]. áʔdar aštíri dularāt mi -lbánk?*
- ◇ *āh, ţáb3an akīd.*
- ○ *3aẓīm. xalāṣ búkra āgi in šāʔ allāh wi nxállaṣ ilʔíṣaṣ di.*
- ◇ *fi -ntiẓār ɧaḍrítak yafándim.*[7]

[1] = مِش بِيِسْحب *miš biyísɧab* = مبِيِسْحبْش *ma-byisɧábš*

[2] حظْر على الحِساب *ɧaẓr 3ála -lɧisāb* **a hold on the account**

[3] مُش *muš* **not** is a variant of مِش *miš.*

[4] يِتْفكّ الحِساب *yitfákk ilɧisāb* **the account is accessible**

[5] = تاني يوْم على طول *tāni yōm 3ála ţūl*

[6] يِمْكِن أسافِر الشّهْر الجّاي *yímkin asāfir iššáhr iggáyy* **I might be traveling next month**

[7] تِنوّرْنا يافنْدِم في أيّ وَقْت. *tinawwárna yafándim, fi ayy[ə] waʔt.* **You're very welcome, sir. Anytime!**

Vocabulary

bank	*bank*	بنْك
the central bank	*ilbánk ilmarkázi*	البنْك المرْكزي
account	*ħisāb*	حِساب
checking account	*gāri*	جاري
savings account	*tawfīr*	توْفير
CD account	*šahāda*	شهادة
interest	*fawāyid*	فَوايِد
earnings	*arbāħ*	أرْباح
rates	*3awāyid*	عَوايِد
monthly	*šáhri*	شهْري
quarterly	*rub3ᵊ sánawi*	رُبْع سنَوي
semi-annually	*nuṣṣᵊ sánawi*	نُصّ سنَوي
annually	*sánawi*	سنَوي
[bank] card	*kart(ᵊ vīza)*	كارْت (فيزا)
debit card	*kart ilxáṣm ilfáwri*	كارت الخصْم الفَوْري
ATM card	*kart il-*[ATM]	كارت الـATM
to withdraw	*sáħab*	سحب
withdrawal	*masħūb*	مسْحوب
to deposit	*áwda3*	أَوْدع
deposit	*idā3*	إيداع

transfer	*taħwīl*	تحْويل
sending	*irsāl*	إرْسال
receiving	*isti?bāl*	اِسْتِقْبال
(bank) teller	*muwáẓẓaf (ilbánk)*	مُوَظّف (البنْك)
bank manager	*mudīr ilbánk*	مُدير البنْك
ATM machine	*mákanit* [ATM]	مكنِةْ ATM
ID card	*biṭā?a*	بِطاقة
passport	*paspōr*	باسْبوْر
credit card	*krēdit kard*	كْريْدِت كارْد
Visa card	*kartᵊ vīza*	كارْت فيزا
Mastercard	*kartᵊ mástar*	كارْت ماسْتر
dollar	*dōlar/dulār*	دوْلار
euro	*yūru*	يورو
pound	*ginēh*	جِنيْهْ
piastre	*?irš (?urūš)*	قِرْش (قُروش)
riyal	*riyāl*	رِيال
dinar	*dinār*	دينار
loan	*qarḍ (qurūḍ)*	قرْض (قُروض)
debt	*dēn (diyūn)*	ديْن (دِيون)
funding	*tamwīl*	تمْويل
installments, payments	*ta?sīṭ*	تقْسيط
request	*ṭálab*	طلب

signature	*ímḍa* *tawqī3*	إمْضا تَوْقيع
information	*bayanāt*	بَيانات
customer service	*xídmit il3úmala*	خِدْمِةْ العُملا
call center	*kōl sántir*	كوْل سنْترِ
activation	*taf3īl*	تفْعيل
bank statement	*kašf*ᵊ *ḥisāb*	كشْف حِساب
address	*3inwān*	عِنْوان
phone number	*ráqam tilifōn*	رقم تِليفوْن
to save up, put aside	*ḥáwwiš*	حوِّش

Expressions

	○	
What are the bank's business hours?	*húwwa -lbánk*ᵊ *biyíftaḥ min kām li-kām?*	هُوَّ البنْك بِيِفْتح مِن كام لِكام؟
What is the call center's phone number?	*ṭáyyib, ʔē ráqam ilkōl sántir?*	طيِّب، أيْه رقم الكوْل سنْترِ؟
I transferred this amount three days ago, but it hasn't been deducted yet from my account.	*ilmáblaɣ da ána miḥawwílu min tálat tiyyām wi líssa ma-txaṣámš*ᵊ *min ḥisābi.*	المبْلغ ده أنا مِحوِّلْه مِن تلاتّ إيّام و لِسّه متْخصمْش مِن حِسابي.
How can I activate this card?	*afá33al ilkárt*ᵊ *da izzāy?*	أفعّل الكارْت ده إزّاي؟

Do the earnings on the CD compound monthly or quarterly?	*ṭab, wi 3awāyid iššahāda di šáhri wálla rub3^ə sánawi?*	طب، و عَوايِد الشّهادة دي شهْري وَلّا رُبْع سنَوي؟
I haven't received bank statements two months in a row.	*kašf ilħisāb miš biyiwṣálli baʔālu marritēn.*	كشْف الحِساب مِش بيِوْصلّي بقالُه مرِّتيْن.
Excuse me, I want to update my mailing address.	*min fáḍlak, 3āyiz aɣáyyar 3inwān ilmuraslāt.*	مِن فضْلك، عايِز أغيرّ عِنْوان المُراسْلات.
I want to clear out this account and close it.	*kunt^ə 3āyiz aṣáffar ilħisāb da w aʔfílu.*	كُنْت عايِز أصفّر الحِساب ده و أقْفِلُه.

◇

You can contact customer service, sir.	*ħaḍrítak múmkin tatawāṣal má3a xídmit il3úmala.*	حضْرِتك مُمْكِن تتَواصل معَ خِدْمِةْ العُملا.
Signing business contracts inside the bank is not allowed.	*mamnū3 kitābit il3uʔūd fi -lbank^ə yafándim.*	ممْنوع كِتابِةْ العُقود في البنْك يافنْدِم.
You should make payments before the 5th of the month.	*ilʔáħsan tisáddid ʔabl^ə yōm xámsa fi -ššahr.*	الأحْسن تِسدِّد قبْل يوْم ٥ في الشّهْر.

Visiting a Museum في المتْحف

The most famous museum in Egypt is undoubtedly المتْحف المصْري *ilmátḫaf ilmáṣri* **the Egyptian Museum**[1] in Tahrir Square. First opening in 1902, the museum has since become overcrowded with too many آثار *asār* **artifacts** and tourists for its modest size. To address this, they will be moving its artifacts to a much larger and more modern home in 2020, المتْحف المصْري الكِبير *ilmátḫaf ilmáṣri -kkibīr* **the Grand Egyptian Museum (GEM)** near الاهْرامات *ilʔahramāt* **the Pyramids** in الجّيزة *iggīza* **Giza**. Of course, there are countless more museums throughout Egypt, not only showcasing Egypt's rich ancient history but also art, textiles, agriculture, railway, military, and so on. Be sure to get the right تذاكِر *tazākir* **tickets** for yourself and others in your group. There are different prices for Egyptian nationals and foreigners, and discounts for students. You may also need a special ticket to enter a premium exhibit area.

[1] The official name is متْحف الآثار المِصْرية *mátḫaf alʔaṭār almiṣríyya* **the Museum of Egyptian Antiquities**.

Asking about Hours of Operation

○ لَوْ سمحْت هُوَّ المتْحف بِيِفْتح[1] أيّام أيْه؟

◇ كُلّ يوْم[2] ما عدا الجُمْعة[3].

○ طيِّب، مِن السّاعة كام لِكام؟[4]

◇ مِن ٩ الصُّبْح لـِ ٥ العصْر.

○ ألْف شُكْر.

○ Excuse me, on which days is the museum open?

◇ Every day except for Friday.

○ All right, and what are the opening hours?

◇ From 9 a.m. until 5 p.m.

○ Thanks a lot.

○ *law samáḫt, húwwa -lmátḫaf biyíftaḫ*[1] *ayyām ʔē?*

◇ *kull*ᵊ *yōm*[2] *ma 3áda -ggúm3a*[3].

○ *ṭáyyib, min issā3a kām li-kām?*[4]

◇ *min tís3a -ṣṣúbḫ*ᵊ *li-xámsa -l3áṣr.*

○ *alf*ᵊ *šukr.*

[1] = شغّال *šaɣɣāl*

[2] = طول الأُسْبوع *ṭūl ilʔusbū3*

[3] = بسّ الجُمْعة لا *bass iggúm3a laʔ*

[4] = مَواعيدُه أيْه؟ *mawa3īdu ʔē?*

Check a museum's hours of operation before you go. Some museums are open seven days a week, while others close on Fridays (and sometimes Saturdays).

2

GOING THROUGH SECURITY

◇ الشّنْطة عَ الجِّهاز مِن فضْلِك، و أيّ مفاتيح أَوْ موبايْل جُوّة الشّنْطة.

o تمام. طيِّب لَوْ سمحْت أشْترِي[1] التّذاكِر مِنيْن؟

◇ شِبّاك التّذاكِر هِناك قبْل البوّابة و الأسْعار مكْتوبة فوْق الشِّبّاك.

◇ Please, put the bag in the machine, and put any keys or cell phone inside the bag.

o Okay. And where can I get tickets, please?

◇ The ticket window is over there before the gate, and the prices are written above the window.

◇ *iššánṭa 3a -ggihāz min fáḍlik, w ayyᵊ mafatīḫ aw mubāyl gúwwa -ššánṭa.*

o *tamām. ṭáyyib law samáḫt aštíri[1], -ttazākir minēn?*

◇ *šibbāk ittazākir hināk ʔabl ilbawwāba wi -lʔas3ār maktūba fōʔ iššibbāk.*

[1] = أجيب *agīb*

③

Taking photos

◇ مِن فضْلك، ممْنوع التّصْوير.

○ بسّ فيه ناس تانْيَة بِتْصوّر عادي.

◇ دوْل معاهُم تذْكرِةْ تصْوير لكِن حضْرِتك تذْكرِةْ دُخول بسّ.

○ طيِّب، أقْدر أشْترِي تذْكرِةْ التّصْوير مِنيْن؟

◇ مِن شِبّاك التّذاكِر اللي اِشْتريْت مِنُّه تذْكرِةْ الدُّخول.

◇ Excuse me, taking photos is not allowed.

○ But I can see others taking photos normally.

◇ They have a ticket for photography. Yours is entrance only.

○ Okay, where can I get a photography ticket?

◇ From the same window you got the entrance ticket from.

◇ *min fáḍlak, mamnū3 ittaṣwīr.*

○ *bassᵊ fī nās tánya bitṣáwwar 3ādi.*

◇ *dōl ma3āhum tazkárit taṣwīr lākin ḫaḍrítak tazkárit duxūl bass.*

○ *ṭáyyib, áʔdar aštíri tazkárt ittaṣwīr minēn?*

◇ *min šibbāk ittazākir ílli ištarēt mínnu tazkárit idduxūl.*

The Ministry of Antiquities has announced that visitors to Egypt's museums and archaeological sites are no longer required to purchase photography tickets as of August 2019. Taking photos using cell phones without flash is now allowed.

4

Getting a Tour Guide

○ مِن فضْلِك، فيه مُرْشِد يِقْدر يِعْمِلِّنا جَوْلة في المتْحف؟
◇ فيه آه مُوَظّفة مُمْكِن تِعْمِلُّكُم جَوْلة كمان نُصّ ساعة.
○ طيِّب، دي هتْكون بِالعربي وَلّا فيه بِلُغات تانْيَة؟
◇ لا هِيَّ بِتْتِعْمِل بِالعربي بسّ مُمْكِن حدّ تاني يِترْجِمْلُكُم لإِنْجِليزي.
○ يا ريْت فِعْلاً.

○ Excuse me, is there a tour guide that can give us a tour of the museum?
◇ There is an employee who can give you a tour in 30 minutes
○ All right. Will it be in Arabic or is it available in other languages?
◇ Well, it's only done in Arabic, but someone else can translate it into English.
○ That would be great.

○ *min fáḍlik, fī múršid yiʔdar yi3millína gáwla fi -lmátḥaf?*
◇ *fī āh muwaẓẓáfa múmkin ti3millúkum gáwla kamān nuṣṣᵊ sā3a.*
○ *ṭáyyib, di hatkūn bi-l3árabi wálla fī bi-luɣāt tánya?*
◇ *laʔ, híyya bittí3mil bi-l3árabi bassᵊ múmkin ḥaddᵊ tāni yitargimlúkum li-ingilīzi.*
○ *ya rēt fí3lan.*

Some museums offer tours in Arabic but rarely in other languages. You may find an unofficial guide, but be sure to agree on the tour price beforehand (and whether that price is for your whole group or per person).

5

ASKING WHERE AN ARTIFACT IS LOCATED

○ لَوْ سمحْت هِيَّ مومْيا رمْسيس التّاني فينْ؟

◇ لا دي في قِسْم خاصّ[1] جُوّة المتْحف معَ مومْياوات تانْيَة نادْرة.

○ طيِّب، دي نِقْدر نِدْخُلّها إزّاي؟

◇ بِتِشْترولْها تذْكرة مُنْفصِلة[2] قبْل الدُّخول.

○ Excuse me, where is the mummy of Ramses II?

◇ That mummy is in a separate section inside the museum among other rare mummies.

○ How can we enter that section then?

◇ You buy a separate ticket for it at its entrance.

○ *law samáḫt, híyya múmya ramsīs ittāni fēn?*

◇ *laʔ, di f qismᵊ xaṣṣ*[1]*, gúwwa -lmátḫaf má3a mumyawāt tánya nádra.*

○ *ṭáyyib, di níʔdar nidxulláha izzāy?*

◇ *bitištirúlha tazkára munfáṣila*[2] *ʔabl idduxūl.*

[1] لِوَحْدُه *li-wáḫdu* **alone, on its own**; مُنْفصِل *munfáṣil* **separated**

[2] لِوَحْدها *li-waḫdáha* **separately**

6

ASKING SOMEONE TO TAKE YOUR PICTURE

○ مِن فضْلك، مُمْكِن تِصوّرْنا؟[1]

◇ آه طبْعاً أكيد. عايْزينْها بِالطّول وَلّا بِالعرْض.

○ لا ياريْت بِالطّول و تِبيِّن معانا العمود ده[2].

◇ مِن عينيّا. أنا أخدْت كذا صورة[3] و إنْتو اِخْتاروا بقى.

○ شُكْراً جِدّاً.

○ Can you take a photo for us, please?

◇ Sure! Do you want it portrait or landscape?

○ Portrait would be better. And please make sure that column is included.

◇ My pleasure... I took a couple of photos so you can choose.

○ Thank you very much.

○ *min fáḍlak, múmkin tiṣawwárna?*[1]

◇ *āh, ṭáb3an akīd. 3ayzínha bi-ṭṭūl wálla bi-l3arḍ.*

○ *laʔ, yarēt bi-ṭṭūl wi tbáyyin ma3āna -l3amūd da*[2].

◇ *min 3ináyya. ána axádtᵊ káza ṣūra*[3] *w íntu -xtāru báʔa.*

○ *šúkran gíddan.*

[1] = (مُمْكِن) تاخُدْلِنا صورة؟ *(múmkin) taxudlína ṣūra?*

[2] و عايْزين العمود ده يِبان *wi 3ayzīn il3amūd da yibān* **and we want that column to be visible**

[3] = صوّرْتُكُم شُوَيِّة صُوَر *ṣawwartúkum šuwáyyit ṣúwar*

○ مِن فضْلك، تذْكرِةْ الدُّخول لِلْأطْفال هِيَّ هِيَّ الكُّبار؟[1]

◇ الطّالِب المصْري بِـ ٥ جِنيْهْ و الطّالِب الأجْنبي بِـ ١٠ جِنيْهْ و لِلكُّبار المصْري بِـ ١٠ جِنيْهْ و الأجْنبي بِـ ٢٠ جِنيْهْ.

○ طيِّب، عايْزين تذْكرْتيْن كُبار أجانِب و معانا واحِد مصْري و إبْنُه صُغيّر.

◇ يِبْقى كِده كُلُّه ٥٥.

○ تمام اِتْفضّل.

◇ طيِّب، معلِشّ اِنْتِظْروني[2] أشوفْلُكُم فكّة لِلْباقي.

○ هُوَّ المتْحف بيِفْتح كُلّ يوْم عادي؟

◇ آه فاتِح[3] كُلّ يوْم.

○ طيِّب، لَوْ جينا الجُّمْعة بيِفْتح عادي[4]؟

◇ آه بيِكون فاتح الجُّمْعة بسّ مِن بعْد الصّلاة تيجوا أحْسن.

○ طيِّب، يِنْفع نِصوّر عادي[5] ولّا ممْنوع؟

◇ لا التّصْوير ممْنوع عشان الفِلاش بيِضُرّ الآثار.

○ تمام طيِّب مُمْكِن أعْرف لَوْ فيه حدّ مُمْكِن يِعْمِلّنا جَوْلة؟

◇ بُصّي حضْرتِك هُوَّ كُلّ أثر مكْتوب تحْتُه كُلّ حاجة عنُّه[6] بِالعربي و الإنْجِليزي.

○ طيِّب، هُوَّ العُمود اللي برّه ده أثر وَلّا اِتْبنى قُريِّب على الطِّراز الفِرْعوْني؟

◇ دي مِسلِّةْ سنوْسِرْت الأوّل.

○ مِسلِّةْ مين؟[7]

◇ واحِد مِن مُلوك[8] الأُسْرة الاِتْناشر. كان بيِحْكُم مصْر مِن ٤٠٠٠ سنة تقْريباً.

- o Excuse me, are the tickets for children the same as for adults?
- ◇ For Egyptian students 5 LE, foreign students 10 LE. For adult Egyptians 10 LE, and foreigners 20 LE.
- o Okay, we would like to buy two adult tickets for foreigners, and we also have an Egyptian adult with his child.
- ◇ Then the total will be 55 LE.
- o Okay, here you are.
- ◇ Okay, please wait here until I find you some change.
- o Is the museum open every day?
- ◇ Yes, it is open every day.
- o So, if we came on a Friday, would it be open as usual?
- ◇ Yes, it's open on Fridays, but you'd best come after the prayers.
- o Can we take photos inside or is it not allowed?
- ◇ No, it's not allowed because the flash affects the antiquities.
- o All right. I'd like to know if there's someone who can give us a tour.
- ◇ Well, every relic has everything about it written underneath it in Arabic and English.
- o What about this column outside? Is it a monument [authentic] or was it built recently on the same pharaonic style [a replica]?
- ◇ It's the obelisk of Snosert I.
- o Whose obelisk?
- ◇ One of the kings from the 12th Dynasty. He ruled Egypt around 4,000 years ago.

- o *min fáḍlak, tazkárt idduxūl li-lʔaṭfāl híyya híyya ikkubār?*[1]
- ◇ *iṭṭālib ilmáṣri bi-xámsa gnēh wi -ṭṭālib ilʔagnábi bi-3ášara gnēh wi li-kkubār ilmáṣri bi-3ášara gnēh wi -lʔagnábi bi-3išrīn ginēh.*
- o *ṭáyyib, 3ayzīn tazkartēn kubār agānib wi ma3āna wāḫid máṣri w íbnu ṣɣáyyar.*
- ◇ *yíbʔa kída kúllu xámsa w xamsīn.*
- o *tamām, itfáḍḍal.*

◇ *ṭáyyib, ma3alíšš intiẓrūni*[2] *ašuflúkum fákka li-lbāʔi.*
○ *húwwa -lmátḫaf biyíftaḫ kullᵊ yōm 3ādi?*
◇ *āh, fātiḫ*[3] *kullᵊ yōm.*
○ *ṭáyyib, law gīna -ggúm3a biyíftaḫ 3ādi*[4]*?*
◇ *āh, biykūn fātiḫ iggúm3a bassᵊ min ba3d iṣṣála tīgu áḫsan*
○ *ṭáyyib, yínfa3 niṣáwwar 3ādi*[5] *wálla mamnū3?*
◇ *laʔ, ittaṣwīr mamnū3 3ašān ilfilāš biyḍúrr ilʔasār.*
○ *tamām ṭáyyib, múmkin á3raf law fī ḫaddᵊ múmkin yi3millína gáwla?*
◇ *búṣṣi ḫaḍrítik húwwa kull ásar maktūb táḫtu kullᵊ ḫāga 3ánnu*[6] *bi-l3árabi wi -lʔingilīzi.*
○ *ṭáyyib, húwwa -l3umūd ílli bárra da ásar wálla -tbána ʔuráyyib 3ála -ṭṭirāz ilfir3ōni?*
◇ *di misállit snōsirt ilʔáwwal.*
○ *misállit mīn?*[7]
◇ *wāḫid min mulūk*[8] *ilʔúsra -lʔitnāšar. kān biyúḫkum maṣr min arba3talāf sána taʔrīban.*

1 = تذْكرةْ دُخول الأطْفال نفْس سِعْر الكُبّار؟ *tazkárit duxūl ilʔaṭfāl nafsᵊ si3r ikkubār?*

2 = اِسْتنّوني *istannūni*

3 = مفْتوح *maftūḫ*

4 = بِيْكون شغّال *biykūn šaɣɣāl*

5 مسْموح بِالتّصْوير؟ *masmūḫ bi-ttaṣwīr?* **Is photography allowed?**

6 معْلومات عنُّه *ma3lumāt 3ánnu* **information about it**

7 معْلِشّ قول تاني كِده؟ *ma3líšš, ʔūl tāni kída.* **Excuse me, say that again.**

8 ملِك فرعوْني مِن... *málik fara3ōni min...* **a pharaoh from...**

Vocabulary

museum	*mátḫaf (matāḫif)*	متْحف (متاحِف)
gate	*bawwāba*	بوّابة
entrance	*duxūl*	دُخول

exit	*xurūg*	خُروج
inspection	*taftīš*	تفْتيش
guard	*ḥáras*	حرس
(food) containers	*awāni*	أواني
cell phone	*mubāyl*	موبايْل
window	*šibbāk*	شِبّاك
ticket	*tazkára (tazākir)*	تذْكرة (تذاكِر)
guide	*múršid*	مُرْشِد
tour	*gáwla*	جَوْلة
orientation, information	*ta3rīf*	تعْريف
photography	*taṣwīr*	تصْوير
camera	*kāmira*	كاميرا
monument, artifact, relic	*ásar (asār)*	أثر (آثار)
historical	*ásari*	أثري
civilization, culture	*ḥaḍāra*	حضارة
period, era, age	*3aṣr (3uṣūr)*	عصْر (عُصور)
Pharaonic, ancient Egyptian	*fir3ōni*	فِرْعوْني
Islamic	*islāmi*	إسْلامي
Coptic	*ʔíbṭi*	قِبْطي
Greek	*yunāni*	يوناني
Roman	*rumāni*	روماني

B.C.	*ʔabl ilmilād*	قبْل الميلاد
A.D.	*ba3d ilmilād*	بعْد الميلاد
statue	*timsāl*	تمِْثال
column	*3amūd*	عمود
obelisk	*misálla*	مِسلّة
mummy	*múmya*	مومْيا
weapons	*aslíɧa*	أسْلِحة
currency	*3úmla*	عُمْلة
tools	*adawāt*	أدَوات
letters	*rasāyil*	رسايِل
papyrus	*bárdi*	برْدي
wooden	*xášabi*	خشبي
mask	*qinā3 (áqni3a)*	قِناع (أقْنِعة)
tomb	*qabr (qubūr)*	قبْر (قُبور)
sarcophagus	*nawūs (nawawīs)*	ناووس (نَواويس)
coffin	*tabūt (tawabīt)*	تابوت (تَوابيت)
statue	*timsāl (tamasīl)*	تمِْثال (تماثيل)
crown	*tāg (tigān)*	تاج (تيجان)
the Pyramids	*ilʔahramāt*	الأهْرامات

Expressions

○		
How long has this museum been open [to the public]?	*húwwa -lmátḫaf da maftūḫ min ímta?*	هُوَّ المتْحف ده مفْتوح مِن إمْتى؟
Is there somewhere I can leave my belongings?	*fī amanāt min fáḍlak, múmkin asīb fīha ḫágti?*	فيه أمانات مِن فضْلك، مُمْكِن أسيب فيها حاجْتي؟
I want two tickets for foreigners.	*law samáḫt, 3āyiz tazkartēn agānib.*	لَوْ سمحْت عايِز تذْكرْتيْن أجانِب.
I want to buy a photography ticket.	*3áyza aštíri tazkárit taṣwīr.*	عايْزة أشْترِي تذْكرِةْ تصْوير.
Can I wait for the next tour?	*múmkin astánna -lgáwla -ggáyya?*	مُمْكِن أسْتنى الجَّوْلة الجّايّة؟

◇		
No leaning on the glass.	*mamnū3 tísnid 3ála -lʔizāz.*	ممْنوع تِسْنِد على الإزاز.
Photography without flash only.	*ittaṣwīr min ɣēr filāš.*	التّصْوير مِن غيْر فِلاش.
This museum is divided into 3 floors.	*ilmátḫaf da munqásim li-tálat adwār.*	المتْحف ده مُنْقسِم لِتلات أدْوار.
It's a historical palace that the state has transformed into a museum.	*da ʔaṣr ásari wi -ddáwla ḫawwilítu mátḫaf.*	ده قصْر أثري و الدَّوْلة حوِّلِتُه متْحف.

At a Mosque

في الجّامع

Cairo is known as مدينةِ الألْف مدْنة *madīnit ilʔálfᵊ mádna* **City of a Thousand Minarets**. There are actually more minarets than that, and many are attached to beautiful, historical mosques that welcome tourists. Some mosques, such as Sultan Hassan Mosque, require a ticket upon entrance for foreign tourists and are closed to tourists during Friday prayers. Modest clothing should be worn inside mosques, and shoes are removed before entering a prayer area. Women should keep their heads covered and be wearing a dress or skirt (not pants). Mosques provide loose skirts and isdals for women, as well as headscarves. Try to avoid passing in front of someone praying so as not to distract them and invalidate their prayer. In any case, there is no need to be nervous about the details of etiquette. People are usually welcoming and hospitable as long as you attempt to show respect for the people and the faith, and small missteps will certainly be excused.

Looking for a Mosque

o مِن فضْلك، جامع الحاكِم بِأمْرِ الله فينْ؟[1]

◇ هتِفْضلي ماشْيَة زيّ ما إنْتي[2] هتْلاقيه آخِر جامِع عَ اليمين قبْل بوّابِةْ الفُتوح.

o تمام، مُتْشكِّرة أوي.

◇ بسّ خلّي بالِك، لازِم تِدْخُلي بِحِجاب[3].

o تمام ما أنا معايا سْكارْف[4].

o Excuse me, where is the Al-Hakim bi-Amr Allah Mosque?

◇ You'll keep walking straight and you'll find it to be the last mosque on your right just before El-Fetouh Gate.

o Okay, thanks a lot.

◇ But keep in mind you have to enter wearing hijab.

o Yes, I have a scarf.

o *min fáḍlak, gāmi3 ilḥākim bi-ʔamrillāh fēn?*[1]

◇ *hatifḍáli mášya zayyᵊ má-nti*[2]*, hatlaʔī āxir gāmi3 3a -lyimīn ʔablᵊ bawwābit ilfutūḥ.*

o *tamām, mutšakkíra áwi.*

◇ *bassᵊ xálli bālik, lāzim tidxúli bi-ḥgāb*[3].

o *tamām, m- ána ma3āya skarf*[4].

1 أَوْصل لِـ_ إزّاي؟ *áwṣal li-__ izzāy?* **How do I get to __?**

2 = على طول *3ála ṭūl* = طوّالي *ṭawwāli* **straight ahead**

3 لازِم تِغطّي شعْرِك و إنْتي داخْلة. *lāzim tiɣáṭṭi šá3rik w ínti dáxla.* **You need to cover you hair when you go in.**

4 طرْحة *ṭárḥa* = إيشارْب *išárb* **headscarf**

2

DRESSING APPROPRIATELY FOR MEN

◇ مِش هَيِنْفع[1] تِدْخُل بِالشّورْت[2] يا أُسْتاذ.

○ طيِّب، أنا مُمْكِن أغطّي نفْسي بِأيْه؟[3]

◇ اِدْخُل عَ اليمين، سيب الجّزْمة عنْد الرّاجِل اللي هِناك ده و هتْلاقي معاه حاجة مُمْكِن تِغطّي بيها نفْسك.

○ تمام، شُكْراً أوي.

◇ You can't enter with shorts, sir.

○ Well, how can I cover up then?

◇ Enter on the right, leave your shoes with that man over there, and you will find he has something you can use to cover yourself with.

○ Okay, thanks a lot.

◇ *miš hayínfa3*[1] *tídxul bi-ššúrtᵊ*[2] *ya ustāz.*

○ *ţáyyib, ána múmkin aɣáţţi náfsi bi-ʔē?*[3]

◇ *ídxul 3a -lyimīn, sīb iggázma 3and irrāgil ílli hnāk da wi hatlāʔi ma3ā ħāga múmkin tiɣáţţi bīha náfsak.*

○ *tamām, šúkran áwi.*

1 = ممْنوع *mamnū3* **forbidden**

2 بِاللِّبْس ده *bi-líbsᵊ da* **with those clothes, wearing that**

3 ألْبِس أيْه؟ *álbis ʔē?* **What should I wear?**

You should always be reverent and keep your voice down inside a mosque, especially in the prayer hall. If there is a sermon, do not talk at all. Make sure your phone is on silent. Take photos discreetly and try not to bother worshippers.

3

DRESSING APPROPRIATELY FOR WOMEN

◇ مَينْفعْش، تِدْخُلي كِده يا أُسْتاذة.

○ ما أنا لابْسة طرْحة!

◇ معلِشّ بسّ حضْرِتِك لابْسة بنْطلوْن.

○ طيِّب، أيْه العمل[1] دِلْوَقْتي؟

◇ حضْرِتِك مُمْكِن تاخْدي جيبة أَوْ إسْدال مِن هِناك[2].

◇ You cannot enter like this, miss.

○ But I'm wearing hijab!

◇ Yes, but you're wearing pants.

○ Well, what to do now?

◇ You can borrow a skirt or isdal from over there.

◇ *ma-yinfá3š, tidxúli kída ya ustāza.*

○ *m- ána lábsa ţárђa!*

◇ *ma3alíšš^ə bass^ə ђaɖrítik lábsa banţalōn.*

○ *ţáyyib, ?ē il3ámal[1] dilwá?ti?*

◇ *ђaɖrítik múmkin táxdi žība aw isdāl min hināk[2].*

[1] = أعْمِل أيْه؟ *á3mil ?ē?* **What should I do?**

[2] مِن جُوّه *min gúwwa* **(from) inside**

Large mosques have a hall which people can reserve to celebrate كتْب الكِّتاب *katb ikkitāb* **marriage contracts**.

Timing Your Visit

◇ معلِش نِسْتأْذِنْكُم تيجوا كمان نُصّ ساعة لِحدّ ما الصّلاة تِخلّص[1].

o طيِّب، نِقْدر نِدْخُل السّاحة؟ مِش هنِدْخُل الجّامع نفْسُه.[2]

◇ كِده كِده شِبّاك التّذاكِر هَيِفْتح بعْد الصّلاة على طول[3].

o تمام خلاص، هنيجي تاني بعْد نُصّ ساعة.

◇ Sorry, come back in 30 minutes when the prayers are over.

o Can we just enter the courtyard area? We won't go inside the mosque.

◇ Anyway, the ticket window [is closed now and] will re-open right after the prayers.

o Okay, we'll come back in half an hour.

◇ *ma3alíšš, nista?zínkum tīgu kamān nuṣṣᵊ sā3a li-ḫáddᵊ ma -ṣṣála txállaṣ*[1].

o *ṭáyyib, ní?dar nídxul issāḫa? miš hanídxul iggāmi3 náfsu.*[2]

◇ *kída kída šibbāk ittazākir hayíftaḫ ba3d iṣṣála 3ála ṭūl*[3].

o *tamām, xalāṣ, hanīgi tāni ba3dᵊ nuṣṣᵊ sā3a.*

[1] بعْد نُصّ ساعة، تِكون الصّلاة خِلْصِت *ba3dᵊ nuṣṣᵊ sā3a, tikūn iṣṣála xílṣit* **in half an hour when the prayers are over**

[2] هنِتْمشّى برّه/حَواليْن الجّامع. *hanitmášša bárra/ḫawalēn iggāmi3.* **We'll walk outside/around the mosque.**

[3] شِبّاك التّذاكِر قافِل دِلْوَقْتي. *šibbāk ittazākir ?āfil dilwá?ti.* **The ticket window is closed now.**

It is typical for streets around mosques to be blocked by people praying during congressional prayers on Fridays and during holidays or in Ramadan, since the average modern mosque in any city, no matter how vast it may be, will never be able to accommodate an entire neighborhood inside its walls.

5

PERFORMING ABLUTION

o مِن فضْلك، فيْن المِيْضة؟[1]

◇ برّه. هتِمْشي يمين هتْلاقيها على شِمالك.

o تمام، مُتْشكّر أوي.

◇ العفو. تَقبّل الله[2]، و جُمْعة مُبارْكة[3] إن شاء الله.

o Excuse me, where is the ablution area?

◇ Outside. You will walk toward the right and you'll find it on your left.

o Okay, thanks a lot.

◇ You're welcome. May God accept [you], and have a blessed Friday, God willing.

o *min fáḍlak, fēn ilmēḍa?*[1]

◇ *bárra. hatímši yimīn, hatlaʔīha 3ála šmālak.*

o *tamām, mutšákkir áwi.*

◇ *il3áfw. taqábbal allāh*[2], *wi gúm3a mubárka*[3] *in šāʔ allāh.*

[1] فيْن الحمّام؟ *fēn ilḥammām?* **Where's the washroom?**; أقْدر أتْوَضّى فيْن؟ *áʔdar atwáḍḍa fēn?* **Where can I perform ablution?**

[2] تَقبّل الله *taqábbal allāh* **May God accept your prayer** is a prayer that Muslims say to each other before or after a prayer.

[3] The response is مِنّا وَ مِنْكُم *mínna wa mínkum* **I wish that for you, too.**

Ablution is a purification ritual that Muslims perform before prayer by washing the face, head, arms, and feet. Visitors who are not participating in the prayer are not expected to perform ablution.

Anyone can request to meet with the imam of the mosque to consult him about religious matters.

6

Prayer section for ladies

o لَوْ سمحْت، فينْ مُصّلى السّيِّدات؟

◇ الباب الجّاي عَ الشِّمال. ثَواني أبْعتْلِك حدّ يِفْتحْهولِك.

o طب، أقْدر أقابِل إمام الجّامع؟

◇ خيرْ فيه حاجة؟

o لا كُنْت عايْزة أسْألُه في فتْوى.[1]

◇ طيِّب، اِتْفضّلي وَرايا أوَصّلِك لِمكْتبُه.

o Excuse me, where is the prayer section for ladies?

◇ Through the next door on the left. Just a moment and I'll send someone to open it for you.

o All right. And can I see the imam?

◇ What's the matter?

o Nothing. I just wanted to ask him about a fatwa.

◇ Okay, follow me. I'll show you his office.

o *law samáɧt, fēn muṣṣála -ssayyidāt?*

◇ *ilbāb iggáyy, 3a -ššimāl. sawāni ab3átlik ɧadd^ə yiftaɧhūlik.*

o *ṭab, áʔdar aʔābil imām iggāmi3?*

◇ *xēr, fī ɧāga?*

o *laʔ, kunt^ə 3áyza asʔálu f fátwa*[1].

◇ *ṭáyyib, itfaḍḍáli warāya awaṣṣálik li-maktábu.*

[1] كُنْت مِحْتاجة فتْوى. *kunt^ə miɧtāga fátwa.* = كُنْت عايْزاه في فتْوى شرْعية. *kunt^ə 3ayzā f fátwa šar3íyya.* **I wanted [to consult] him on a matter of religious law.**

Historic mosques usually have a vast courtyard in the middle where everyone can move around, and then separate sections for males and females when it comes to prayers. Modern mosques are usually much smaller, with a women's section on the second floor. If the women's section is closed, you can request it be opened for you.

Extended Dialogue

○ لَوْ سمحْت، نِروح جامِع الأزْهر إزّاي؟[1]

◇ هتِمْشوا زيّ ما إنْتو كِده لِحدّ نفق المُشاة. مدْخل الجّامِع بعْديه بِحاجة بسيطة[2].

○ تمام، مُتْشكِّرين أوي. نِقْدر نِدْخُل عادي؟

◇ آه عادي. اِتْفضّلوا معايا طيِّب. أنا كِده كِده رايِح.

○ شُكْراً جِدّاً.

◇ على أيْه! بسّ هتِقْلعوا الجِّزم برّه و تِلْبِسوا إسْدال أَوْ حاجة.

○ بسّ إحْنا معناش[3].

◇ لا مِش مُشْكِلة. هُمّا بِيِبْقوا مُوَفّرين. أهُم[4]، تِقْدروا تاخْدوا اِسْدالات و جيبات مِنْهُم.

○ طيِّب، نِقْدر نِصوّر[5] عادي جُوّه؟

◇ آه صوّروا بِراحِتْكُم[6] في السّاحة طالما مِش وَقْت صلاة أَوْ خُطْبة.

○ طيِّب، إحْنا معانا واحْدة مُسْلِمة و حابّة تِصلّي. تِقْدر تِصلّي فينْ؟

◇ مُمْكِن تِدْخُل مكان السّيِّدات اللي عَ اليمين ده.

○ طيِّب، فيه مكان هِيَّ تِقْدر تِتْوَضى فيه؟[7]

◇ آه بسّ برّه.

○ طيِّب، خلّينا نْروح كُلِّنا الحمّام أحْسن بعْديْن نِدْخُل مرّة واحْدة.

◇ تمام، زيّ ما تْحِبّوا بسّ أديكو[8] عِرِفْتوا الأماكِن و النِّظام.

○ تمام، مُتْشكِّرين جِدّاً لِذوْقك.

◇ العفْو! على أيْه؟

o Excuse me, how can we get to Azhar Mosque?

◇ You'll keep going in this direction until the pedestrian tunnel. The entrance of the mosque is just a bit after it.

o Okay, thanks a lot. Is it okay to enter it?

◇ Oh yes. Please, come along with me then. I'm going that way anyway.

o Thanks a lot.

◇ Not at all. But you will need to take off your shoes and wear isdal or something.

o But we don't have those.

◇ No problem. They will provide them. There they are! You can take either an isdal or a skirt from them.

o And can we take photos inside?

◇ Yes, you can take as many photos as you wish in the courtyard as long as it is not the time for prayers or a sermon.

o Okay. And we have a Muslim lady with us and she would like to pray. Where can she pray?

◇ She can enter the ladies' section on the right over there.

o Okay. And is there somewhere she can perform ablution?

◇ Yes, but it's outside.

o Okay, we'd better all go to the bathroom first and then come back in.

◇ Okay, as you wish. And now you know where you can find everything.

o Yes, thanks a lot for your kindness!

◇ You're welcome! It's nothing!

o *law samáɧt, nirūɧ gāmi3 ilʔázhar izzāy?*[1]

◇ *hatímšu zayyᵊ má-ntu kída l-ɧaddᵊ náfaʔ ilmušā. mádxal iggāmi3 ba3dī b-ɧāga basīṭa*[2].

o *tamām, mutšakkirīn áwi. níʔdar nídxul 3ādi?*

◇ *āh, 3ādi. itfaḍḍálu ma3āya ṭáyyib. ána kída kída rāyiɧ.*

o *šúkran gíddan.*

◇ *3ála ʔē! bassᵊ hatiʔlá3u -ggízam bárra wi tilbísu isdāl aw ɧāga.*

○ *bass íḫna ma-3anāš*[3].

◇ *laʔ, miš muškíla. húmma biyíbʔu muwaffarīn. áḫum*[4], *tiʔdáru táxdu isdalāt wi žibāt mínhum.*

○ *ṭáyyib, níʔdar niṣáwwar*[5] *3ādi gúwwa?*

◇ *āh, ṣawwáru b-raḫítkum*[6] *fi -ssāḫa ṭālama miš waʔtᵊ ṣála aw xúṭba.*

○ *ṭáyyib, íḫna ma3āna wáḫda muslíma wi ḫábba tṣálli. tíʔdar tiṣálli fēn?*

◇ *múmkin tídxul makān issayyidāt ílli 3a -lyimīn da.*

○ *ṭáyyib, fī makān híyya tíʔdar titwáḍḍa fī?*[7]

◇ *āh, bassᵊ bárra.*

○ *ṭáyyib, xallīna nrūḫ kullína -lḫammām áḫsan ba3dēn nídxul márra wáḫda.*

◇ *tamām, zayyᵊ ma tḫíbbu, bass adīku*[8] *3iríftu -lʔamākin wi -nniẓām.*

○ *tamām, mutšakkirīn gíddan li-zōʔak.*

◇ *il3áfw. 3ála ʔē?*

[1] = جامع الأزْهر منِيْن؟ *gāmi3 ilʔázhar minēn?*

[2] = بمِسافة قُصيرّة *bi-masāfa ʔuṣayyára*

[3] = مِش معانا *miš ma3āna*

[4] هيِبْقى فيه جُوّه. *hayíbʔa fī gúwwa.* **They'll be inside.**

[5] = ناخُد صُوَر *nāxud ṣúwar*

[6] = زيّ ما إنْتو عايْزين *zayyᵊ má-ntu 3ayzīn* **as you want**

[7] = فيه مكان لِلوُضوء؟ *fī makān li-lwuḍūʔ?*

[8] آدي *ādi* **voilà, here is...**; أديك *adīk* / أديكي *adīki* / أديكو *adīku* **Here you are!**

Vocabulary

(large) mosque	*gāmi3*	جامِع
small mosque, masjid	*másgid*	مسْجِد
small "storefront" mosque (inside another building without a minaret)	*záwya*	زاوْيَة
minaret	*mádna (mídan)*	مدْنة (مِدن)
dome	*ʔúbba (ʔúbab)*	قُبّة (قُبب)
courtyard	*sāɧa* *ṣaɧn*	ساحة صحْن
column	*3amūd*	عمود
gate	*bawwāba*	بوّابة
tickets	*tazākir*	تذاكِر
shoe rack, shoe area	*makān iggízam*	مكان الجِّزم
charity box	*sandūʔ iṣṣadaʔāt*	صنْدوق الصّدقات
administration office	*máktab ilʔidāra*	مكْتب الإدارة
hijab, veil	*ɧigāb*	حِجاب
woman wearing hijab, covered woman	*muɧággab*	مُحجّب
headscarf	*ṭárɧa*	طرْحة
khimar (long head-scarf that also covers upper torso)	*ximār*	خِمار
niqab (covers entire face except the eyes)	*niqāb*	نِقاب

woman in niqab	*muntáqiba*	مُنْتقِبة
abaya	*3abāya*	عبايَة
women's prayer gown	*isdāl*	إسْدال
skirt	*žība*	جيبة
to visit	*zār*	زار
Muslim (male)	*múslim*	مُسْلِم
Muslim (female)	*muslíma*	مُسْلِمة
ablution (ritual cleaning before prayer)	*wuḍūʔ*	وُضوء
to perform ablution	*itwáḍḍa*	اِتْوَضّ
ablution washroom	*mēḍa*	ميْضة
washroom, restroom	*ɦammām*	حمّام
prayer area[1]	*muṣálla*	مُصلّى
women's section (of a mosque)	*muṣálla -ssayyidāt*	مُصلّى السّيِّدات
call to prayer	*azān* *adān*	أذان أدان
muezzin (person who does the call to prayer)	*muʔázzin*	مُؤذِّن
qibla (prayer direction toward Mecca)	*ʔíbla*	قِبْلة
to pray (a ritual prayer)	*ṣálla*	صلّى
ritual prayer	*ṣála*	صلاة

obligatory prayer	*ṣalāt ilfarīḍa*	صلاةْ الفريضة
voluntary prayer	*ṣalāt ittaṭáwwu3*	صلاةْ التّطوُّع
prayer for guidance	*ṣalāt ilʔistixāra*	صلاةْ الاِسْتِخارة
prayer of need	*ṣalāt ilḥāga*	صلاةْ الحاجة
dawn prayer	*ṣalāt ilfágr*	صلاةْ الفجْر
Duha prayer (voluntary morning prayer)	*ṣalāt iḍḍúḥa*	صلاةْ الضُّحى
noon prayer	*ṣalāt iḍḍúhr*	صلاةْ الضُّهْر
afternoon prayer	*ṣalāt il3áṣr*	صلاةْ العصْر
sunset prayer	*ṣalāt ilmáɣrib*	صلاةْ المغْرِب
evening prayer	*ṣalāt il3íša*	صلاةْ العِشا
Tahajjud prayer (voluntary night prayer)	*ṣalāt ittahággud*	صلاةْ التّهجُّد
holiday prayer	*ṣalāt il3īd*	صلاةْ العيد
prayer rug	*siggādit ṣála* *miṣallíyya*	سِجّادِةْ صلاة مِصلّية
people who are praying	*muṣallīn*	مُصلّين
prayer, invocation	*dú3a* *dá3wa*	دُعاء دعْوَة
chanting (repetition of short prayers)	*zikr (azkār)*	ذِكْر (أذْكار)
imam (prayer leader)	*imām*	إمام
pulpit	*mínbar*	مِنْبر

sermon	*xúṭba*	خُطْبة
Friday	*gúm3a*	جُمْعة
Friday prayer	*ṣalāt iggúm3a*	صلاةْ الجُّمْعة
halaqa (study circle)	*ḥálaʔa*	حلقة
lesson	*dars*	درْس
Quran	*qurʔān*	قُرْآن
recitation	*tilāwa*	تِلاوَة
sunna (a tradition of the Prophet)	*súnna*	سُنّة
fatwa (a religious opinion)	*fátwa*	فتْوى
fatwa council	*dār ilʔífta*	دار الإفْتا
reward, merit	*sawāb*	ثَواب
Ramadan	*ramaḍān*	رمضان
Taraweeh prayers (during Ramadan)	*ṣalāt ittarawīḥ*	صلاةْ التّراويح
to fast	*ṣām*	صام
fast(ing)	*ṣōm* *ṣiyām*	صوْم صِيام
breaking fast	*fiṭār* *ifṭār*	فِطار إفْطار
funeral	*ganāza*	جنازة
funeral prayer	*ṣalāt igganāza*	صلاةْ الجّنازة
tomb	*ḍarīḥ*	ضريح

Expressions

○		
What direction do we pray in?	*híyya -lʔíbla izzāy/minēn?*	هِيَّ القِبْلة إزّاي/مِنينْ؟
How much time is left until the midday prayer?	*húwwa bāʔi ʔaddᵊ ʔē 3ála ṣalāt iḍḍúhr?*	هُوَّ باقي قدّ أيْه على صلاةْ الضُّهْر؟
Where can I make an ablution?	*áʔdar atwáḍḍa fēn?*	أقْدر أتْوَضى فينْ؟
Where is the women's prayer section?	*fēn muṣálla -ssayyidāt?*	فينْ مُصلّى السّيِّدات؟
I'd like [to borrow] a skirt, please.	*3áyza žība law samáħti.*	عايْزة جيبة لَوْ سمحْتي.
May I have an isdal, please?	*múmkin isdāl min fáḍlik?*	مُمْكِن إصْدال مِن فضْلِك؟

◇		
The sermon has just started.	*ilxúṭba líssa bádʔa.*	الخُطْبة لِسّة بادْئة.
There is some maintenance going on inside the mosque.	*fī tarmimāt fi -ggāmi3.*	فيه ترْميمات في الجّامِع.
There are copies of the Quran and books in the library over there.	*fī maṣāħif wi kútub fi -lmaktába ílli hināk.*	فيه مصاحِف و كُتُب في المكْتبة اللي هِناك.
Charity boxes are next to the gate on your way out.	*ṣanadīʔ iṣṣadaʔāt gamb ilbāb w ínta xārig.*	صناديق الصّدقات جمْب الباب و إنْتَ خارِج.

There is a marriage ceremony after the evening prayer.	*fī katbᵊ kitāb ba3d il3íša.*	فيه كتْب كِتاب بعْد العِشا.
Take an isdal to put on.	*xúdi isdāl tilbisī.*	خُدي إسْدال تِلْبِسيه.
Women are on the upper floor.	*issayyidāt iddōr ílli fō?.*	السّيِّدات الدّوْر اللي فوْق.
There is a room for children upstairs.	*fī ōḍa li-l?aṭfāl fō?.*	فيه أوْضة لِلأطْفال فوْق.

[1] مُصلّى *muṣálla* can refer to the prayer hall inside a mosque, or to any area not in a mosque that is set up for prayers.

At a Language Institute في مركز تعْليم لُغة

A simple internet search will bring up a host of private language institutes in Cairo and Alexandria that specialize in teaching عربي *3árabi* **Arabic** to non-native speakers. If you are going to Egypt specifically to study Arabic for a limited time, it might be a good idea to enroll in a course online so that everything is organized and you know when you need to arrive for the first study term and when to book your return flight for. But if you are going to be in Egypt for an extended time, there are advantages in waiting until you arrive to find the best school and course for your needs. In any case, whenever possible, try to get word-of-mouth recommendations from current or former students. Most schools have programs in both عامّية *3ammíyya* **Egyptian Colloquial Arabic (ECA)** and فُصْحى *fúşħa* **Modern Standard Arabic (MSA)**. Some schools also have specialized (media, business, literature, etc.) courses in MSA. Non-secular institutes will also offer a third variety of Arabic: عربي القُرْآن *3árabi -lqurʔān* **Quranic Arabic** (sometimes called Classical Arabic). Some schools can provide you with a language partner or tutor, who gets paid per hour, so that you can practice the language more and even go on excursions (to a museum, restaurant, etc.) together.

1

INQUIRING ABOUT COURSES

o كُنْت عايْزة أعْرف كورْسات العربي اللي عنْدُكُم في المركز.

◇ فُصْحى وَلّا عامّية؟[1]

o مُمْكِن آخُد فِكْرة عن الاِتْنينْ؟

◇ سَواء فُصْحى أَوْ عامّية، الاِتْنينْ بِيِبْقوا ١٢ مُسْتَوَي، كُلّ مُسْتَوى ٢٤ ساعة.

o I would like to find out about the Arabic courses you give at your center.

◇ MSA or colloquial?

o Can you tell me about both?

◇ Well, whether MSA or colloquial, both have 12 levels of 24 hours each.

o *kuntᵊ 3áyza á3raf kursāt il3árabi -lli 3andúkum fi -lmárkaz.*

◇ *fúṣḫa wálla 3ammíyya?*[1]

o *múmkin āxud fíkra 3an ilʔitnēn?*

◇ *sawāʔ fúṣḫa aw 3ammíyya, ilʔitnēn biyíbʔu itnāšar mustáwa, kullᵊ mustáwa arbá3a w 3išrīn sā3a.*

[1] = عربي وَلّا مصْري؟ *3árabi wálla máṣri?* = فُصْحى وَلّا عامّي؟ *fúṣḫa wálla 3ámmi?*

Egyptian Arabic is a giant among Arabic dialects. It has more native speakers than any other variety of Arabic. (The population of Egypt is now around 100 million, with an annual growth rate around 2%.) It is also, arguably, the most widely understood dialect of Arabic outside of Egypt (i.e., throughout the Arab world) thanks to the popularity of Egyptian media, music, and cinema–Egypt is seen as the Arab Hollywood.

2

ARRANGING PRIVATE LESSONS

○ مِن فضْلك، كُنْت عايز مجْموعة لينا إحْنا الاِتْنينْ بسّ.

◇ بسّ ده كِده هَيِبْقى بْرايْفِت و هَيِبْقى سِعْرُه أعْلى مِن الكّورْس العادي.

○ تمام مفيش مُشْكِلة، بسّ أهمّ حاجة يِبْقى بعْد الضُّهْر.

◇ طيِّب، خلّيني أشوف لَوْ فيه مَواعيد مُناسْبة و أكلِّمك أبلّغك.

○ Excuse me, I'd like a group just for the two of us.

◇ But that would be considered a private course and will cost more than a regular course.

○ Okay, no problem. But most importantly, it should be in the afternoon.

◇ Well, let me check if there are available times, and I'll call and let you know.

○ *min fáḍlak, kuntᵊ 3áyza magmū3a līna íḫna -lʔitnēn bass.*

◇ *bassᵊ da kída hayíbʔa* [private] *wi hayíbʔa sí3ru á3la min ikkúrs il3ādi.*

○ *tamām, ma-fīš muškíla, bass ahámmᵊ ḫāga yíbʔa ba3d iḍḍúhr.*

◇ *ṭáyyib, xallīni ašūf law fī mawa3īd munásba w akallímak aballáɣak.*

Of course, ECA is not uniform throughout Egypt. It varies slightly from one region to another. However, if there is a "standard," it is that of middle-class Cairenes, and this is what you will be taught in ECA courses (and in Lingualism materials, such as this book). Alexandrian urban ECA differs only slightly, so that, if you learn ECA in Cairo, you will have no issues understanding someone from Alexandria, and vice versa. In the countryside of the Delta region, you will notice some more differences, but صِعيدي *ṣi3īdi* the **Upper Egyptian** dialect is markedly distinct from Cairene. There are also Bedouin dialects in Sinai and the Western Desert. Two groups speak non-Arabic languages in addition to Egyptian Arabic. Nubians in Upper Egypt speak Nubian (Nobiin), which is classified as a Sudanic language. Residents of the Siwa Oasis in the Western Desert speak Siwi, a Berber language.

3

Canceling a private lesson

- ○ معلِشّ أنا مِش هقْدر آجي الكّورْس النّهارْده و عايِز ألْغي الحِصّة.
- ◇ حضْرِتك أنْهي مجْموعة؟
- ○ لا أنا عنْدي بْرايْفِت النّهارْده معَ أُسْتاذ كريم السّاعة ٤.
- ◇ هُوَّ حضْرِتك كان لازِم تِبلّغْنا قبْلها بِيوْم فا كِده الحِصّة دي هتِتْحِسِب عليْك.
- ○ تمام أنا كِده كِده مِش هقْدر آجي بسّ بلّغي أُسْتاذ كريم عشان مَيِجيش عَ الفاضي.

- ○ I'm sorry, but I won't be able to make it to the course today and would like to cancel the lesson.
- ◇ Which group are you in?
- ○ No, I have a private lesson at 4 p.m. today with Mr. Karim.
- ◇ Well, you should have notified us a day ahead. Now you'll be charged for the lesson.
- ○ That's okay. I won't be able to make it anyway. Just let Mr. Karim know so that he doesn't come in [to work] for nothing.

- ○ *ma3alíšš, ána miš háʔdar āgi -kkurs innahárda wi 3āyiz álɣi -lɧíṣṣa.*
- ◇ *ɧaḍrítak ánhi magmū3a?*
- ○ *laʔ, ána 3ándi* [private] *innahárda má3a ustāz karīm, issā3a arbá3a.*
- ◇ *húwwa ɧaḍrítak kān lāzim tiballáɣna ʔabláha b-yōm, fa kída -lɧíṣṣa di hatitɧísib 3alēk.*
- ○ *tamām, ána kída kída miš háʔdar āgi, bassᵊ balláɣi ustāz karīm 3ašān ma-yigīš 3a -lfāḍi.*

4

PAYING FOR A COURSE

○ مِن فضْلِك، كُنْت عايِز أدْفع كورْس العامّية المُسْتَوى التّالِت.

◇ تمام هِيَّ الحِصّة الأولى هتِبْدأ بُكْره إن شاء الله.

○ تمام ٤٥٠، مِش كِده؟

◇ آه بِالظّبْط.٤٥٠ لِلكّورْس و ٥٠ لِلْكِتاب.

○ Excuse me, I'd like to pay for the Colloquial course, level 3.

◇ Okay, the first lesson will be tomorrow, God willing.

○ Yes, 450 LE, right?

◇ Yes, exactly. 450 LE for the course and 50 for the book.

○ *min fáḍlik, kuntᵊ 3āyiz ádfa3 kurs il3ammíyya -lmustáwa -ttālit.*

◇ *tamām, híyya -lḫíṣṣa -lʔūla hatíbdaʔ búkra in šāʔ allāh.*

○ *tamām, rub3umíyya w xamsīn, miš kída?*

◇ *āh, bi-ẓẓábṭ. rub3umíyya w xamsīn li-kkúrs, wi xamsīn li-kkitāb.*

5

Finishing a Course

◇ طيِّب، إحْنا كِده المرّة الجّايّة هتْكون آخِر حِصّة[1] إن شاء الله.
○ طب و المُسْتَوى اللي بعْدُه هَيِبْدأ إمْتى؟
◇ الأوِّل بسّ هَيْكون فيه اِمْتِحان مُدِّتُه ساعْتينْ و مِن ١٠٠ درجة.
○ و ده هَيْكون اِمْتى؟
◇ بعْد آخِر حِصّة بِأُسْبوع و النّتيجة بِتِطْلع بعْدها بِأُسْبوع. بعْدِها[2] بِنْجمّع مجْموعة لِلْمُسْتَوى اللي بعْدُه.

◇ Okay, next time will be our final class, God willing.
○ When will the next level start?
◇ Well, first there will be a two-hour exam out of 100 points.
○ When will that be?
◇ One week after the final lesson and the results will come out a week after that. Then we start making a group for the next level.

◇ *ṭáyyib, íḩna kída -lmárra -ggáyya hatkūn āxir ḩíṣṣa*[1] *in šāʔ allāh.*
○ *ṭab wi -lmustáwa -lli bá3du hayíbdaʔ ímta?*
◇ *ilʔáwwil bassᵊ haykūn fī imtiḩān muddítu sa3tēn wi min mīt dáraga.*
○ *wi da haykūn ímta?*
◇ *ba3dᵊ āxir ḩíṣṣa bi-ʔusbū3 wi -nnatīga btíṭla3 ba3dáha*[2] *b-ʔusbū3. ba3dáha bingámma3 magmū3a li-lmustáwa -lli bá3du.*

[1] هنْخلّص المرّة الجّايّة *hanxállaṣ ilmárra -ggáyya* **we will finish next time (next class)**

[2] = و بعْديْن *wi ba3dēn*

6

FINAL ASSESSMENT

○ أُسْتاذة سارة، معلِش مُمْكِن أعْرف درجْتي؟[1]

◇ إسْمِك أيْه؟

○ سانْدْرا ويلْيامْز.

◇ سانْدرا، إنْتي جِبْتي ٩٥ ما شاء الله. لازِم تِكمِّلي المُسْتَوى الجّايّ.

○ بِجدّ مُسْتَوايا كُوَيِّس؟

◇ جِدّاً... و بقى عنْدِك حصيلةْ كلِمات كُوَيِّسة جِدّاً. متْوَقّفيش بقى.[2]

○ Ms. Sara, can I find out what my grade is, please?

◇ What's your name?

○ Sandra Williams.

◇ Sandra, you got 95. Wow! You should continue on ot the next level.

○ Really? Is my level good?

◇ Very good. And you have acquired a great amount of vocabulary. Don't stop!

○ *ustāza sāra, ma3alíšš, múmkin á3raf darágti?*[1]

◇ *ísmik ʔē?*

○ [Sandra Williams].

◇ [Sandra], *ínti gíbti xámsa w tis3īn ma šāʔ allāh. lāzim tikammíli -lmustáwa -ggayy.*

○ *bi-gáddᵊ mustawāya kuwáyyis?*

◇ *gíddan... wi báʔa 3ándik ђaṣīlit kalimāt kuwayyísa gíddan. ma-twaʔʔafīš báʔa.*[2]

[1] مُمْكِن أعْرف جِبْت كام في الاِمْتِحان؟ *múmkin á3raf gibtᵊ kām fi -lʔimtiђān?* **Can I find out what I got on the exam?**

[2] اِسْتمِرّي على كِده! *istamírri 3ála kída!* **Keep it up!**

◇ صباح الخيرْ! أنا مِسْتِر[1] وائِل. هدرِّسْلُكُم العامّية المصْرية المُسْتَوى الرّابِع و كُنْت حابِب اتْعرّف بيكُم.

○ أنا إسْمي روْزْماري روْك.

◇ مِنيْن يا روْزي؟

○ مِن امْريكا.

◇ عظيم! و بِتِتْعلِّمي مصْري ليْه؟

○ أنا بشْتغل هِنا في عقْد مُدِّتُه خمس سِنين فا عشان كِده مِحْتاجة اتْعلِّم المصْري عشان اعْرف اتْعامِل.

◇ حِلْو جِدّاً و حضْرِتك؟

○ أنا إسْمي مارْك مِن بِريطانْيا و بحضّر ماجِسْتيرْ في اللُّغة العربية بسّ حابِب اتْعلِّم المصْري برْضُه.

◇ حِلْو جِدّاً! طيِّب خلّيني الاوِّل اقولُّكُم الكّورْس هَيِمْشي إزّاي.

○ آه هل هَيِبْقى فيه اِخْتِلاف عشان إحْنا بِرايْفِت؟

◇ لا خالِص هُمّا هُمّا الـ ٢٤ ساعة مرّتيْن في الأُسْبوع لِمُدِّةْ شهْر و نُصّ و كُلّ مرّة ساعْتيْن.

○ بيِبْقوا السّاعْتيْن على بعْض؟ مفيش بْريْك[2]؟

◇ إحْنا هنبْدأ بِالظّبْط إن شاء الله كُلّ مرّة ٤ بِالدِّقيقة. نِشْتغل لِحدّ ٥ اِلّا ١٠ و ناخُد بْريْك و بعْديْن نِكمِّل.

○ هل هناخُد مَواضيع جِديدة وَلّا هنكْمِّل مِن نفْس الكِّتاب؟

◇ إحْنا هنبْدأ في كِتاب جِديد. المفْروض يِكون معاكُم دِلْوَقْتي و هناخُد فيه ٦ وَحدات.

○ أنا جِبْت الكِّتاب فِعْلاً معايا. هُوَّ ٢٤ وِحْدة.

◇ ده بِيْغطّي ٤ مُسْتَوَيات[3] و اوِّل مرّة هناخُد اِسْتِماع و قِرايَة[4]، و المرّة التّانْيَة مُحادْثة و كِتابة فا الوِحْدة تِخْلص في مرِّتيْن.

o حِلْو التّقْسيم ده فِعْلاً عشان المُسْتَوى اللي فات مكانْش ماشي بِنِظام[5].

◇ لا إن شاء الله نمْشي عَ الخِطّة دي[6]. و خلّينا نِبْدأ مِن دِلْوَقْتي. هنِبْدأ في الاِسْتِماع و نِصحْصح الدُّنْيا كِده. جاهْزين؟

◇ Good morning! I'm Mr. Wa'el, and I will be teaching you Colloquial Egyptian, level 4. I would like to get to know you.

o My name is Rosemary Rock

◇ Where are you from, Rosie?

o From the U.S.

◇ Great! And why are you learning Egyptian Arabic?

o I'm working here on a 5-year contract. That's why I need to learn Egyptian Arabic, to be able to get by.

◇ Very nice. And what about you?

o My name is Mark, from the U.K., and I'm pursuing a Master's Degree in Arabic, but I would like to learn the Egyptian dialect, as well.

◇ Excellent! Okay, let me first tell you how the course will go.

o Yeah, will there be any difference since we're a private group?

◇ No, not at all. They're the same, 24 hours [with classes] twice a week for a month and a half. Each class is two hours long.

o Two continuous hours? No break?

◇ We start right at 4 p.m. everytime, God willing, and then stop at 4:50 [ten to five], take break, then continue.

o Are we going to take on new topics, or will we move on with the same book?

◇ We will start in a new book. You should have it now, and we will do six units.

- I already bought it, and it has 24 units.
- ◇ It covers four levels. First, we will do the reading and listening [sections], and in the following class, writing and conversation. So, a unit is completed in two classes.
- Nice plan... because the previous level was not that systematic.
- ◇ Hopefully, we will stick to this plan. Let's start now. We will start with the listening to refresh a little bit. Are you ready?

◇ *ṣabāḥ ilxēr! ána místar*[1] *wāʔil. hadarrislúkum il3ammíyya -lmaṣríyya -lmustáwa -rrābi3 wi kuntᵊ ḥābib at3árraf bīkum.*

O *ána ísmi* [Rosemary Rock].

◇ *minēn ya rōzi?*

O *min amrīka.*

◇ *3aẓīm! wi bitit3allími máṣri lē?*

O *ána baštáɣal hína f 3aʔdᵊ muddítu xámas sinīn, fa 3ašān kída miḥtāga at3állim ilmáṣri 3ašān á3raf at3āmil.*

◇ *ḥilwᵊ gíddan wi ḥaḍrítak?*

O *ána ísmi markᵊ min biriṭánya wi baḥáḍḍar mažistēr fi -llúɣa -l3arabíyya, bassᵊ ḥābib at3állim ilmáṣri bárḍu.*

◇ *ḥilwᵊ gíddan! ṭáyyib, xallīni -lʔáwwil aʔullúkum ikkúrsᵊ hayímši -zzāy.*

O *āh, hal hayíbʔa fī -xtilāf 3ašān íḥna* [private]*?*

◇ *laʔ, xāliṣ. húmma húmma -lʔarbá3a w 3išrīn sā3a marritēn fi -lʔusbū3 li-múddit šahrᵊ wi nuṣṣᵊ wi kullᵊ márra sa3tēn.*

O *biyíbʔu -ssa3tēn 3ála ba3ḍ? ma-fīšᵊ* [break][2]*?*

◇ *íḥna haníbdaʔ bi-ẓẓábṭ in šāʔ allāh kullᵊ márra arbá3a bi-ddiʔīʔa. ništáɣal li-ḥáddᵊ xámsa ílla 3ášara wi nāxud* [break] *wi ba3dēn nikámmil.*

O *hal hanāxud mawaḍī3 gidīda wálla hankámmil min nafs ikkitāb?*

◇ *íḥna haníbdaʔ fi ktāb gidīd. ilmafrūḍ yikūn ma3ākum dilwáʔti wi hanāxud fī sittᵊ waḥadāt.*

O *ána gibt ikkitāb fi3lan ma3āya. húwwa arbá3a w 3išrīn wíḥda.*

◇ *da biyɣáṭṭi árba3 mustawiyyāt*[3] *w áwwil márra hanāxud istimā3 wi ʔirāya*[4]*, wi -lmárra -ttánya muḥádsa wi kitāba fa -lwíḥda tíxliṣ fi marritēn.*

○ *ḫilw, itta?sīm da fí3lan 3ašān ilmustáwa -lli fāt ma-kánšᵊ māši bi-nẓām*[5].

◇ *la?, in šā? allāh nímši 3a -lxíṭṭa di*[6]. *wi xallīna níbda? min dilwá?ti. haníbda? fi -l?istimā3 wi nṣáḫṣaḫ iddúnya kída. gahzīn?*

[1] You should address a male teacher with مِسْتر *místar,* optionally followed by his first name, as in this dialogue. For a female teacher, it's ميسّ *miss.*

[2] = اِسْتِراحة *istirāḫa*

[3] بيِخْلص في أرْبع مُسْتَويّات. *biyíxlaṣ fi árba3 mustawiyyāt.* **It is completed over four levels.**

[4] = قِراءة *qirā?a*

[5] مكانْش مُنظّم *ma-kánšᵊ munáẓẓam* **was not well-organized**

[6] = نِطبّق الخِطّة دي *niṭábba? ilxíṭṭa di* = نِنفِّذ السِّسْتِم ده *nináffiz issístim da*

Vocabulary

institute, school	*má3had (ma3āhid)* *márkaz (marākiz)*	معْهد (معاهِد) مرْكز (مراكِز)
course	*kurs* *dáwra*	كورْس دَوْرة
intensive course	*kurs mukássaf*	كورْس مُكثّف
to enroll	*ištárak*	اِشْترك
enrollment	*ištirāk*	اِشْتِراك
level	*mustáwa*	مُسْتَوى
Arabic	*3árabi*	عربي
the Arabic Language	*lúɣa 3arabíyya*	لُغة عربية

Standard Arabic, MSA	*fúṣɧa*	فُصْحى
Colloquial Arabic	*3ammíyya* *3ámmi*	عامّية عامّي
Egyptian (Colloquial) Arabic	*máṣri*	مصْري
teacher (male)	*mudárris*	مُدرِّس
teacher (female)	*mudarrísa*	مُدرِّسة
to teach	*dárris*	درِّس
student (male)	*ṭālib*	طالِب
student (female)	*ṭālíba*	طالِبة
class, session	*ɧíṣṣa*	حِصّة
to cancel	*láɣa*	لغى
to start	*báda?*	بدأ
to learn	*it3állim*	اِتْعلِّم
to study, to be a student	*dáras*	درس
to study, do homework	*zākir*	ذاكِر
to take (a course, etc.)	*áxad*	أخد
level	*mustáwa*	مُسْتَوى
placement test	*imtiɧān taɧdīd mustáwa*	اِمْتِحان تحْديد مُسْتَوى
beginner	*mubtádi?*	مُبْتدِئ
(level) basic, elementary	*ibtidā?i*	اِبْتِدائي

intermediate	*mutawássiṭ*	مُتَوَسِّط
advanced	*3āli*	عالي
to improve, get better	*itɦássin*	اِتْحسِّن
to make progress in	*itʔáddim fi*	اِتْقدِّم في
to practice	*itdárrab*	اِتْدرّب
book	*kitāb (kútub)*	كِتاب (كُتُب)
unit, chapter	*wíɦda (waɦadāt)*	وِحْدة (وَحدات)
method(ology)	*mánhag (manāhig)*	منْهج (مناهِج)
listening	*istimā3*	اِسْتِماع
to listen to	*símí3*	سِمِع
speaking, conversation	*muɦádsa*	مُحادْثة
to speak	*itkállim*	اِتْكلِّم
writing	*kitāba*	كِتابة
to write	*kátab*	كتب
reading	*ʔirāya*	قِرايَة
to read	*ʔára*	قرا
passage, text	*qíṭ3a (qíṭa3)*	قِطْعة (قِطع)
test, exam	*imtiɦān*	اِمْتِحان
certification	*šahāda*	شهادة
degree	*dáraga*	درجة
to succeed	*nígiɦ*	نِجِح

success	*nagāɧ*	نجاح
photocopy	*núsxa (núsax)*	نُسْخة (نُسخ)
topic	*mawḍū3*	مَوْضوع
fees	*rusūm*	رُسوم
price, fee, tuition	*táman*	تمن
private	[private]	بْرايْفِت
group	*magmū3a*	مجْموعة
class time, scheduled time	*ma3ād*	معاد
break, rest time	[break] *istirāɧa*	بْريْك اِسْترِاحة
lecture hall	*qā3a*	قاعة
classroom	*faṣl*	فصْل
test, exam	*imtiɧān*	اِمْتِحان
restroom	*ɧammām*	حمّام
canteen	*bufēh*	بوفيْه

Expressions

○

Can you call me next month since I won't be able to start this month?	*múmkin tikallímni -ššahr iggáyyᵊ 3ašān miš há3raf ábda? ma3ākum iššáhrᵊ da?*	مُمْكِن تِكلِّمْني الشّهْر الجّاي عشان مِش هعْرف ابْدأ معاكُم الشّهْر ده؟

I want to change to a new class, please.	*kuntᵊ 3āyiz abáddil ilmagmū3a btá3ti.*	كُنْت عايِز أبدِّل المجْموعة بِتاعْتي.
I want an intensive course because I'm here temporarily.	*3āyiz kursᵊ mukássaf 3ašān misāfir.*	عايِز كورْس مُكثّف عشان مِسافِر.
Who will be teaching the next level?	*mīn ílli haydárris ilmustáwa -ggidīd?*	مين اللي هَيْدرِّس المُسْتَوى الجِّديد؟
Is there a placement test?	*fī imtiħān taħdīd mustáwa?*	فيه اِمْتِحان تحْديد مُسْتَوى؟
I want to join Mr. Khaled's class.	*3āyiz ábʔa fi magmū3it místar xālid.*	عايِز أبْقى في مجْموعِةْ مِسْتر خالِد.

Your placement results indicate that you need to start in level 2.	*natīgit taħdīd ilmustáwa bitʔūl ínnak lāzim tíbdaʔ min ilmustáwa -ttāni.*	نتيجِةْ تحْديد المُسْتَوى بِتْقول إنّك لازِم تِبْدأ مِن المُسْتَوى التّاني.
There will be a test at the end of each level.	*hayíbʔa fī imtiħān fi nihāyit kullᵊ mustáwa.*	هَيِبْقى فيه اِمْتِحان في نِهايِةْ كُلّ مُسْتَوى.
You can register in the course now and start whenever you want.	*múmkin tíħgiz ikkúrsᵊ dilwáʔti wi tíʔdar tibtídi fi -lwáʔt ílli yināsib.*	مُمْكِن تِحْجِز الكّورْس دِلْوَقْتي و تِقْدر تِبْتِدي في الوَقْت اللي يِناسْبك.

Dealing with Bureaucracy التّعامُل معَ الرّوتين الحُكومي

This chapter deals in particular with renewing visas, a shared experience by any foreigner who wishes to stay in Egypt long-term. In July 2019, just days before the publication of this book, it seems the Passports, Emigration & Nationality Administration moved from the Mogamma building in Tahrir Square to a new headquarters in a more modern facility in the Abbasseya district of Cairo. Visiting the overcrowded and outdated monstrosity that is the Mogamma to renew a visa had long been a bureaucratic nightmare for foreigners staying in Egypt. The Administration boasts that the new location has brought the process into modern times, with digital queuing, electronic visa systems, and new 'smart residence cards.' Optimistically, this is all very good news and, frankly, long overdue. It also means that the details in the dialogues in this chapter are no longer reflective of the new procedures you will encounter in Abbasseya. However, the vocabulary and many phrases are still applicable and will hopefully come in handy if you find yourself getting your visa renewed in Egypt. And if you do, please email us to let me know about your experiences in the new headquarters and how the procedures have changed, which will be appreciated and help me update this chapter for future editions of the book.

GETTING AN APPLICATION FORM

○ مِن فضْلك، متِعْرفْش أجيب مِنينْ اِسْتِمارِةْ حُصول على تأْشيرة؟[1]

◇ مُمْكِن تِلاقيهُم[2] في شِبّاك ١٢.

○ شِبّاك ١٢؟

◇ آه هتْلاقيه هِناك أهُه. هتِحْتاجي تِروحي هِناك و تمْضي الاِسْتِمارة دي مِن الظّابِط. شايْفة الطّابور الطّويل؟ متِقْلقيش بيِمْشي بِسُرْعة.

○ Excuse me, do you know where I can get a visa application form?

◇ You can find them at window 12.

○ Window 12?

◇ Yes, it's right over there. You need to go over there and get this form signed by the police officer. See the long line? Don't worry; it moves quickly.

○ *min fáḍlak, ma-ti3ráfš agīb minēn istimārit ḥuṣūl 3ála taʔšīra?*[1]

◇ *múmkin tilaʔīhum*[2] *fi šibbāk itnāšar.*

○ *šibbāk itnāšar?*

◇ *āh, hatlaʔī hināk ahú. hatiḥtāgi trūḥi hināk wi tímḍi -lʔistimāra di min izẓābiṭ. šáyfa iṭṭabūr iṭṭawīl? ma-tiʔlaʔīš, biyímši b-súr3a.*

[1] اِسْتِمارِةْ التّأْشيرة مِنينْ؟ *istimārit ittaʔšīra mnēn?* **Where are the visa application forms?**

[2] شوف كِده... *šūf kída...* **Look...**; اِسْأل... *ísʔal...* **Ask...**

2

GETTING AN APPLICATION FORM

○ سلامُ عليْكُم كُنْت عايْزة اِسْتِمارة أمْلاها.

◇ آهُه اِتْفضّلي، بسّ خلّصي و هاتيها تاني عشان أمْضيهالِك.

○ Hi, I need a form to fill out.

◇ Here you go. Please bring it back here when you're done so I can sign it.

○ *salāmu 3alēkum, kuntᵊ 3áyza -stimāra amlāha.*

◇ *ahú, itfaḍḍáli. bassᵊ xallásِi wi hatīha tāni 3ašān amḍihālik.*

3

GETTING PASSPORT PHOTOS AND PHOTOCOPIES

○ عايْزة صورْتينْ خلْفية بيْضا لِلْباسْبوْر لَوْ سمحْت.

◇ التِّسع صُوَر بِـ ١٥ جِنيْه.

○ تمام.

◇ اِتْفضّلي اُقْعُدي هِناك. مِن فضْلِك اِقْلعي النّضّارة عشان الصّورة.[1] اِرْفعي دقْنِك سيكا[2]... تمام.

○ هُوَّ أنا يِنْفع أصوّر وَرق هِنا برْضُه؟[3]

◇ لا مِش مِن هِنا... اِرْجعي لِلْمدْخل الرّئيسي. هتْلاقي محلّ النّاحْيَة التّانْيَة مِن السّلالِم.

○ I need two passport photos with a white background, please.

◇ It's 15 LE for 9 photos.

○ Okay.

◇ Have a seat over there. Please remove your glasses for the photo.... Tilt your chin up a bit... Okay.

○ Can I get photocopies done here too?

◇ No, not here. Go back into the main rotunda. There's a shop on the other side of the stairs.

○ *3áyza ṣurtēn xalfíyya bēḍa li-lpaspōr, law samáḥt.*

◇ *ittísa3 ṣúwar bi-xamastāšar ginēh.*

○ *tamām.*

◇ *itfaḍḍáli uʔ3údi hināk. min fáḍlik. iʔlá3i -nnaḍḍāra 3ašān iṣṣūra.*[1] *irfá3i dáʔnik sīka*[2]*... tamām.*

○ *huww-ána yínfa3 aṣáwwar wáraʔ hína bárḍu?*[3]

◇ *laʔ, miš min hína... irgá3i li-lmádxal irraʔīsi. hatlāʔi maḥáll innáḥya ittánya min issalālim.*

[1] أستأذنك تِقْلعي النّضّارة؟ *astaʔzínak tiʔlá3i -nnaḍḍāra?* **Could you take off your glasses?** / [2] سيكا *sīka* **a little bit** (slang) = شُوَيّة *shuwáyya* = سِنّة *sínna* / [3] فيه تصْوير وَرق هِنا؟ *fī taṣwīr wáraʔ hína?* = عنْدُكو تصْوير وَرق؟ *3andúku taṣwīr wáraʔ?*

4

RENEWING A VISA

◇ اِتْفضّل.

○ أنا مِحْتاج أمِدّ[1] الفيزا بِتاعْتي تلات شُهور مِن فضْلِك. اِتْفضّلي.

(hands clerk passport and visa application)

◇ طيِّب، هحْتاج صورة خلْفية بيْضا و صورة مِ الباسْبوْر.[2]

○ آه تمام. أنا معايا،[3] معلِشّ... اِتْفضّلي.

◇ تمام. خُد ده و اِنْزِل لِشِبّاك ٤٣.

◇ Yes?

○ I need to extend[1] my visa three months, please. Here you are.

(hands clerk passport and visa application)

◇ I also need a passport photo with a white background and photocopies of your passport.

○ Ah, yes, I have them here. Sorry... Here you are.

◇ Okay, take this and go down to window 43.

◇ *itfáḍḍal.*

○ *ána miḥtāg amídd[1] ilvīza btá3ti tálat šuhūr, min fáḍlik. itfaḍḍáli.*

(hands clerk passport and visa application)

◇ *ṭáyyib, haḥtāg ṣūra xalfíyya bēḍa wi ṣūra mi -lpaspōr.[2]*

○ *āh, tamām. ána ma3āya.[3] ma3alíšš... itfaḍḍáli.*

◇ *tamām. xud da w ínzil li-šibbāk talāta w arbi3īn.*

[1] Although many people think of this as extending the duration of their current visa, technically they are getting a new visa, not an extension.

[2] لَوْ كِده هنِعْمِل فيزا جِديدة و هتْكون مُدِّتْها تلات شُهور. *law kída haní3mil vīza gdīda w hatkūn muddítha tálat šuhūr.* **So, we'll issue a new visa which is valid for three months.**

[3] مَوْجود يافنْدِم. *mawgūd, yafándim.* **I have them, ma'am.**

5

PAYING FOR THE VISA

(hands clerk invoice received at window 12)

o اِتْفضّلي.

◇ ١١٠٥ جِنيْهْ مِن فضْلك.[1]

o اِتْفضّلي.

◇ اِتْفضّل.[2]

o و بعْديْن؟[3]

◇ خُد ده وَدّيه تاني لِشِبّاك ١٢.

(hands clerk invoice received at window 12)

o Here you are.

◇ 1105 LE, please.

o Here you are.

◇ And here you are.

o And now?

◇ Take that back to window 12.

(hands clerk invoice received at window 12)

o *itfaḍḍáli.*

◇ *alfᵊ míyya w xámsa gnēh, min fáḍlak.*[1]

o *itfaḍḍáli.*

◇ *itfáḍḍal.*[2]

o *wi ba3dēn?*[3]

◇ *xud da, waddī tāni li-šibbāk itnāšar.*

1 ١١٠٥ جِنيْهْ فكّة بسّ. *alfᵊ míyya w xámsa gnēh, fákka bass.* **1105 LE in exact change.**

2 معاك خمْسة و تاخُد عشرة؟ *ma3āk xámsa, wi tāxud 3áša̧ra?* **Do you have five and I'll give you ten?**

3 أروح فيْن دِلْوَقْتي؟ *arūḥ fēn dilwáʔti?* **Where do I need to go now?;** أيْه المطْلوب بعْد كِده؟ *ʔē ilmaṭlūb ba3dᵊ kída?* **What is the next step?**

6

Finishing up

◇ طيِّب، خلاص كِده[1]. تعالى بُكْره تاني قبْل السّاعة ٩.

○ ٩ الصُّبْح تمام؟

◇ آه ٩ بِالظّبْط. متِتْأخّرْش.[2]

○ تمام، حاضِر. شُكْراً!

◇ Okay, that's it. Come back tomorrow before 9 a.m.

○ 9 a.m.? Okay.

◇ But not after. Don't be late!

○ Okay, got it. Thank you!

◇ *ţáyyib, xalāş kída*[1]*. ta3āla búkra tāni ʔabl issā3a tís3a.*

○ *tís3a -şşúbɧ*ᵊ *tamām?*

◇ *āh, tís3a bi-zzábţ. ma-titʔaxxárš.*[2]

○ *tamām, ɧāɖir. šúkran!*

[1] = كِده تمام *kída tamām*

[2] تعالى بدْري. *ta3āla bádri.* **Come early.**

7

Picking up your visa

○ أنا هِنا عشان أسْتِلِم باسْبوْري.[1]

◇ اِسْتنّى رقمك مِن فضْلك.

○ بسّ الرّقم عَ الشِّبّاك ٤٥ و أنا رقمي ٤٤. خايِف أكون فوِّتّ رقمي وَلّا حاجة.

◇ لا متِقْلقْش، الأرْقام مِش بِالتّرْتيب. النّاس بِتْقدِّم مجْموعات. اُصْبُر بسّ و إحْنا هنِنْدَهْ على رقمك كمان شُوَيّة.[2]

○ طيِّب، تمام.

○ I'm here to pick up my passport.

◇ Just wait for your number, please.

○ But the number on the board is 45, and I'm 44. I'm worried I missed my number.

◇ Don't worry. The numbers aren't in order. People are grouped together. Just be patient and we'll call your number soon.

○ Ah, okay.

○ *ána hína 3ašān astílim paspōri.*[1]

◇ *istánna ráqamak, min fáḍlak.*

○ *bass irráqam 3a -ššibbāk xámsa w arbi3īn w ána ráqami arbá3a w arbi3īn. xayf akūn fawwítt^ə ráqami wálla ḥāga.*

◇ *laʔ, ma-tiʔláʔš, ilʔarqām miš bi-ttartīb. innās bitʔáddim magmu3āt. úṣbur bass^ə w íḥna haníndah 3ála ráqamak kamān šuwáyya.*[2]

○ *ṭáyyib, tamām.*

[1] جايّ أَسْتِلِم باسْبوري. *gayy astílim paspōri.* **I've come to pick up my passport.**

[2] و لمّا ييجي رقمك هنِنْدَهْ عليْك *wi lámma yīgi ráqamak haníndah 3alēk* **and when your number comes up, we'll call for you**

○ كُنْت عايْزة اِسْتِمارةْ فيزا مِن فضْلِك.

◇ روحي على شِبّاك ١٢.

○ فينْ معلِشّ شِبّاك ١٢ ده؟

◇ شايْفة الطّابور[1] اللي هِناك ده؟

○ يا نْهار أبْيَض![2] ده طَويل خالِص.

◇ لا متِقْلقيش[3] بيِمْشي بِسُرْعة[4]. أَوْ تعالي بُكْره مِن بدْري أحْسن.

○ لا خلّيني أحاوِل أنْجِز النّهارْده.

◇ طيِّب، روحي هِناك و اِخْتِمي الاِسْتِمارة مِن الظّابِط.

(goes to get an application form and get it stamped)

◇ رِجِعْتي بِسُرْعة آهُه[5].

○ آه الحمْدُ لله كانِت مِتيَسّرة[6]... اِتْفضّلي.

◇ طيِّب، هاتيلي باسْبوْرك بقى.

○ آه لا مُؤاخْذة معلِشّ. اِتْفضّلي الباسْبوْر آهُه.

◇ روحي صوّريه و اِتْصوّري صورة خلْفية بيْضا و هاتيهومْلي بقى.

(goes to get a photo and photocopies done and returns)

○ تمام كِده؟

◇ آه آخِر حاجة تِروحي تِدْفعي الرُّسوم دي مِن شِبّاك ٤٣.

○ بسّ الشِّبّاك يِكون فاتِح دِلْوَقْتي؟[7]

◇ معلِشّ يا تِلْحقيه يا لا[8]. لَوْ كِده خُدي الحافْظة أهي و اِدْفعي بُكْره مِن بدْري.

○ طيِّب، بعْد ما بدْفع أقْدر أسْتِلِم الفيزا بعْد قدّ أيْه؟

◇ بعْديها بيِوْم على طول.[9]

o خلاص أنا هشوف لَوْ هلْحق الشِّبّاك دِلْوَقْتي أدفع و آجي بُكْره أسْتِلِمِ إن شاء الله.

◇ تمام أهمّ حاجة بسّ تيجي مِن بدْري.

o طيِّب، و لَوْ مَيِنْفعْش معايا بُكْره أقْدر آجي بعْد بُكْره؟

◇ لا مِش بِنِشْتغل الجُمْعة. لَوْ كِده تعالي السّبْت بقى.

o I would like a visa application form, please.

◇ Go to window 12.

o Where is that, please?

◇ You see that line over there?

o Oh my goodness! It's so long.

◇ Don't worry, it moves quickly. Or you could come back early tomorrow.

o No, let me try to finish this today.

◇ Okay now, go there and get your form stamped from the officer.

(goes to get an application form and get it stamped)

◇ You came back quickly!

o Yes, thank God it went smoothly. Here you are.

◇ Okay, bring me your passport then.

o Oh yeah, sorry. Here is my passport.

◇ Okay, now go photocopy it and get a photo of yourself with a white background and bring them to me.

(goes to get a photo and photocopies made and returns)

o Okay. Now?

◇ Yes, the last thing: you go pay these fees at window 43.

o But is that window open now?

◇ Well, you may or may not make it in time. If that's the case, you can take the invoice and pay tomorrow morning.

o Okay, after I pay, how long will it be until I get my visa?

◇ The following day.

○ Okay, I'll go and see if the window is still open, pay now, and come collect it tomorrow, God willing.

◇ Yes, the most important thing is that you come early.

○ All right, and what if I can't make it tomorrow? Can I come the day after tomorrow?

◇ No, we don't work on Fridays. In that case, come on Saturday then.

○ *kuntᵊ 3áyza -stimārit vīza, min fáḍlik.*

◇ *rūḫi 3āla šibbāk itnāšar.*

○ *fēn ma3alíššᵊ šibbāk itnāšar da?*

◇ *šáyfa -ṭṭabūr*[1] *ílli hināk da?*

○ *ya nhār ábyaḍ!*[2] *da ṭawīl xāliṣ.*

◇ *laʔ, ma-tiʔlaʔīš*[3]*, biyímši b-súr3a*[4]*. aw ta3āli búkra min bádri áḫsan.*

○ *laʔ, xallīni aḫāwil ángiz innahárda.*

◇ *ṭáyyib, rūḫi hināk w ixtími -lʔistimāra min iẓẓābiṭ.*

(goes to get an application form and get it stamped)

◇ *rigí3ti b-súr3a ahú.*[5]

○ *āh, ilḫámdu li-llāh kānit mityassára*[6]*... itfaḍḍáli.*

◇ *ṭáyyib, hatīli paspōrik báʔa.*

○ *āh, la muʔáxza, ma3alíšš. itfaḍḍáli -lpaspōr ahú.*

◇ *rūḫi ṣawwarī wi -tṣawwári ṣūra xalfíyya bēḍa wi hatihúmli báʔa.*

(goes to get a photo and photocopies done and returns)

○ *tamām kída?*

◇ *āh, āxir ḫāga, tirūḫi tidfá3i -rrusūm di min šibbāk talāta w arbi3īn.*

○ *bass iššibbāk yikūn fātiḫ dilwáʔti?*[7]

◇ *ma3alíšš, ya tilḫaʔī ya laʔ.*[8] *law kída xúdi -lḫáfẓa ahí w idfá3i búkra min bádri.*

○ *ṭáyyib, ba3dᵊ ma bádfa3, áʔdar astílim ilvīza ba3dᵊ ʔaddᵊ ʔē?*

◇ *ba3dīha bi-yōm 3ála ṭūl.*[9]

○ *xalāṣ, ána hašūf law hálḫaʔ iššibbāk dilwáʔti ádafa3 w āgi búkra astílim in šāʔ allāh.*

◇ *tamām, ahámmᵊ ḫāga bassᵊ tīgi min bádri.*

○ *ṭáyyib, wi law ma-yinfá3šᵊ ma3āya búkra, áʔdar ági ba3dᵊ búkra?*

◇ *laʔ, miš biništáɣal iggúm3a. law kída ta3āli -ssabtᵊ báʔa.*

[1] = الصّفّ *iṣṣáff*

² يا خبر! = *ya xábar!* = يا خبر أبْيَض! *ya xábar ábyad!* = يا نْهاري! *ya nhāri* =

³ متْخافيش *matxafīš* **don't be afraid**

⁴ بيِخْلص على طول *biyíxlaṣ 3ála ṭūl* =

⁵ شُفْتي بقى؟ أديكي مغِبْتيش. *šúfti báʔa? adīki ma-ɣbitīš* **See? You weren't gone long.**

⁶ كانِت مِتْسهِّلة *kānit mitsahhíla* = عدِّت *3áddit* =

⁷ بسّ يا ترى هلاقيهُم شغّالين دِلْوَقْتي؟ *bassᵊ yatára halaʔīhum šaɣɣalīn dilwáʔti?* **But I wonder, will it be open now?**

⁸ إنْتي و حظِّك بقى. *ínti w ḫáẓẓik báʔa.* **It depends on your luck.** (i.e., Give it a shot.)

⁹ تاني يوْم على طول *tāni yōm 3ála ṭūl* **the next day**

Vocabulary

The Mogamma (lit. The Complex)	*ilmugámma3*	المُجمّع
the Mogamma in Tahrir	*mugámma3 ittaḫrīr*	مُجمّع التّحْرير
Passports, Emigration & Nationality Administration	*maṣláḫit iggawazāt wi -lhígra wi -gginsíyya*	مصْلحِةْ الجّوازات و الهِجْرة و الجِّنْسية
ground floor	*iddōr ilʔárḍi*	الدّوْر الأرْضي
first floor	*iddōr ilʔáwwal*	الدّوْر الأوّل
window, counter	*šibbāk*	شِبّاك
tourist visa	*vīza siyāḫa*	فيزا سِياحة
residency (visa)	*iqāma*	إقامة
form	*istimāra*	اِسْتِمارة
application	*ṭálab*	طلب

paperwork	*taxlīṣ wára?*	تخْليص وَرق
to process	*xállaṣ*	خلّص
fees	*rusūm*	رُسوم
stamp	*xitm*	خِتْم
invoice (for payment)	*ḫáfẓa*	حافْظة
receipt (of payment)	*waṣl (wuṣulāt)*	وَصْل (وُصُلات)
official, clerk	*muwáẓẓaf*	مُوَظّف
(police) officer	*ẓābiṭ*	ظابِط
place of residence	*maḫáll iqāma*	محلّ إقامة
reason for travel	*sábab issáfar*	سبب السّفر
duration	*múdda*	مُدّة
to extend	*madd*	مدّ
to apply	*?áddim*	قدِّم
to receive	*istálam*	اِسْتلم
to finish	*xállaṣ*	خلّص
to wait	*istánna*	اِسْتنّى
line, queue	*ṭabūr* *ṣaff*	طابور صفّ
turn	*dōr*	دوْر
number	*ráqam (arqām)*	رقم (أرْقام)
fingerprinting	*báṣmit il?aṣābi3*	بصْمِة الأصابِع

Expressions

○		
Where's the restroom?	*ilḫammām fēn?*	الحمّام فينْ؟
What do I need to do now?	*ilmafrūḍ á3mil ʔē dilwáʔti?*	المفْروض أعْمِل أيْه دِلْوَقْتي؟
I'm sorry. I don't understand.	*ána āsif, ma3alíšš. miš fāhim.*	أنا آسِف معلِشّ. مِش فاهِم.
Can I enter here?	*áʔdar ádxul hína?*	أقْدر أدْخُل هِنا؟
I brought five passport photos with me, just in case.	*ána gibt xámas ṣúwar paspōr iḫtiyāṭi.*	أنا جِبْت خمس صُوَر باسْبوْر اِحْتِياطي.

◇		
You're getting a new visa, not an extension.	*hani3mílak taʔšīra gdīda, miš hanmiddílak.*	هنِعْمِلك تأْشيرة جِديدة مِش هنْمِدِّلك.
The period of validity of the new visa will be from the date the new visa is issued, for three months.	*múddit saryān ittaʔšīra -ggidīda hatkūn min tarīx iṣdār ilvīza li-múddit tálat šuhūr.*	مُدِّةْ سرْيان التّأْشيرة الجِّديدة هتْكون مِن تاريخ إصْدار الفيزا لِمُدِّةْ تلات شُهور.

Dealing with the Police مع البوليس

You will see police officers all over the country. They wear white uniforms in the summer and black ones in the winter. And you will likely have to talk to a police officer at some point. Maybe you took a photo in the wrong place. Maybe you just look like a potential threat. Address a police officer respectfully using يا حضْرِةْ الظّابِط *ya ḫádrit izzābiṭ* **officer** or يافنْدِم *yafándim* **sir** and the formal pronoun حضْرِتك *ḫadrítak* **you** to ensure that the conversation gets off to the right start. In touristic areas (downtown, near museums, etc.), there are special tourist police whose job is to protect and assist tourists. If you get pickpocketed, for example, look around for tourist police. Know that traffic police, on the other hand, have no authority over issues other than traffic and will be of little help. God forbid, you are arrested or even taken to a police station under suspicion of a crime. If so, keep your cool, and try to contact a friend or lawyer to come to your aid. And good luck!

Reporting a Theft

○ لَوْ سمحْت كُنْت عايْزة أبلّغ عن سِرْقة[1].

◇ سِرْقِةْ أيْه بِالظّبْط؟[2]

○ شنْطِةْ سفر. كانِت في تاكْسي أخدْني مِن المطار.

◇ طيِّب، معاكي رقم التّاكْسي؟[3]

○ آه اِتْفضّل.

○ I want to report a theft, please.

◇ What was stolen exactly?

○ My suitcase. It was in the taxi that took me from the airport.

◇ Well, do you have the taxi number?

○ Yes, here it is.

○ *law samáḫt, kuntᵊ 3áyza abállaɣ 3an sírʔa*[1].

◇ *sírʔit ʔē bi-zzábṭ?*[2]

○ *šánṭit sáfar. kānit fi táksi axádni min ilmaṭār.*

◇ *ṭáyyib, ma3āki ráqam ittáksi?*[3]

○ *āh, itfáḍḍal.*

[1] أنا اتْسرقْت. *ána -tsaráʔt.* **I was robbed.**

[2] = أيْه اللي اِتْسرق بِالظّبْط؟ *ʔē ílli -tsáraʔ bi-zzábṭ?*

[3] أخدْتي رقم التّاكْسي؟ *axádti ráqam ittáksi?* **Did you take down the taxi('s license plate) number?**

Emergency Numbers in Egypt

Police	**122**
Tourist Police	**126**
Traffic Police	**128**
Fire Brigade	**180**
Ambulance	**123**

2

REPORTING A CRIME

◇ طيِّب، إنْتي اِدّيتي مُفْتاح شقِّتِك لِحدّ؟[1]

o لا مفيش حدّ معاه مُفْتاح الشّقّة غيْر اللي مِأجّرة مِنُّه[2].

◇ طيِّب، سِبْتي[3] باب الشّقّة مفْتوح مثلاً و إنْتي نازْلة؟

o لا خالِص. أنا رِجِعْت لقيْت المنْظر زيّ ما إنْتَ شايِف[4] و الفِلوس مسْروقة.

◇ Well, have you given the key to your apartment to anyone?

o No one has the keys except the person I'm renting from.

◇ Okay, did you leave the door open when you left?

o No, not at all. I came back to find this scene, as you can see, and the money stolen.

◇ *ṭáyyib, ínti -ddīti muftāḫ ša??ítik li-ḫádd?*[1]

o *la?, ma-fīš ḫadd[ə] ma3ā muftāḫ iššá??a ɣēr ílli m?aggára mínnu*[2].

◇ *ṭáyyib, síbti*[3] *bāb iššá??a maftūḫ másalan w ínti názla?*

o *la?, xāliṣ. ána rigí3t[ə] la?ēt ilmánẓar zayy[ə] má-nta šāyif*[4] *wi -lfilūs masrū?a.*

[1] حدّ معاه مُفْتاح شقِّتِك؟ *ḫadd[ə] ma3ā muftāḫ ša??ítik?* **Does anyone have the key to your apartment?**

[2] = صاحِب الشّقّة *ṣāḫib iššá??a* **the landlord**

[3] نِسيتي *nisīti* **you forgot**

[4] = لقيْت الشّقّة بِالمنْظر ده *la?ēt iššá??a bi-lmánẓar da*

3

DEALING WITH A RANSOM

o حضْرِتك أنا شغّال في السِّفارة و اللّابْتوْب بِتاعي عليْه بَيانات مُهِمّة جِدّاً.

◇ طيِّب و اللي سرقوه مِنّك اِتْواصْلوا معاك[1]؟

o طالْبين فِدْيَة عِشْرين ألْف دوْلار عشان يِرجّعوه.

◇ طيِّب، خلّينا نِحوِّل القضية على المباحِث الإلِكْترونية و هُمّا هَيْقوموا بِاللازِم[2].

o I work at the embassy, and my laptop contains extremely important documents.

◇ And have those who stole it from you contacted you?

o They're asking for a 20,000-dollar ransom to return it.

◇ Okay, let's transfer this case to the electronic crimes division, and they will handle everything.

o *ђaḑrítak, ána šaɣɣāl fi -ssifāra wi -llaptōp bitā3i 3alē bayanāt muhímma gíddan.*

◇ *ţáyyib, w ílli saraʔū mínnak itwáşlu ma3āk*[1]*?*

o *ţalbīn fídya 3išrīn alfᵊ dōlar 3ašān yiragga3ū.*

◇ *ţáyyib, xallīna nђáwwil ilʔaḑíyya 3ála -lmabāђis ilʔiliktruníyya wi húmma hayʔūmu bi-llāzim*[2].

[1] = كلِّموك *kallimūk*

[2] = هَيِتْصرّفوا *hayitşarráfu*

4

BEING DETAINED

○ مُمْكِن أعْرف أنا هِنا ليْه؟[1]

◇ حضْرِتك مُتّهم[2] بِبيْع دولارات في السّوق السّوْدا و إنْتَ هِنا عشان نِحقّق معاك.

○ لا حضْرِتك، أنا كُنْت مِحْتاج أغيرّ دولارات و حدّ عرض يِشْترِيهُم. أنا مِحْتاج أكلِّم المُحامي بِتاعي[3].

○ Can I know why I'm here?

◇ You're accused of selling dollars on the black market, and you're here to be questioned.

○ No, Officer. I needed to change some dollars and someone offered to buy them. I need to call my lawyer.

○ *múmkin á3raf, ána hína lē?*[1]

◇ *ɦadrítak muttáham*[2] *bi-bē3 dularāt fi -ssūʔ issōda w ínta hína 3ašān niɦáʔʔaʔ ma3āk.*

○ *laʔ, ɦadrítak, ána kuntᵊ miɦtāg ayáyyar dularāt wi ɦaddᵊ 3áraḍ yištirīhum. ána miɦtāg akállim ilmuɦāmi btā3i*[3].

[1] أنا مُتّهم بِأيْه؟ *ána muttáham bi-ʔē?* **What am I accused of?**; أيْه تُهْمِتي؟ *ʔē tuhmíti?* **What's the accusation/charge?**

[2] مُشْتبَه *muštábah* **suspected**

[3] مِحْتاج أرْجع لِلمُحامي *miɦtāg árga3 li-lmuɦāmi* **I need to get ahold of my lawyer.**

5

TRAFFIC FINE

o حضرتِك أنا معْرفْش إنّ الرّكْنة هِنا ممْنوع[1].

◇ رُخصك و خمْسين جِنيْه غرامة.

o أنا لِلْأسف نِسيت رُخْصِةْ القِيادة.

◇ طيِّب، رُخْصِةْ العربية بقى مِن فضْلك، و انْزِلّي.

o Sir, I didn't know parking wasn't allowed here.

◇ Your papers and a 50-LE fine.

o I have unfortunately lost my driver's license.

◇ I see. Then the automobile registration, please, and step out of the vehicle.

o *ḥaḍrítak, ána ma-3ráfš inn irrákna hína mamnū3*[1].

◇ *rúxaṣak wi xamsīn ginēh ɣarāma.*

o *ána li-lʔásaf nisīt rúxṣit ilqiyāda.*

◇ *ṭáyyib, rúxṣit il3arabíyya báʔa, min fáḍlak, w inzílli.*

[1] = مكُنْتِش اعْرف إنّ ممْنوع اركِن هِنا. *ma-kúntiš á3raf innᵊ mamnū3 árkin hína.*

6

Traffic accident

○ مِن فضْلك، يا حضْرِةْ الظّابِط هُوَّ اللي خِبط فِيّا[1] مِن وَرا يِبْقى هُوَّ الغلْطان[2].

◇ بسّ إنْتَ[3] وِقِفْت فجْأة برْضُه.

○ ما حضْرِتك شُفْت السِّتّ اللي عدِّت قُدّامي. لَوْ مكُنْتِش وِقِفْت كُنْت خبطْتها[4].

◇ طيِّب، تِحِبّوا تِخلّصوا المَوْضوع وِدِّي[5] وَلّا نِعْمِل محْضر؟

○ Excuse me, officer, he is the one who crashed into me from behind. Therefore, he's in the wrong.

◇ But you stopped all of a sudden, too.

○ You saw yourself the lady who crossed in front of me. If I hadn't stopped, I would have run her over.

◇ Okay, would you like to end this dispute in a friendly[4] manner or shall we make a report?

○ *min fáḍlak, ya ḫáḍrit iẓẓābiṭ, húwwa -lli xábaṭ fíyya*[1] *min wára, yíbʔa húwwa -lɣalṭān*[2].

◇ *bass ínta*[3] *wiʔíftᵊ fágʔa bárḍu.*

○ *ma ḫaḍrítak šuft issítt ílli 3áddit ʔuddāmi. law ma-kúntiš wiʔíft, kuntᵊ xabaṭtáha*[4].

◇ *ṭáyyib, tiḫíbbu txalláṣu -lmawḍū3 wíddi*[5], *wálla ní3mil máḫḍar?*

[1] = خبطْني *xabáṭni* = دخل فِيّا *dáxal fíyya*

[2] = الغلْطة غلْطِتُه *ilɣálṭa ɣalṭítu*

[3] = ما إنْتَ (اللي) *má-nta (-lli)*

[4] = كُنْت دُسْتها *kuntᵊ dustáha*; كان زماني مَوِّتّها *kān zamāni mawwittáha* **I would have killed her**; كُنْت طيرّْتها *kuntᵊ ṭayyartáha* **I would have sent her flying**

[5] وِدّي *wíddi* **friendly** implies that the two parties resolve the dispute between themselves without involving the police and filing an official report.

○ لَوْ سمحْت أنا عايِز أقدِّم بلاغ في بيّاع في محلّ.

◇ عملّك أيْه؟

○ سرق مِنّي فِلوس مِن الشّنْطة.

◇ المبْلغ كام؟[1]

○ ٥٠٠٠ يورو.

◇ طيِّب، خلّينا نِروح لِلْقِسْم بقى.

○ أيْوَه، فينْ أقْرب قِسْم شُرْطة؟

◇ تعالى وَرايا. نِروح نِعْمِل المحْضر هِناك. معاك باسْبوْرك؟

○ آه معايا الباسْبوْر.

◇ طيِّب و المحلّ ده فينْ[2] بِالظّبْط؟

○ في خان الخليلي. و ده الكّيس بتاعُه. أنا مُتأكِّد إنُّه هُوَّ اللي سِرق مِنّي[3].

◇ اِحْكيلي اللي حصل بِالظّبْط طيِّب.

○ أنا كُنْت بتْكلِّم معَ اِتْنينْ بيّاعينْ، واحِد مِنْهُم عينيْه خضْرا و شعْرُه إسْوِد.

◇ تمام و بعْديْن؟

○ فجْأة ده اِخْتفى و بقيْت بفاصِل و أتِّفِق معَ التّاني بسّ. بعْدها بِشْوَيّة دخل واحِد كَإنُّه زُبون بِنفْس مُواصفات[4] البيّاع اللي خرج بسّ مِغيرّ لِبْسُه[5].

◇ أبو عِيون خضْرا و شعْر إسْوِد؟

○ بِالظّبْط، هُوَّ ده. بسّ لابِس كَإنُّه سايِح و حسّيْت بِحركة في شنْطِتي و بعْديْن البيّاع الأوّلاني فِضِل يوَرّيني حاجات تانْيَة و يِشتِّتْني[6].

◇ إنْتَ شاكِك إنُّهُم معَ بعْض[7] يَعْني؟

o أنا مِش شاكِك، أنا مُتأكِّد. لإِنّ أوِّل ما البيّاع اِبْتدى يِشتِّتْني كان التّاني خد الفِلوس و فصّ ملْح و داب[8].

◇ عُموماً هتِدْخُل تِعْمِل محْضر بِالكلام ده كُلُّه و اِكْتِب كُلّ التّفاصيل و اِوْصِف لِحضْرِةْ الظّابِط مكان المحلّ بِالظّبْط.

o Excuse me, I want to report a salesperson in a shop.

◇ What did he do to you?

o He stole money out of my bag.

◇ How much?

o 5000 euros.

◇ Okay, let's go to the police station then.

o All right. Where is the nearest police station?

◇ Come with me. We'll go file a report. Do you have your passport on you?

o Yes, I have my passport.

◇ And where is this shop exactly?

o In Khan El-Khalili. Here's the plastic bag from the shop. I'm sure he's the one who stole it.

◇ Can you tell me what happened exactly?

o I was talking to two salesmen, and one of them had green eyes and black hair.

◇ Okay, and then?

o All of a sudden, he disappeared while I was haggling with the other one. Then, a few moments later, someone came in as if he were a customer, but he had the same look as the salesman who left earlier but he had changed his clothes.

◇ The one with green eyes and black hair?

o Exactly, that one. He was dressed like a tourist, and I felt some movement in my bag, and then the first salesman started to show me other stuff to distract me.

◇ Do you suspect they're together?

- I don't suspect; I'm certain of it. Because the moment the salesman started distracting me, the other took the money and vanished.
- ◇ In any case, you will file a report stating all this. Write out all the details and describe to the officer the location of the shop.

- *law samáḥt, ána 3āyiz aʔáddim balāɣ fi bayyā3 fi maḥáll.*
- ◇ *3amállak ʔē?*
- *sáraʔ mínni flūs min iššánṭa.*
- ◇ *ilmáblaɣ kām?*[1]
- *xamastalāf yūru.*
- ◇ *ṭáyyib, xallīna nrūḥ li-lʔísmᵊ báʔa.*
- *áywa, fēn aʔrab ʔismᵊ šúrta?*
- ◇ *ta3āla warāya. nirūḥ ní3mil ilmáḥḍar hinãk. ma3āk paspōrak?*
- *āh, ma3āya -lpaspōr.*
- ◇ *ṭáyyib, wi -lmaḥállᵊ da fēn*[2] *bi-ẓẓábṭ?*
- *fi xān ilxalīli. wi da -kkīs bitā3u. ána mutaʔákkid ínnu húwwa -lli sáraʔ mínni*[3].
- ◇ *iḥkīli -lli ḥáṣal bi-ẓẓábṭᵊ ṭáyyib.*
- *ána kuntᵊ batkállim má3a -tnēn bayya3ēn, wāḥid mínhum 3inē xáḍra wi šá3ru íswid.*
- ◇ *tamām, wi ba3dēn?*
- *fágʔa, da -xtáfa wi baʔēt bafāṣil w attífiʔ má3a -ttāni bass. ba3dáha bi-šwáyya dáxal wāḥid ka-ínnu zubūn bi-náfsᵊ muwaṣafāṭ*[4] *ilbayyā3 ílli xárag, bassᵊ mɣáyyar líbsu*[5].
- ◇ *ábu 3iyūn xáḍra wi ša3r íswid?*
- *bi-ẓẓábṭ, húwwa da. bassᵊ lābis ka-ínnu sāyiḥ, wi ḥassēt bi-ḥáraka fi šanṭíti wi ba3dēn ilbayyā3 ilʔawwalāni fíḍil yiwarrīni ḥagāt tánya wi yišattítni*[6].
- ◇ *ínta šākik innúhum má3a ba3ḍᵊ*[7] *yá3ni?*
- *ána miš šākik, ána mutaʔákkid. li-ínn áwwil ma -lbayyā3 ibtáda yšattítni kān ittāni xad ilfilūs wi faṣṣᵊ malḥᵊ w dāb*[8].
- ◇ *3umūman, hatídxul tí3mil máḥḍar bi-kkalām da kúllu w íktib kull ittafaṣīl w íwṣif li-ḥáḍrit iẓẓābiṭ makān ilmaḥállᵊ bi-ẓẓábṭ.*

[1] سرق كام؟ *sáraʔ kām?* **How much did they steal?**

[2] مكانه فينْ؟ *makānu fēn?* **Where is it?**; عِنْوانه أيْه؟ *3inwānu ʔē?* **What's the address?**

[3] = سرقْني *saráʔni*

[4] = نفْس شكْل *nafsᵊ šakl*

[5] = هُدومُه *hudūmu*

[6] = يِتوّهْني *yitawwáhni*

[7] = مِتّفِقين معَ بعْض *mittifiʔīn má3a ba3ḍ*

[8] idiom (lit. a grain of salt and it desolved) **vanished into thin air**

Vocabulary

police station	*ʔism*	قِسْم
police post	*núʔṭa*	نُقْطة
police officer	*ẓābiṭ*	ظابِط
police officer (lower ranking)	*amīn šúrṭa*	أمين شُرْطة
soldier (lower ranking than a police officer)	*3askári*	عسْكري
report, complaint (first step to a court case)	*máɦḍar*	محْضر
report (doesn't have to lead to a court case; could be done by phone)	*balāɣ*	بلاغ
to report	*bállaɣ*	بلّغ
to accuse (of)	*ittáham (bi-)*	اِتّهم (بِـ)
suspect; accused	*muttáham*	مُتّهم
criminal	*múgrim*	مُجْرِم
suspected of	*muštábah bi-*	مُشْتبَهْ (بِـ)

to steal; to rob	*sáraʔ*	سرق
theft	*sírʔa*	سِرْقة
thief	*ḩarāmi*	حرامي
pickpocket, cutpurse	*naššāl*	نشّال
fraud, trickery	*naşb*	نصْب
murder	*ʔatl*	قتْل
murderer	*ʔātil*	قاتِل
swindler, con man	*naşşāb*	نصّاب
forger, counterfeiter	*muzáwwir*	مُزوِّر
forgery	*tazwīr*	تزْوير
bribe	*rášwa*	رشْوَة
kidnapping	*xaţf*	خطْف
ransom	*fídya*	فِدْيَة
court case	*ʔaḑíyya*	قضية
interrogation	*taḩʔīʔ*	تحْقيق
court testimony	*aʔwāl*	أقْوال
driver's license	*rúxşa*	رُخْصة
penalty, fine	*muxálfa*	مُخالْفة
traffic ticket	*muxálfit murūr*	مُخالْفِة مُرور
fine	*ɣarāma*	غرامة
revoking one's driver's license	*saḩbᵊ rúxşa*	سحْب رُخْصة

traffic police	*šúrṭit ilmurūr*	شُرْطِةْ المُرور
antiquities police	*šúrṭit ilʔasār*	شُرْطِةْ الآثار
tourism police	*šúrṭit issiyāɦa*	شُرْطِةْ السِّياحة
witness	*šāhid*	شاهِد
judge	*ʔāḍi*	قاضي
court	*maɦkáma*	محْكمة
session	*gálsa*	جلْسة
judgment	*ɦukm*	حُكْم
proof	*dalīl*	دليل
arrest (of)	*i3tiʔāl ʔabdᵊ (3ála)*	اِعْتِقال قبْض (على)
complaint	*šákwa*	شكْوى
detective	*muháʔʔiʔ*	مُحقِّق
prosecutor	*wakil niyāba*	وكيل نِيابة

Expressions

○

This lady tried to rob me.	*issíttᵊ di ɦáwlit tisráʔni.*	مِن فضْلك، السِّتّ دي حاوْلِت تِسْرقْني.
This man has changed his car's license plate number.	*irrāgil da mɣáyyar arqām 3arabītu.*	الرّاجِل ده مِغيرّ أرْقام عربيتُه.
I want to file an official complaint.	*kuntᵊ 3āyiz aʔáddim šákwa.*	كُنْت عايِز أقدِّم شكْوى.

I want to report a nuisance.	*3āyiz á3mil máɧɖar iz3āg.*	مِن فضْلك، عايِز أعْمِل محْضر إزْعاج.
I want to report a big fight with gun shots.	*3āyiz abállaɣ 3an xināʔa kbīra wi fī ɖarb*^{ə} *nār.*	عايِز أبلّغ عن خِناقة كِبيرة و فيه ضرْب نار.
I want to follow up with the official complaint I made two months ago.	*kunt*^{ə} *3āyiz atābi3 ilmáɧɖar ílli 3amáltu min šahrēn.*	كُنْت عايِز أتابِع المحْضر اللي عملْتُه مِن شهْريْن.
	◇	
You will be interrogated.	*ínta hatitɧáwwil li-ttaɧʔīʔ.*	إنْتَ هتِتْحوِّل لِلتّحْقيق.
We're here to arrest __.	*maʈlūb ilʔábɖ*^{ə} *3ála __.*	مطْلوب القبْض على ــــ.
Photography is illegal in this area.	*mamnū3 ittaʂwīr hína.*	ممْنوع التّصْوير هِنا.

Dealing with Difficulties لَوْ فيه مُشْكِلة

The people. The culture. The food. The history. The weather...?? There's a lot to love about Egypt. But, of course, every place has its own issues that foreigners (and locals) have to deal with... or, at least, put up with. Bureaucracy. Corruption. Incompetence. Cheating. Beggars. Harassment. We all have our lists of the advantages and disadvantages of living in Egypt. Of course, the majority of Egyptians are incredibly welcoming and helpful; however, there are those who might take advantage of the language and culture barriers. So, below and on the following pages of this chapter are things any foreigner in Egypt needs to know:

Double and triple check information. People like to go the extra mile in helping you with directions... even if they're not 100% sure themselves. Before walking too far, ask someone else to make sure you're actually going the right way.

Red tape is no joke in Egypt. Again, you'll need to double and triple any step that needs to be done for certain documents, for instance, to save lots of unneeded steps. One civil servant will tell you that you only need to bring A, B, and C. Then when you go back, someone else will tell you that you don't need B, but you need D and E. Keep calm and carry on!

①

Dealing with beggars

◇ أيّ حاجة لله يا بيْه.

○ الله يِسهِّلّك.[1]

◇ أنا بجْري على أرْبع عِيال و بتْعالج بِخمسْتلاف جِنيْهْ في الشّهْر.[2]

○ ربِّنا يِرْزُقك و يِشْفيك.[3]

◇ Anything for God's sake, sir.

○ May God make it easier for you.

◇ I'm responsible for four children, and my monthly medications cost 5000 LE.

○ May God heal you and provide for you.

◇ *ayyᵊ ḫāga li-llāh ya bēh.*

○ *allāh yisahhíllak.*[1]

◇ *ána bágri 3ála árba3 3iyāl wi bat3āliq bi-xamastalāf ginēh fi -ššahr*[2].

○ *rabbína yirzúʔak wi yišfīk.*[3]

[1] = الله يِعْطيك. *allāh yi3ṭīk* = الله يُرْزُقك. *allāh yurzúʔak* = الله يِحنِّن عليْك. *allāh yiḫánnin 3alēk.*

[2] = علاجي بْيِتْكلِّف خمسْتلاف كُلّ شهْر. *3ilāgi byitkállif xamastalāf kullᵊ šahr.*

[3] ربِّنا الرّزّاق. *rabbína -rrazzāʔ* = ربنا الشّافي *rabbína -ššāfi*

Egypt is awash with "professional" beggars who are ready to play on your sympathy to get a بقْشيش *baʔšiš* **handout**. (This is very unfortunate for the rare few who are legitimately in such hard times that they resort to begging to survive.) The frauds will fake blindness and other handicaps, hide limbs inside clothing, and generally try to make themselves seem as pitiful as possible. Begging children are particularly irresistible, but they are often sent out by handlers who hide out nearby and take their earnings from them. Let your conscience be your guide when giving money, but know that giving money, especially to children, not only [continued on the next page]...

2

Dealing with someone cutting in line

○ لَوْ سمحْتي، ده دوْري.
◇ ما إنْتي سِبْتيه و مِشيتي.
○ حضْرِتِك أنا كُنْت في الحمّام و قايْلة لِلّي وَرايا إنُّه دوْري عشان محدِّش يُقف مكاني.

○ Excuse me, it's my turn.
◇ But you left and went away.
○ I was in the bathroom and I told the person standing behind me to hold my place and not let anyone take it.

○ *law samáђti, da dōri.*
◇ *má-nti sibtī wi mšīti.*
○ *ђaḍrítik, ána kuntᵊ fi -lђammām wi ʔáyla lí-lli warāya ínnu dōri 3ašān ma-ђáddiš yúʔaf makāni.*

If you walk up to a counter or ticket window and patiently wait for the clerk to ask to help you... and specifically *you* because you were *next,* well, you'll be waiting a long time while others come up and push right past you holding money in outstretched arms and shouting their orders. Take a cue from the locals, be assertive, and make yourself heard. You will otherwise be doomed to persistent frustration. After all, when in Rome...

[continued from the previous page] ... perpetuates the problem and strengthens the mafia, but you will also likely be surrounded by a dozen more beggars immediately and every time you pass by the same spot. If you really want to help, give food, but most likely it's not what they're looking for anyway. You can give children sweets you have on you.

3

Dealing with harassment

◇ أيْه يا عسل يا جميل![1]

○ اِحْترِم نفْسك[2] و لَوْ قرّبْت أكْتر مِن كِده هتِنْدِم[3].

◇ أيْه ده و بِتِتْكلّمي عربي كمان؟ ما تيجي معايا طيِّب.

○ إنْتَ هتِمْشي و تِتْلمّ وَلّا أفْضحك و أوَدّيك في داهْيَة[4]؟

◇ What's up, gorgeous!

○ Behave, and if you get any closer, you'll regret it.

◇ Wow, and you speak Arabic, too? Come with me!

○ Will you leave and save yourself or shall I make a scene here and make sure you go to hell?

◇ *ʔē ya 3ásal ya gamīl*[1]*!*

○ *iḫtírim náfsak*[2] *wi law ʔarrábt áktar min kída hatíndam*[3]*.*

◇ *ʔē da wi bititkallími 3árabi kamān? ma tīgi ma3āya ṭáyyib.*

○ *ínta hatímši wi titlámm wálla -fḍáḥak w awaddīk fi dáhya*[4]*?*

[1] يا قُطّة! *ya ʔúṭṭa!* **Hey, pussy cat!**; يا مُزّة! *ya múzza!* **Hey, hottie!** / [2] = لِمّ نفْسك *limmᵊ náfsak* / [3] هصوّت و ألِمّ عليْك الشّارِع. *haṣáwwat w alímmᵊ 3alēk iššāri3.* **I'll scream and make a scene in the street!** (lit. get the street the gather around you).; هتْشوف هعْمِل فيك أيْه. *hatšūf há3mil fīk 2ē.* **You'll see what I'll do to you!**; هَوَرّيك اللي هعْمِلُه. *hawarrīk ílli ha3mílu.* **I'll show you what I'll do!** / [4] في سِتّين داهْيَة *fi sittīn dáhya* **to the depths of hell** (lit. sixty hells) • Ladies, unfortunately, you're bound to encounter harassment at some point. A man might follow you down the street a ways, remark on your appearance as you pass by, catcall, or even hiss. In most cases, they're annoying but harmless. A harasser will rarely take it further than that, especially if others are around. The best thing is to ignore him or shame him loudly, which will usually make him back off before more attention is drawn to him. However, if you do feel physically threatened, make sure you shout loud enough so that people nearby notice that something is wrong. They will likely gather around to help. You may proceed to report the harasser to the police if you want. (See also **Mido: In Egyptian Arabic**, chapter 5.)

4

COMPLAINING IN A RESTAURANT

○ لَوْ سمحْت الأكْل فيه رمْلة.

◇ مفيش الكّلام ده حضْرِتِك. إحْنا أكْلِنا زيّ الفُلّ[1].

○ يَعْني أنا بكْدِب مثلاً؟

◇ معْرفْش حضْرِتِك. بسّ دي أوّل مرّة حدّ يِشْتِكي[2] مِن الأكْل بِتاعْنا.

○ طيِّب، متِزْعلْش بقى لمّا أنزِّل الكّلام ده على الإنْترْنِت[3].

○ Excuse me, the food has some sand in it.

◇ No way, miss. Our food is perfectly good.

○ So, I'm making this up?!

◇ I don't know, miss, but this is the first time anyone has complained about our food.

○ Well, don't be upset if I post about this online!

○ *law samáħt, ilʔáklᵊ fī rámla.*

◇ *ma-fīš ikkalām da, ħadrítik. íħna aklína zayy ilfúll*[1].

○ *yá3ni ána bákdib másalan?*

◇ *ma-3ráfšᵊ ħadrítik. bassᵊ di áwwil márra ħaddᵊ yištíki*[2] *min ilʔáklᵊ bitá3na.*

○ *ṭáyyib, ma-tiz3álšᵊ báʔa lámma -názzil ikkalām da 3ála -lʔíntarnat*[3].

1 زيّ الفُلّ *zayy ilfúll* **perfect** (lit. like a jasmine flower)

2 = عُمْر ما حدّ اِشْتكى *3umrᵊ ma ħadd ištáka* **no one's ever complained**

3 لمّا أقدِّم فيك شكْوى *lámma -ʔáddim fīk šákwa* **when I make an official complaint against you**; لمّا أبلّغ عنْكُم حِمايةْ المُسْتهْلِك *lámma -bállaɣ 3ánkum ħimāyit ilmustáhlik* **when I report you to the consumer protection agency**

If you encounter bad customer service at a shop or restaurant, one effective method is to report them to the consumer protection agency (Call 19588 or visit a post office to fill out a form.) or simply post the issue on social media. The negative publicity that can go viral on social media can be more effective than anything else for a business.

5

DEALING WITH AN PERSISTENT SALESPERSON

◇ مِش عايِز تِشْتِري[1] حاجة يا بيْه؟

o لا شُكْراً.

◇ تعالى شوف بسّ. الأسْعار عنْدي حاجة تانْيَة خالِص.

o ريّح نفْسك[2]. أنا مِش جايّ أشْترِي أساساً.

◇ Don't you want to buy anything, sir?

o No, thanks.

◇ Just come and see for yourself. My prices are out of this world.

o Save your breath. I'm not here to buy anyway.

◇ *miš 3āyiz tištíri*[1] *ђāga ya bēh?*

o *laʔ, šúkran.*

◇ *ta3āla šūf bass. ilʔas3ār 3ándi ђāga tánya xāliṣ.*

o *ráyyaђ náfsak*[2]. *ána miš gayy aštíri asāsan.*

[1] تِنفّعْنا *tinaffá3na* **you give us business**

[2] متِتْعِبْش نفْسك *ma-tit3íbš náfsak* **don't wear yourself out**

Besides pesky salespeople, you may encounter touts on the street who can be just as annoying. They'll try to get you to follow them to their "uncle's" perfume or papyrus shop or be your local tour guide. They may even be upfront about this. But, as a rule, it's better to simply say لا شُكْراً! *lā šúkran!* **No, thank you!** and keep walking. Another popular technique to get your attention and start engaging with you is by saying something like "You dropped your wallet!" Ignore them and keep walking.

Keep in mind that many disagreements stem from innocent misunderstandings, and it's always good to give your waiter (or whoever you're dealing with) the benefit of the doubt and consider whether the confusion is because of differing cultural expectations or even (... likely?) because of a mistake you made in your Arabic.

6

DEALING WITH A SALESPERSON WHO'S TRYING TO RIP YOU OFF

○ سِعْرها كام دي مِن فضْلك؟

◇ ٩٠ دوْلار.

○ لا يا راجِل![1] هات مِ الآخِر[2] و اِدّيني السِّعْر الحقيقي مِش بِتاع السُّيّاح.

◇ يا نْهار أبْيَض! ده إنْتَ مصْري بقى. اللي إنْتَ عايْزُه يا باشا.

○ How much is this, please?

◇ 90 dollars.

○ Oh, please! What's your final offer? Give me the real price, not the one for tourists.

◇ Oh my goodness! You must be an Egyptian then. Whatever you wish, sir.

○ *si3ráha kām di, min fádlak?*

◇ *tis3īn dōlar.*

○ *lā, ya rāgil![1] hāt mi -lʔāxir[2] w iddīni -ssi3r ilḫaʔīʔi, miš bitā3 issuyyāḫ.*

◇ *ya nhār ábyaḍ! da -nta máṣri báʔa. íll- ínta 3áyzu ya bāša.*

[1] = يا سلام! *ya salām!* = لا يا شيْخ! *lā ya šex!* = لا والله! *lā wallāhi!* The phrase is translated as a sarcastic "Oh, please!" in the translation above, but it could also be "Oh, come... on!" or "Seriously?!" or any other expression to show exasperation and disbelief.; فاكِرْني مِش فاهِم مثلاً؟ *fakírni miš fāhim másalan?* **Do you think I'm stupid or something?**

[2] = آخْرك كام؟ *áxrak kām?*

Some sellers will double prices when dealing with foreigners. Always ask an Egyptian acquaintance about expected prices before making a significant or frequent purchase.

Extended Dialogue

◦ شارِع فيْصل؟

⬥ فيْن في شارِع فيْصل؟

◦ عِنْد الطَّوابِق كِده.

⬥ ماشي اِتْفضَّلي.

◦ أسْتأْذِنك تِشغَّل العدَّاد.

⬥ اِصْطبحْنا و اِصْطبِح الملِك لله،[1]

◦ أفنْدِم؟

⬥ لا مفيش. مِش شغّال.

◦ طيِّب، هتاخُد كام مِن هِنا لِهِناك؟

⬥ يا سِتّي نِتْحرَّك بسّ و بعْديْن نِشوف متِقْلِقيش.

◦ طيِّب، تمام!

(taxi approaches Tawabe')

◦ هنْزِل هِنا مِن فضْلك.

⬥ تحْت أمْرِك يا أُسْتاذة.

◦ حِسابْنا كام بقى ياسْطى؟

⬥ خلِّي عليْنا![2]

◦ ربِّنا يِكْرِمك. كام بسّ؟

⬥ ١٥٠ جِنيْه.

◦ ١٥٠ إزّاي يَعْني؟ إنْتَ فاكِرْني مِش عارْفة الأسْعار؟

⬥ هِيَّ ١٥٠ جِنيْه و اِنْزِلي وَقَّفي أيّ تاكْس اِسْألِيه.

◦ المِشْوار ده بالظَّبْط يِعْمِله ٥٠ - ٦٠ جِنيْه.

⬥ ٥٠ مين يا سِتّ؟ إنْتي... إنْتي جايّة مِن سِنَةْ كامْ؟[3]

◦ طيِّب، هتاخُدْهُم ولّا نِطْلع عَ القِسْم نِسْألْهُم هِناك؟

◇ أنا مبتْهدِّدْش يا ماما. هُوَّ كان مِشْوار إسْوِد أساساً أنا غلْطان إنيّ خدْتِك.

o طيِّب، تمام أوي كِده... الفِلوس عنْدك أهُه عَ الكّنبة و ده اللي عنْدي.

o Feisal street?
◇ Where exactly on Feisal?
o Near Tawabe'.
◇ Okay, get in.
o Would you please turn on the meter?
◇ Oh, jeez!
o Excuse me?
◇ Nothing... It's not working.
o Okay, how much will you take from here to there?
◇ Let's start moving first, lady, and then we'll see. Don't worry.
o Very well then.

(taxi approaches Tawabe')

o I'll get out here, please.
◇ As you wish, ma'am.
o How much is the fare, sir?
◇ It's okay... you keep it!
o Thanks a lot... how much is it, please?
◇ 150 LE.
o How is it 150 LE? You think I don't know fares?
◇ It's 150 LE, and you can get out and ask any taxi passing by.
o This trip costs exactly something between 50-60 LE.
◇ 50 what, woman?! What year are you from?
o All right, will you take it or shall we go to the police station and ask them?
◇ I won't be intimidated, lady! It was a stupid trip in the first place. I shouldn't have stopped for you!

○ Okay, very well then... Here's your money on the back seat, and that's that.

○ *šāri3 fēṣal?*
◇ *fēn fi šāri3 fēṣal?*
○ *3and iṭṭawābiʔ kída.*
◇ *māši, itfaḍḍáli.*
○ *astaʔzínak tišáyɣal il3addād.*
◇ *iṣṭabáḥna wi -ṣṭábaḥ ilmúlkᵊ li-llāh.*[1]
○ *afándim?*
◇ *laʔ, ma-fīš. miš šaɣɣāl.*
○ *ṭáyyib, hatāxud kām min hína li-hināk?*
◇ *ya sítti nitḥárrak bass, wi ba3dēn nišūf ma-tiʔlaʔīš.*
○ *ṭáyyib, tamām!*

(taxi approaches Tawabe')

○ *hánzil hína, min fáḍlak.*
◇ *taḥtᵊ ámrik ya ustāza.*
○ *ḥisábna kām báʔa yásṭa?*
◇ *xálli 3alēna!*[2]
○ *rabbína yikrímak. kām bass?*
◇ *míyya w xamsīn ginēh.*
○ *míyya w xamsīn izzāy yá3ni? ínta fakírni miš 3árfa -lʔas3ār?*
◇ *híyya míyya w xamsīn ginēh, w inzíli waʔʔáfi ayyᵊ taks isʔalī.*
○ *ilmišwār da bi-ẓẓábṭᵊ yi3mílu xamsīn - sittīn ginēh.*
◇ *xamsīn mīn ya sittᵊ ínti? ínti gáyya min sánat kām?*[3]
○ *ṭáyyib, hataxúdhum wálla níṭla3 3a -lʔismᵊ nisʔálhum hināk?*
◇ *ána ma-bathaddídšᵊ ya māma. húwwa kān mišwār íswid asāsan. ána ɣalṭān ínni xádtik.*
○ *ṭáyyib, tamām áwi kída... ilfilūs 3ándak ahú 3a -lkánaba wi da -lli 3ándi.*

[1] = أَسْتَغْفِر الله العظيم. *astáɣfir allāh il3aẓīm.* (lit. I ask God for forgiveness!) = يا فتّاح يا عليم يا رزّاق يا كريم! *ya fattāḥ, ya 3alīm, ya razzāʔ, ya karīm!* (lit. O facilitator, omniscient, provider, generous one!) These are invocations to God, but in this context, they are used to express frustration.

[2] خلّيها = wallāhi ábadan! والله أبداً! = ma-fīš ɦāga wallāhi! مفيش حاجة والله! = خلّينا المرّة دي! xallīna -marrā-di! Such phrases are not to be taken literally. (See book 1, p. 4, note 3.)

[3] إنْتي عايْشة في العصْر الحجري؟ ínti 3áyša fi -l3aşr ilɦágari? **Are you living in the stone age?**

Taxi drivers are notorious for overcharging foreigners. Make sure your taxi driver turns on his meter (or better yet, use a rideshare service like Uber). Be careful, even when agreeing to a flat rate. I've had taxi drivers, claiming at the end of the trip that the agreed fare was per person or actually in dollars.

Vocabulary

to verbally harass, catcall	*3ākis*	عاكِس
verbal harassment	*mu3áksa*	مُعاكْسة
to sexually harass someone (verbally or physically)	*itɦárraš*	اِتْحرّش
sexual harassment	*taɦárruš*	تحرُّش
to push	*za??*	زقّ
lack of manners, crudeness	*?íllit ádab*	قِلّةْ أدب
bad service	*xídma wíɦša*	خِدْمة وِحْشة
to cheat, swindle, deceive	*ɣašš*	غشّ
to report	*bállaɣ*	بلّغ
report	*balāɣ*	بلاغ
complaint	*šákwa*	شكْوى
to scream, cry out	*şáwwat*	صوّت

situation	*máwqif (mawāqif)* *máwʔif (mawāʔif)*	مَوْقِف (مَواقِف)
accident	*ɦádsa*	حادْثة
fight, argument	*xināʔa*	خِناقة

Expressions

○		
Help!	*ilɦaʔūni!*	اِلْحقوني!
Thief!	*ɦarāmi!*	حرامي!
Police!	*šúrţa!*	شُرْطة!
No, thanks!	*la šúkran!*	لا شُكْراً!
Enough already!	*xalāş!*	خلاص!
In your dreams!; When pigs fly!	*fi -lmíšmiš!*	في المِشْمِش!
Behave yourself!	*iɦtírim náfsak!* *itlámm!* *limm náfsak!*	اِحْترِم نفْسك! اِتْلمّ! لِمّ نفْسك!
Shame on you!	*3ēb 3alēk!* *itkísif 3ála dámmak!*	عيْب عليْك! اِتْكِسِف على دمّك!
Shame on you, at your age!	*3ēb 3ála sínnak!*	عيْب على سِنّك!
That man over there is bothering us.	*irrāgil ílli hināk da biyḑaylíʔna.*	الرّاجِل اللي هِناك ده بِيْضايِقْنا.
I want to report a case of sexual harassment.	*3áyza abállaɣ 3an taɦárruš.*	عايْزة أبلّغ عن تحرُّش.

Someone is following and verbally harassing us.	*fī wāḫid māši warāna wi biy3akísna.*	فيه واحِد ماشي وَرانا و بيْعاكِسْنا.
My papers haven't been issued for more than a month now.	*ána wáraʔi ma-xlíṣšᵊ min šahr.*	أنا وَرقي مخْلِصْش مِن شهْر.
I've been standing in line forever.	*ána wāʔif fi -ṭṭabūr min bádri.*	أنا واقِف في الطّابور مِن بدْري.
Excuse me, can you make some room (for me to pass)?	*law samáḫtᵊ múmkin issíkka?*	لَوْ سمحْت مُمْكِن السِّكّة؟
Look where you're going!; Hey, watch out!	*miš tiḫāsib ṭáyyib?*	مِش تِحاسِب طيِّب؟
(to a taxi driver) You're taking [us] for a long ride when the trip is actually short!	*ínta bitlíffᵊ kitīr raɣm inn issíkka ʔuṣayyára!*	إنْتَ بِتْلِفّ كِتير رغْم إنّ السِّكّة قُصيّرة!
We're not stupid. Are you going to give us reasonable prices or shall we leave?	*laʔ, íḫna miš húbal. hatiddīna as3ār 3ídla wálla nímši?*	لا إحْنا مِش هُبل. هتِدّينا أسْعار عدْلة وَلّا نمْشي؟
Don't think you're going to outsmart us!	*ínta hatitšáṭṭar 3alēna wálla ʔē?*	إنْتَ هتِتْشطّر علينْا وَلّا ايْه؟
This is a suitable price, and I will not pay a penny more!	*ḫilwᵊ kída, wi miš hádfa3 mallīm ziyāda.*	حِلْو كِده و مِش هدْفع ملّيم زِيادة.

www.ingramcontent.com/pod-product-compliance
Lightning Source LLC
Chambersburg PA
CBHW052054110526
44591CB00013B/2202
* 9 7 8 1 9 4 9 6 5 0 0 5 1 *